CREATED FROM NAFTA

The Structure, Function, and Significance of the Treaty's Related Institutions

Joseph A. McKinney

M.E. Sharpe
Armonk, New York
London, England

Library of Congress Cataloging-in-Publication Data

McKinney, Joseph A., 1943–
    Created from NAFTA : the structure, function, and significance of the treaty's related
institutions / Joseph A. McKinney.
        p. cm.
    Includes bibliographical references and index.
    ISBN 0-7656-0466-3 (hardcover : alk. paper)
    ISBN 0-7656-0467-1 (paperback : alk. paper)
    1. Free trade—North America. 2. Canada. Treaties, etc. 1992 Oct. 7. 3. North
America—Economic integration. I. Title.

KDZ945.A41992 M37 2000
382′.917—dc21   99-087440

Printed in the United States of America

The paper used in this publication meets the minimum requirements of
American National Standard for Information Sciences
Permanence of Paper for Printed Library Materials,
ANSI Z 39.48-1984.

∞

BM (c)   10   9   8   7   6   5   4   3   2   1
BM (p)   10   9   8   7   6   5   4   3   2   1

Dedicated to the memory of my
esteemed friend and colleague
Professor Glen E. Lich
who first stimulated my interest in regional studies

Table of Contents

Acronyms   ix

Preface   xi

1 Development of the North American Free Trade Agreement   3

2 NAFTA-Related Institutions in the Context of Theory   14

3 The Free Trade Commission   24

4 Commission for Labor Cooperation and National
   Administrative Offices   33

      Appendix 4.1 North American Agreement on
                    Labor Cooperation   53

5 North American Commission for Environmental
   Cooperation   90

      Appendix 5.1 Recommendations of the Independent
                    Review Committee   118

      Appendix 5.2 North American Agreement on
                    Environmental Cooperation   123

6 Border Environment Cooperation Commission and
   North American Development Bank   161

Appendix 6.1 Charter of North American Development Bank and Border Environment Cooperation Commission   178

7 Other Dispute Settlement Mechanisms   223

8 Summary and Conclusions   236

Bibliography   245

Web Pages of NAFTA-Related Institutions   253

Index   255

Acronyms

APEC	Asia Pacific Economic Cooperation
BECC	Border Environment Cooperation Commission
BEIF	Border Environment Infrastructure Fund
CAIP	Community Adjustment and Investment Program
CDFAIT	Canadian Department of Foreign Affairs and International Trade
CEC	Commission for Environmental Cooperation
CLC	Commission for Labor Cooperation
ECE	Evaluation Committee of Experts
EPA	Environmental Protection Agency
EU	European Union
GAC	Governmental Advisory Committee
GATT	General Agreement on Tariffs and Trade
IBWC	International Boundary and Water Commission
IDCP	Institutional Development Cooperation Program
JPAC	Joint Public Advisory Committee
NAAEC	North American Agreement on Environmental Cooperation
NAALC	North American Agreement on Labor Cooperation
NAC	National Advisory Committee
NADB	North American Development Bank
NAFTA	North American Free Trade Agreement
NAO	National Administrative Offices
NGO	Nongovernmental Organization
NLRB	National Labor Relations Board
PDAP	Project Development Assistance Programs
USCAIP	United States Community Adjustment and Investment Program

USDOC	United States Department of Commerce
USDJ	United States Department of Justice
USDOL	United States Department of Labor
USGAO	United States General Accounting Office
USITC	United States International Trade Commission
USTR	United States Trade Representative
WTO	World Trade Organization

Preface

The North American Free Trade Agreement (NAFTA) has been one of the more controversial pieces of trade legislation in recent history. Not only did it link in a regional economic integration scheme countries of widely disparate size, but it also brought together countries having very different income levels, legal traditions, regulatory regimes, and cultural traditions. Because of these differences, apprehensions about the agreement have been significant in all three of the member countries.

Many attempts have been made to assess the economic effects of the NAFTA agreement. This has been no simple task given the complications introduced by the peso crisis that beset Mexico a little less than a year after the agreement came into effect. Nevertheless, the economic effects of NAFTA have received frequent and rigorous analyses.

Much less studied has been the institutional structure that was established as a result of the NAFTA agreement. In part this can be attributed to the fact that the institutions were slow in getting organized and are still very young in terms of their operation. In part it is due to the fact that the NAFTA-related institutions are so small in comparison to other regional institutions that many doubt their real significance. Yet, in the long run the institutions that were created as a result of NAFTA may well have an impact that overshadows the significant effects of trade liberalization.

In this volume I have attempted to set the NAFTA-related institutions into context, to provide an overview of their activities, and to make some observations concerning their significance. Given the number of institutions that have taken shape as a result of the NAFTA agreement, an in-depth treatment of them would have been impossible in a single volume. Therefore, I have not attempted to give an exhaustive treatment of any of the institutions but, rather, to provide an overview of all of them in one reference volume. The reader who desires detailed knowledge of any of the institutions will need to look elsewhere. For most of the institutions an almost overwhelming amount of information is available on their web sites. I have attempted to synthesize enough of this information for each of the institutions to provide at least a rudimentary description of their structure, their functions, and their significance.

In the first chapter, I place the NAFTA-related institutions in their historical context by briefly describing the events that led to the signing of the NAFTA agreement and, subsequently, to the negotiation of supplemental agreements on labor and environmental cooperation.

In Chapter 2, I attempt to place the NAFTA-related institutions in theoretical context by relating them to some of the major theories of international institutions. I believe that the institutions' significance cannot be understood without at least some reference to this literature. In this venture I am out of my professional domain, and I beg the indulgence of experts in this subject area who may resent the intrusion of an amateur into their professional space. I must express profound gratitude to Professor Janet Adamski of the Baylor University Department of Political Science for having taken a look at this chapter and for correcting some of my more egregious errors. At the same time she must be absolved of any guilt by association, as I was not able to follow through on all of her valuable suggestions.

In the remaining chapters of the book, I consider the structure and functioning to date of the major NAFTA-related institutions and make at least a preliminary assessment of their effectiveness and of their significance.

A generous research grant from the Embassy of Canada in Washington, D.C., made possible visits to Washington, Montreal, and Ottawa to talk with officials at some of the institutions and with members of governmental agencies, nongovernmental organizations, and other scholars. Further research support from the Department of Economics at Baylor University funded visits to Dallas, San Antonio, Los Angeles, and Juarez, Mexico, to visit the headquarters of other institutions. These on-site visits were a valuable part of the research, and I am grateful to the organizations that made it possible.

At the various institutions I was received graciously and assisted in important ways. In particular, I would like to thank Sarah Richardson of the Commission for Environmental Cooperation Secretariat in Montreal; Kevin Banks of the Commission for Labor Cooperation Secretariat in

Dallas; Annie M. Alvarado and George E. Longoria of the North American Development Bank staff in San Antonio; Hugh Loftus, director of the North American Development Bank, Los Angeles Branch; and Ricardo Castanon and Edgardo C. Tovilla of the Border Environment Cooperation Commission staff in Juarez. I am grateful to all of them for their assistance. None of them, of course, should be held responsible for any misinterpretations that I may have made of the information that they provided.

For assistance with proofreading, I thank my friend, Arthur Milton, and my graduate assistant, Ben Williams. For assistance with the bibliography and other aspects of manuscript preparation, I am most grateful to Julie Lastrape, office manager in the McBride Center for International Business at Baylor University. Finally, to my wife, Nancy, I owe a debt of gratitude for her patience, understanding, and moral support during late nights at the office and neglected tasks at home as the book came to fruition.

CREATED FROM NAFTA

1

Development of the North American Free Trade Agreement

The foundations of the North American Free Trade Agreement (NAFTA) can be traced to the U.S. Congress's passage of the Trade and Tariff Act of 1984. In this legislation Congress indicated a willingness to negotiate free trade agreements between the United States and other interested countries. Prior to that time the United States had been the leading proponent of multilateralism in international trade. Granted, the United States had supported and even encouraged regional economic integration in Western Europe. However, the motivation there was geopolitical—to strengthen Western European countries and to encourage political cooperation among them in order to thwart the spread of communism on the European continent. In its own trade policy the United States had espoused a preference for the multilateral trading system with its underlying principles of nondiscrimination and national treatment.

The change in U.S. trade policy during the 1980s arose partly from frustration over lack of progress within the General Agreement on Tariffs and Trade (GATT) in addressing issues of particular concern to the United States. These issues included restrictions on trade in agricultural products, insufficient protection of intellectual property, the use of subsidies in international trade, and restrictions on trade in services. Being frustrated at the multilateral level, the United States moved in the direction of bilateral agreements hoping that progress there could provide a demonstration effect that would carry over into the broader arena.

Also, during the 1980s the U.S. economy was suffering the ill effects of an overvalued dollar. A combination of stringent monetary policy and expansionary fiscal policy had driven real interest rates to new heights, strengthening the U.S. dollar relative to other currencies. This made it difficult for firms in the United States to compete with those of other countries. Consequently, the United States began to apply protectionist measures. It used the contingent protection instruments of antidumping penalties and countervailing duties more aggressively, and devised nontariff trade barriers such as voluntary export restraints. Congress mandated certain unilateral protection measures such as the Super 301 and Special 301 provisions of the Omnibus Trade and Competitiveness Act of 1988 to deal with perceived unfairness in international trade.

Although these measures applied by the United States were targeted primarily toward Japan, Canada watched these developments with great concern because it was highly dependent on trade with the United States. Restricted access to its largest market would have been costly to Canada, requiring much adjustment and denying Canadian industries the benefits of economies of scale. Therefore Canada, which had previously been leery of a bilateral free trade agreement with the United States, began to rethink its position.

At the so-called Shamrock Summit in Quebec in March of 1985, President Ronald Reagan and Prime Minister Brian Mulroney discussed the possibility of a free trade agreement between Canada and the United States. They tasked their trade ministers to study the desirability of such an agreement, and when the trade ministers came back with an affirmative report, the political processes were set in motion to consummate the agreement (Merkin 1990, 47).

A free trade agreement between the United States and Canada was not uncontroversial in either country. During the previous century free trade agreements between the United States and Canada had been considered on several occasions, but one party or the other had always backed away. Plans for such an agreement in the 1980s were almost blocked in the Senate Finance Committee of the U.S. Congress. A motion to disapprove the request for a free trade agreement garnered much support. After a struggle the vote on the motion ended in a tie, which meant that the negotiations were not disapproved (ibid.). Consequently, negotiations for a U.S.–Canada free trade agreement began early in 1986, and President Reagan and Prime Minister Mulroney signed the agreement on 2 January 1988.

In Canada the notion of a free trade agreement with the United States stirred up heated debate. Some Canadians feared that closer relations with the United States would be a threat both to Canada's national sovereignty and to her cultural identity. Questions arose about whether Canadians would be able to maintain their national health system and other social services if Canadian firms were free to locate south of the border where the corporate tax burden was perceived to be lower. In the summer of 1988 opposition leader John Turner came out against the free trade agreement, forcing a national election. The Conservative Party prevailed, however, and the free trade agreement went into effect on 1 January 1989.

By the late 1980s the Canadian public had come to appreciate the fact that the relatively small size of the protected Canadian market hindered the development of efficient industries. Some recognized as well that protection distorted investment patterns. U.S. firms invested in Canada to get behind the trade barriers, while Canadian firms invested in the United States to avoid the uncertainty of continued access to the foreign market of overwhelming importance to them. Trade with the United States had by this time come to account for almost 80 percent of Canada's foreign trade and about 20 percent of Canadian gross domestic product.

The U.S.–Canada free trade agreement broke new ground in a number of areas where frustration with the multilateral system had existed. It liberalized agricultural trade substantially. It established a "bill of rights" for service providers, assuring national treatment of service firms, increased market access, increased mobility of business professionals, and greater transparency with regard to regulation of service industries. It specified that national treatment would be extended to U.S. and Canadian firms investing in each other's markets. The agreement greatly improved dispute settlement by establishing a process that took disputes out of the political arena so that there was a chance for cooling off and settlement on a more reasoned basis. It made disputes over the use of trade remedies such as antidumping penalties and countervailing duties subject to binding arbitration by binational panels. It required that any changes in trade remedy laws name the other country specifically and conform both to GATT rules and to the purposes of the agreement (Hart 1990, 15–32).

At the same time that a free trade agreement between the United States and Canada was being considered and negotiated, remarkable changes were occurring in Mexico. During the postwar period Mexico had followed an import substitution model of economic development that involved greatly restricted access to the Mexican market. While a few trade restrictions had been lifted during the José López Portillo administration in the 1970s, as recently as 1980 Mexico had considered and rejected membership in GATT. Mexico had long resisted GATT membership, believing that it might place limitations on the country's freedom to establish its industrial policy (Weintraub 1984, 84–91).

However, in the early 1980s a dramatic drop in the price of petroleum (which in 1980 accounted for 80 percent of Mexico's export earnings) had placed Mexico in dire financial straits. As export earnings plummeted, external debt mounted. Even before the fall in the price of petroleum, Mexico had been borrowing heavily abroad. Between 1970 and 1981, Mexico's current account deficit had increased from 3 percent to 5 percent of gross domestic product, and was financed by external borrowing based on optimistic projections of future oil revenues (Weintraub 1988, 9). In addition, nationalization of Mexico's banks by López Portillo shortly before he left office in 1982 had caused capital flight and a reduced inflow of foreign investment.

The combined effect of declining export earnings and reduced capital inflows meant that in 1982 Mexico could no longer meet its foreign debt obligations. The country was faced with two choices: it could either default on its foreign obligations, or accept the advice of international institutions to abandon the import substitution model and earn the foreign exchange to service its debt through more outward-oriented policies.

Mexico began a dramatic unilateral trade policy liberalization in 1985, and joined GATT in 1986. The authorities slashed import tariffs, reducing the maximum tariff rate to 20 percent, and the weighted average tariff rate to 11 percent. They also greatly reduced import-licensing requirements, abolished official import reference prices, and liberalized foreign investment regulations (USITC 1990, 2.2–2.3).

As part of this trade policy liberalization, Mexico signed a bilateral trade agreement with the United States, its largest trading partner, in 1985. While limited in scope, that agreement laid the groundwork for future events. The initial agreement was followed in 1987 by a framework of principles and procedures for consultation regarding trade and investment relations. This framework agreement eventually led to negotiations for reduced trade restrictions on steel, alcoholic beverages, and textiles. Consultations were held on matters such as investment regulations, intellectual property protection, and pending unfair trade cases against Mexico (ibid., 2.3–2.4).

When Mexican President Carlos Salinas de Gortari visited the United States in October 1989, he and President George Bush signed a new Understanding Regarding Trade and Investment Facilitation Talks agreement. This agreement contained an action plan mandating that the two countries would identify within a month certain topics as potential subjects for future bilateral negotiations. Petrochemicals and "standards, regulation, testing and certification" were chosen (ibid., 2.6). Talks held in March 1990 had the stated purpose of determining whether such negotiations actually would be held. Instead, the talks in March centered on prospects for a more comprehensive agreement.

In a 1989 *Business Week* interview, President Salinas had given little indication that Mexico was interested in a free trade agreement with the United States (Baker and Weiner 1989, 50–54). However, the leaders of Mexico clearly perceived that economic progress of the country would be greatly enhanced by inflows of foreign capital, including Mexican flight capital. Mexico had wooed Japan as a potential supplier of capital, but without much success. Mexico also had considered Western Europe a promising source of foreign investment. However, the collapse of the Soviet Union and changes in Eastern Europe diverted attention of European Union countries to the east. The Mexican administration is said to have concluded in early 1990 that a free trade agreement with the United States was the best way to send a signal to the world that Mexican economic reforms were genuine and irreversible (Orme 1993, 21–23). Such a signal was necessary for establishing a climate of stability and confidence essential for attracting foreign capital.

On 11 June 1990 President Bush and President Salinas committed their countries to negotiate a free trade agreement. Canada had little intrinsic interest in free trade with Mexico, since the U.S.–Canada free trade agreement had been unpopular with much of the Canadian public, and because Canada's trade with Mexico was minuscule in any case. Also, Canada had apprehensions that some of the hard-won concessions gained in the previous agreement with the United States could possibly be eroded in new negotiations. However, Canada faced a dilemma. If the United States negotiated a free trade agreement with Mexico, while already having one with Canada, that would have developed a "hub and spoke" system with the United States at the center. Firms would have had an incentive to locate in the United States rather than in Canada in order to have unrestricted access to the entire North American market.

Consequently, on 5 February 1991 Canada agreed to enter into formal negotiations with the United States and Mexico to establish a North American Free Trade Agreement. Mexico was not overjoyed at the prospect of Canada's joining the negotiations, thinking that would complicate the negotiations, but acceded to the wishes of the other two countries on the issue.

Mexico's reasons for wanting free trade with the United States, in addition to the hope of attracting foreign capital, mirrored those of Canada in many respects. While Mexico was not quite as dependent on the U.S. market as Canada, still about two-thirds of Mexico's foreign trade was conducted with the United States. Therefore, success for Mexico's recently more outward-oriented industrialization strategy required continued access to the U.S. market.

Taking into account trade preferences received, Mexico faced relatively low trade barriers in the U.S. market even before the trade agreement. However, Mexico realized that strong dependence on the U.S. market made the country vulnerable to changes in U.S. trade policy. For example, in 1987 a dispute between the United States and Mexico over intellectual property issues caused the number of products eligible for entry to the United States under the Generalized System of Preferences to be reduced. Mexico realized, as well, that as the country's stronger export orientation caused greater penetration into the U.S. market, the risk of trade barriers being imposed would rise. Mexico also had some apprehension about trade diversion to Canada as a result of the U.S.–Canada free trade agreement since about 20 percent of Mexico's exports were directly competitive with Canadian products in the U.S. market (McKinney 1990).

The U.S. government responded favorably to Mexico's request for a free trade agreement for reasons already mentioned, but also because of the presumption that a free trade agreement would in some sense "lock in" the economic reforms that had taken place in Mexico. Having the reforms permanently in place not only would improve the prospects for greater prosperity in Mexico, but also would provide a stable environment more suitable for investment in Mexico. The greater cooperation with Mexico also had the potential for improving a political relationship that had in the past too often been characterized by rancor and mistrust.

On 12 June 1991, almost exactly one year after President Bush and President Salinas had agreed to free trade negotiations, the negotiations began in Toronto. For the most part the NAFTA agreement was patterned after the U.S.–Canada free trade agreement, incorporating Mexico into its provisions. Mexico, however, did insert a large number of reservations and exceptions into the agreement that slowed its liberalization of both trade and investment. That is not too surprising given the differences in economic development between Mexico on one hand, and Canada and the United States on the other.

The NAFTA agreement broke new ground in a number of areas, and in that way had a positive demonstration effect for the concurrent multilateral negotiations in the Uruguay Round. Protections accorded intellectual property by the agreement set a new international standard. The investment provisions placed limitations on the use of trade-related investment measures such as local content regulations and export performance requirements, and generally extended national treatment to investments from partner countries. The agreement also substantially liberalized trade in services, including telecommunications, financial, and transportation services. Surprising progress was made toward liberalizing agricultural trade, a sector that is always problematic for trade negotiators. On the other hand, the NAFTA agreement contained trade-distortive rule of origin requirements, particularly in the case of automobiles, textiles, and clothing.

Since the NAFTA agreement was patterned after the U.S.–Canada free trade agreement, negotiations proceeded rather quickly. The historic agreement was signed on 17 December 1992, less than a year and a half after the negotiations began. However, that was by no means the end of the story.

During the 1992 presidential campaign, Bill Clinton had expressed some reservations about the NAFTA accord. While he eventually promised not to reopen negotiations on the basic agreement if elected, he did promise to negotiate supplementary accords to deal with environmental and labor concerns, and to put in place safeguard measures to deal with import surges.

Environmental issues had been slowly making their way onto the international trade agenda quite apart from NAFTA. A working group on trade and environment had been established in GATT in 1971, but did not meet for several years. In 1979 the GATT agreement on technical barriers to trade formally gave countries the right to depart from international trade rules in order to prevent degradation of the environment. Nevertheless, under the terms of the GATT agreement, countries were not to discriminate against products from other countries based upon how the products from those countries were produced, if the products themselves did not harm the importing country's environment. In a highly controversial case, a GATT dispute settlement panel ruled that the United States could not apply trade restrictions on tuna caught using drift nets that in the process killed dolphins (GATT 1994). The fact that Mexico had brought this case to the GATT raised questions among environmental groups about Mexico's sensitivity to environmental issues.

Not all environmental groups opposed NAFTA. Mexico had passed its first comprehensive environmental legislation in 1988, and its environmental regulations were generally not deficient. Major problems existed, however, in the areas of inspection, monitoring, and enforcement of regulations. Since these problems were commonly acknowledged to result largely from a lack of resources, some environmental groups concluded that the increased prosperity that a free trade agreement might bring could have positive effects on Mexico's environment. On the whole, however, environmentalists were apprehensive about entering into a free trade agreement with Mexico.

As concerns about NAFTA's effects on the environment became apparent, the Bush administration had taken several steps while the agreement was being negotiated to try to address these concerns. Some provisions of the NAFTA agreement were designed to provide assurances that it would not degrade the environment. Member countries retained the right to apply any sanitary and phytosanitary measures they deem necessary, so long as these standards have a scientific basis and are applied nondiscriminatorily. In situations where the terms of an international environmental agreement conflict with the provisions of NAFTA, the international agreement takes precedence. NAFTA countries are encouraged to harmonize upward their health, safety, and pollution control regulations. Furthermore, in order to prevent "pollution havens" from developing, the member countries committed themselves not to lower their environmental or other standards in order to attract investment.

Several parallel measures were introduced to address environmental concerns. In February 1992 an integrated environmental plan for the U.S.–Mexico border areas was announced. This plan built upon the 1983 Border Environment Agreement (La Paz Agreement) to focus specifically upon the environmental problems along the U.S.–Mexico border. The 1992 border plan established a twenty-four–member border environmental advisory committee composed of representatives of different areas along the border. Also, in September 1992 the trade ministers of North America formed a North American commission of the environment to advise on regional environmental issues. Neither this institution nor the border plan was formally linked to NAFTA, however (USGAO 1993, 113–18).

If environmental issues were a controversial aspect of NAFTA, labor issues were more so. Labor's concerns about the agreement had their source in the fact that Mexico was at a very different level of economic development than either the United States or Canada. Wage rates in Mexico were only about one-seventh of their level in the United States. In addition, organized labor had concerns about labor rights and working conditions in Mexico. Labor feared that lower wage rates and labor standards in Mexico would give Mexican firms an unfair cost advantage, causing displacement of workers in American industry through competition from products produced in Mexico. Concerns also existed that with trade barriers removed companies would flee to Mexico, or at least that their threats to do so would weaken labor's bargaining position.

The Bush administration proposed to address these concerns indirectly through the terms of the NAFTA agreement. Safeguard measures in the agreement would temporarily restore tariff protection in the case that import surges adversely affected employment in an industry. Stringent rules of origin for certain industries would assure that foreign firms did not use Mexico as an export platform for the U.S. market. Finally, trade restrictions would be phased out gradually, taking up to fifteen years for certain sensitive industries. This gradual phase-out of trade barriers would minimize the displacement of labor by allowing time for trade-affected industries to adjust to the competition from partner country producers, and by allowing for reduction of employment in affected industries through normal turnover and attrition as opposed to layoffs.

As in the case of the environment, the United States and Mexican governments engaged in certain parallel measures dealing with labor even as the NAFTA agreement was being negotiated. In 1991 the United States negotiated a memorandum of understanding with Mexico (as did Canada in 1992). This agreement between the U.S. Department of Labor and the Mexican Secretariat of Labor and Social Welfare called for cooperation on a wide range of labor issues. Included among these were resolution of labor conflicts, health and safety regulations of concern to labor, working conditions, labor standards and enforcement, and the collection of labor statistics. Under terms of the 1991 memorandum of understanding the United States assisted Mexico in a number of ways. For example, the U.S. Department of Labor's Bureau of Labor Statistics advised Mexican officials on methods of data collection and analysis. Also, the Occupational Safety and Health Administration (OSHA) provided technical assistance and training to Mexican counterparts on workplace health and safety issues (ibid., 118–123).

In September 1992 the United States and Mexico signed a new memorandum of understanding that extended the original agreement and established a new consultative commission on labor matters. This consultative commission was intended to be a permanent institution to address labor issues of mutual concern to the United States and Mexico. The memorandum also provided for discussions on the subject of possibly harmonizing workplace safety regulations (ibid.).

None of these measures made any headway toward garnering the support of organized labor for the NAFTA agreement. The initiatives were perceived, perhaps accurately, as a ploy to soften labor's opposition to the NAFTA agreement. They were not perceived as having a lasting impact on the issues that worried labor most concerning the free trade agreement. These issues were that increased trade might lower wages and employment in the United States, and that firms might move production plants to Mexico to take advantage of lower wages there.

Realizing the deep-seated concerns of both environmental and labor groups with regard to the NAFTA agreement, Bill Clinton was careful during the 1992 presidential campaign not to give his unqualified endorsement to the agreement. In a speech at North Carolina State University Clinton promised, if elected, to negotiate supplementary agreements dealing with environmental issues, labor issues, and safeguard measures. With strong support from both labor and environmental groups Clinton was elected. Negotiations on the side agreements began in March 1993, shortly after Clinton was inaugurated, and culminated with trinational agreements signed in August 1993.

The supplemental agreements provided for the establishment of a North American commission on environmental cooperation and a North American commission on labor cooperation. They formalized procedures for consultation and cooperation among the countries of North America on environmental and labor issues. Further, they established mechanisms for dispute settlement on environmental and labor issues, and provided for the possibility of trade sanctions to be imposed on member countries found not to be enforcing their own environmental or labor laws (as described more fully in Chapters 4 and 5 of this book). While these agreements did not satisfy labor and environmental groups in the United States, they provided enough political cover for the members of Congress to get the NAFTA agreement approved. NAFTA went into effect on 1 January 1994.

2

NAFTA-Related Institutions in the Context of Theory

The North American Free Trade Agreement (NAFTA), by removing trade restrictions and reducing other impediments to economic integration, increases the economic interdependence among the countries of North America. As economic interrelationships among the countries become more intense, and particularly as they move beyond border restrictions to deal with matters of domestic regulation, an increasing number of issues arise that require resolution in one way or another. A number of new North American institutions have been put in place to deal with this increased level of interaction and to help the countries of North America to attain their common interests.

Several different theories have been developed to explain the existence of, and the functioning of, international institutions. One school of thought sees such institutions as growing naturally out of the demands of increased economic interdependence. The fact that countries are interacting more frequently with each other creates a demand for simplifying procedures as manifested in rules, procedures, and dispute settlement mechanisms. According to this view of international institutions, the greater the degree of economic interdependence, the greater will be the need for, and the demand for, institutions to facilitate cooperation (Keohane 1983). The institutions can be particularly important to the weaker states in the relationship by providing them with "voice opportunities" to make their views known and to give these views some effect (Grieco 1994).

Within North America, the level of economic interdependence has steadily increased. Geographical proximity provides powerful incentives for regional expansion of international trade and investment. Despite the apprehensions of Canada concerning excessive dependence on the U.S. market, and despite attempts during the Pierre Trudeau administration to pursue a "third option" of export diversification, by the mid-1980s Canada depended on the United States for about three-fourths of its international trade. Mexico, because of its trade barriers resulting from import-substituting industrialization policies, was not quite so dependent on the United States. Even for Mexico, however, the U.S. market accounted for about two-thirds of its external trade. As for the United States, Canada was by far its largest trading partner, and Mexico its third largest. Clearly, to the extent that economic interdependence creates a demand for international institutions, North America was fertile ground for their development.

The neorealist school of political thought has viewed relations among states as anarchic in the sense that the participants are self-interested sovereign states with no international authority to impose agreements or to enforce cooperation (Waltz 1979). According to this theory, cooperation is likely only if a hegemon exists that has sufficient prestige, and is willing to devote sufficient resources, to provide the necessary leadership. Countries may find themselves in prisoners' dilemma situations, where if they all cooperated there would be substantial gains for all, but if not all cooperate those that defect reap the gains while others lose.

Alternatively, in the case of negative externalities such as environmental pollution, while all states could benefit from policies that would reduce the externalities, it may be in the interest of any individual country to "free ride" at the expense of other countries. The negative externalities could be decisions of a country that have unfavorable effects on other countries. In the absence of an international legal authority to impose a solution in such cases, hegemony by a powerful state that is willing and able to provide leadership is one possible way to correct the externalities and thereby prevent a suboptimal situation (Kindleberger 1981). The development of international institutions is another possible solution.

While it cannot be denied that by virtue of its sheer economic size and power the United States acts in some respects as hegemon within North America, in many ways it does not. Both Canada and Mexico have jealously guarded their national sovereignty. Although the United States has possessed the power to infringe upon the national sovereignty of its neighbors, seldom has it demonstrated the desire to do so. Consequently, both Canada and Mexico have exercised considerable policy independence. That being the case, a need has existed, particularly in areas such as the externalities of environmental pollution, for institutions that would facilitate cooperation and help the countries reach agreement on important issues. While multilateral institutions have served this function to some degree, certain issues having particular relevance to the North American region, such as air quality or the preservation of biodiversity, call for regional institutions to address them.

In recent years, the theory of international organizations has drawn insights from economic theory and game theory to explain the formation and activities of international organizations in the absence of hegemony. The new theories explain how nation states can find it in their own interest, for a variety of reasons, to form and participate in international organizations.

Because nation states are sovereign, they potentially can disregard property rights or deny legal liability. International institutions cannot be expected to prevent this by exercising legal authority over their members since the institutions typically possess no such authority. Nevertheless, the existence of institutions can greatly increase the likelihood of cooperation among states by establishing working relationships among them, so that they have a clearer idea of what to expect from each other, and so that they can adapt more easily to new situations (Keohane 1984, 89).

The institutions created by NAFTA certainly have the potential for making a major contribution in this regard. Before the NAFTA agreement, no trilateral institutions existed in North America, and the level of trilateral cooperation was low. Because of the institutions created in North America as a result of NAFTA, which are discussed at some length in later chapters of this book, an extensive network of working relationships is being established relating to a wide variety of issues. Many of the institutions created focus on trade facilitation, but others deal with environmental and labor concerns. As a result of these institutions, the countries of North America should develop much better information about matters of concern to their continental partners, formulate a much better idea of what to expect of each other, and therefore maintain a higher level of mutual trust. This trust likely will develop through the iterative process of negotiations and the long time horizon that the process inculcates (Axelrod 1983).

Furthermore, international organizations alter transactions costs in international relations in several ways. The existence of secretariats can lower the cost of governments getting together to negotiate agreements, and can act as a catalyst for agreements. Governments can, by the nature of the institution established, agree ahead of time on what types of bargains are forbidden and what types are desirable, without having to render that decision each time a new issue arises. In this way, the existence of institutions increases transactions costs for undesirable agreements, since mechanisms for challenging these agreements will be in place. It also reduces transactions costs for desirable agreements since the member states will have agreed ahead of time on certain parameters for desirable agreements (ibid., 90). The end result is a lower probability that the principles that the institutions were founded to uphold will be violated.

Within the framework of the NAFTA agreement, specific provisions have been established for settling disputes over interpretations of the agreement, or to deal with failure to live up to the terms of the agreement. Policymakers know ahead of time which actions are likely to be challenged and which are not. Therefore, because of the existence of the institutions, with their various dispute settlement provisions, member countries are more likely to adhere to the underlying principles of the free trade agreement.

In addition, international institutions make possible economies of scale in decision making. Once an institution has been formed to deal with certain types of issues, the cost of each additional issue decreases because the mechanisms for dealing with such issues have already been established. Furthermore, experience gained in dealing with earlier issues enable later ones to be dealt with more efficiently.

International institutions also provide potential economies of scope. When an institution deals with different types of issues, the possibility exists for trade-offs among issues, and side-payments among members, which make possible agreements that would be unattainable in the absence of the institution (ibid., 91). For example, agreement in international trade negotiations is often more easily obtained in a comprehensive round of trade talks than in sectoral negotiations because countries can make concessions to trading partners in one sector in order to gain concessions in a different sector. Linkages among issues within an institutional context reduce the costs of reaching agreements on different types of issues, and raise the costs of failing to live up to the terms of an agreement because failure to do so affects several other issues as well.

The NAFTA-related institutions provide both economies of scale and

economies of scope in decision making among the North American countries. Each of the institutions deals with a variety of somewhat different,
though related, issues. Experience in dealing with certain issues lowers
the cost of dealing with related issues as they arise. The linkage of issues within an institutional context also fosters agreement. For example,
agreement among the NAFTA countries to accelerate tariff phaseout on
a wide variety of products was made possible by the fact that the Free
Trade Commission could consider the situation in many sectors simultaneously. In doing so, it could find the concessions in certain sectors in
one country that opened the door for concessions in other sectors by the
partner countries.

Another function of institutions that may facilitate cooperation is the
provision of reliable information. When the parties to a potential agreement do not have access to the same information and do not completely
trust each other, reaching an agreement will be difficult. Also, agreement is unlikely when the parties are uncertain about whether the other
country will be able, or willing, to follow through on commitments made
(ibid., 92–96).

A major function of the NAFTA-related institutions is the provision
of reliable information. Both the Commission for Labor Cooperation
(CLC) and the Commission for Environmental Cooperation (CEC) consider one of their major functions to be the provision of accurate information on labor markets and environmental conditions in North America.
Also, both the North American Agreement on Labor Cooperation
(NAALC) and the North American Agreement on Environmental Cooperation (NAAEC) contain provisions for assuring that the member
countries do, in fact, enforce their own environmental and labor legislation. These provisions were motivated by a perception that, while
Mexico's environmental and labor laws were commendable, these laws
were not always enforced adequately by Mexican authorities.

The establishment of institutional rules narrows the range of expected
behavior, thereby reducing uncertainty, which is so important to a favorable business climate. Monitoring of compliance with an agreement
reduces the chances that a country will not follow through on its terms.
Knowledge that there will be compliance monitoring reduces the chances
that a country will enter into an agreement on which it cannot follow
through, and makes other countries more comfortable about entering
into an agreement with it. An institution that has a research staff with
effective oversight can make information available from an unbiased

source, so that the parties can act on it without questioning its veracity (ibid., 92–102).

In the case of NAFTA, an agreement would not have been possible without provisions for compliance monitoring. Assurances that Mexico would be held accountable for enforcement of its labor and environmental laws was crucial to obtaining the necessary political support in the United States for the agreement's approval. Assurance that administrative agencies in the United States could be challenged on whether they were accurately and fairly applying trade remedy laws was essential for Canada's approval of the agreement.

The personal relationships established between the officials and staff members involved in international institutions also increase the levels of communication and trust, and decrease the likelihood of deception. Furthermore, institutions can bring together networks of experts (epistemic communities) who are recognized authorities on particular policy issues. These respected experts can help to define the mutual interests of the member states, can suggest solutions to policy conflicts, and can help to set the agenda for negotiations. In fact, participation in the epistemic communities may create mutual interests among the members so that they come to divide their loyalties between the group and the states from which they come. In this way cooperation is enhanced, particularly when the issues are highly technical in nature (Haas 1992, 2–3).

Both the CEC and the CLC are assisted by national advisory committees and governmental advisory committees comprised of experts on the issues with which they deal. In addition, the CEC is assisted by a joint public advisory committee, and on highly technical environmental issues makes frequent use of scientists who are experts on the particular matters at issue. Without this input, the level of cooperation among the countries of North America on sensitive labor and environmental issues would be diminished.

International institutions can also reduce transactions costs among states through their signaling function. The establishment of an institution to focus on a particular issue, or set of issues, can send a signal to other states that the member states are genuinely committed to a particular course of action. The establishment of the institution, with its rules and norms, can to some extent "lock in" a policy direction, thereby reducing uncertainty about what future policies will be. The increased path dependence reduces future bargaining costs and facilitates cooperation (Martin and Simmons 1998, 746).

Certainly the signaling function of NAFTA, with its associated institutions, was one of the main benefits of the agreement for Mexico. As explained in Chapter 1, Mexico keenly appreciated the need to attract foreign capital to help fund its economic transition and to make its economy more efficient. Mexico had engaged in unilateral trade liberalization and significant economic reforms during the 1980s. However, most of these changes had been implemented by the country's powerful president, and could potentially have been reversed by a succeeding president. The request for a free trade agreement with the United States was perceived by international capital market participants as a means of "locking in" the recent policy direction. By reducing uncertainty about what future policies would be, Mexico succeeded in becoming a more attractive location for foreign capital investment. In addition, future bargaining costs between Mexico and the other countries of North America were reduced, and the level of cooperation among them enhanced.

Sometimes, even when all states recognize that cooperation would be mutually beneficial, cooperation may be forestalled by concerns of countries that they may not get their "fair share" of the benefits.* Institutions can play a positive role in this situation as well. A secretariat that operates with a reasonable degree of independence, and with procedures that are transparent enough to instill confidence, can report on the actions of the member states. The distribution of benefits from an agreement can be estimated and made public. In this way suspicions can be allayed, and if adjustments in an agreement are needed to attain a more equitable distribution of the benefits of cooperation, an objective basis for such adjustments is at hand (ibid., 745).

As will be seen in later chapters, whether the labor secretariat and the environmental secretariat have yet been able to perform this function to a significant degree in North America is open to question, but at least

---

*Joseph M. Grieco (1995) points out that less powerful states within a region are more likely to participate in regional institutions when there is perceived relative stability in their capabilities relative to the other partners. When that is the case, they perceive less threat to their status and more likelihood that their relative gains will be at least as great as those of their partners. In the case of North America, at the time that Mexico agreed to participate in the NAFTA-related institutions its economy was responding favorably to previously instituted reforms, and there existed a high level of confidence in the stability in the country's relative capabilities.

the potential is there for doing so. While the institutions of NAFTA are very young and their potential is far from being realized, their existence even now probably does help to allay fears among the member countries concerning the distribution of benefits (or distribution of costs, as the case may be). For example, the Commission on Environmental Cooperation (CEC) recently issued a document in which, after studying the pattern of specialization resulting from NAFTA, it provided assurances that no evidence existed to suggest that Mexico was becoming a "pollution haven" for North American industries. Indeed, it found the reverse, that heavily polluting industries are shrinking in Mexico and lesser-polluting industries expanding. Studies such as this, to the extent that they are perceived as being from impartial sources, can help to allay fears about possible adverse effects of economic integration.

International institutions can sometimes help with the attainment of objectives that would be difficult or impossible to attain because of domestic political considerations. In the area of trade policy, producer interests that wish to avoid the costs of trade liberalization are often much better focused and organized than are consumer interests where the benefits are diffused over the population at large. Transfer of the issue to an international organization may cause consumers and exporters to be more aware of their interests in the trade liberalization, and therefore can potentially result in a more balanced political process (ibid., 748).

Likewise, the costs of trade liberalization often are incurred within a relatively short period of time, whereas the benefits accrue indefinitely into the future. Politicians thinking of reelection may have a difficult time taking the longer view even if they realize that long-term benefits greatly outweigh the costs. The same dilemma can arise in areas such as pollution control. These problems of time-inconsistency provide an incentive for politicians to shift consideration of such issues to the level of an international institution to deflect some of the political heat (ibid.).

Certainly in the North American case, the existence of the NAFTA institutions helps to overcome the time-inconsistency problem. Instances of trade liberalization that involved significant short-term costs and would have been impossible in isolation were approved as part of the overall NAFTA package. Protectionist measures such as abuse of antidumping and countervailing duty provisions have been reduced because of the oversight of administrative agencies by dispute settlement panels. In many areas the existence of institutionalized dispute settlement procedures provides the opportunity to take issues out of the political setting and have them dealt with on a more objective basis.

One can conceive of other instances in which international institutions might possibly compensate for shortcomings of the domestic political system. Where domestic political institutions are not well developed, or where their functioning is impaired by problems of corruption, societal preferences may not find accurate expression through the domestic political system. A transferring of responsibilities to an international institution, where transparency exists and where other member countries can influence decisions, may compensate to some extent for domestic political deficiencies. This line of reasoning presupposes that agreements reached at the international institutional level will be effectively implemented by all of the member countries, an assumption that may not always be warranted. For that reason, enforcement mechanisms and provisions for monitoring compliance are necessary.

One final strand of the theory of international institutions that may well have relevance to the North American case is constructivism. In contrast to most of the other theories, this theory starts with states viewing each other neutrally rather than adversarily. This theory posits that systemic interaction may in itself transform the interests of states. Through the interaction states realize their mutual interests, and this leads them to cooperate in pursuit of common goals (Wendt 1994).

Real potential exists for interaction within the NAFTA-related institutions to transform the interests of the member states. Particularly in the area of environmental policies, as more complete information is gathered on the ecological effects to the region of certain pollutants, or of threats to biodiversity, the commonality of interests among the member states should become more apparent and their level of cooperation increase.

In conclusion, we can say that several different strands of the theory of international institutions help to provide a rationale for the NAFTA-related institutions. Certainly the increasing interdependence of the NAFTA countries has created some demand for regional rules, procedures, and dispute settlement mechanisms. Lack of complete trust among the member countries makes the rules and enhanced information provided by institutions all the more important as ways to reduce uncertainty and to raise the comfort level of the member states, particularly given the size disparities of North American countries. Interaction within the institutions has the potential for convincing states of their mutuality of interests, thereby enhancing cooperation. The secretariats of the institutions can act as catalysts for, and reduce the costs of, negotiations toward regional agreements. Furthermore, the existence of the NAFTA-related institutions has enabled Mexico to signal financial markets that its economic reforms are permanent, and the United States and Canada to signal concerned publics that labor and environmental concerns will be given due consideration. In the chapters that follow, the activities of the NAFTA-related institutions to date are summarized, and their effectiveness is assessed.

3

The Free Trade Commission

The governing body of NAFTA, the Free Trade Commission, shall "supervise the implementation of the agreement" and "oversee its further elaboration" (NAFTA 1992, 20–1). The commission also is charged with helping to resolve disputes arising from the application of NAFTA, and for overseeing the activities of the various committees, working groups, and other subsidiary bodies created by the agreement.

The NAFTA agreement specifies that the Free Trade Commission will comprise cabinet-level officials of the three countries or their designees. Not surprisingly, the trade ministers of the three countries have been designated for this role: Canada's minister of foreign trade, the U.S. trade representative, and Mexico's secretary of trade and industrial development.

The Free Trade Commission is assisted in its duties by the NAFTA secretariat, which is composed of Canadian, U.S., and Mexican sections that are located in their respective capital cities. While it assists the commission in a variety of ways, the NAFTA secretariat has particular responsibilities with regard to dispute resolution processes, as discussed later in this chapter.

Free Trade Commission Meetings

The Free Trade Commission is supposed to meet at least once a year, and has done so in every year except 1996. The chairing of the meetings rotates among the member nations. Generally, the location of the meetings is in the country of the chairperson for that year, although on occasion the meetings have been held in conjunction with international meetings outside of North America.

The commission held its inaugural meeting in Mexico City on 14

January 1994, just two weeks after the NAFTA agreement took effect. At that meeting, the commission added two working groups (on investment and services, and government procurement) to the eight committees and six working groups that had already been designated in the agreement. It also staffed various leadership positions and discussed dispute settlement procedures (CEC 1997b, 21).

At its first meeting the Free Trade Commission also agreed in principle to establish a NAFTA coordinating secretariat to serve as a clearinghouse and repository of NAFTA documents and to assist on technical matters. The NAFTA coordinating secretariat is to be in addition to the national sections of the NAFTA secretariat located in each of the individual countries. The NAFTA secretariat currently consists of national sections in each of the member countries. The proposed NAFTA coordinating secretariat would be a trinational institution that would help to coordinate the activities of the national sections and would serve as repository for NAFTA documents. Plans were made to locate this organization in Naucalpan, a suburb of Mexico City, so that Mexico would host one of NAFTA's trinational institutions. The secretariat of the Commission for Environmental Cooperation is located in Montreal, and the secretariat of the Commission for Labor Cooperation in Dallas, Texas (although it has recently announced plans to move to Washington, D.C.). Therefore, Mexico was due to receive the coordinating secretariat, with an American as executive director. However, because of funding problems, first in the United States and then in Mexico, as of mid-1999 the NAFTA coordinating secretariat had yet to materialize.

In addition to its official meeting in 1994, the Free Trade Commission also met unofficially twice during that year. The first of these meetings took place in March in Marrakesh, Morocco, in connection with the final session of the Uruguay round of multilateral trade negotiations. The second unofficial meeting was held in connection with the Asia Pacific Economic Cooperation (APEC) meeting in Bogor, Indonesia, in September 1994 (ibid., 22).

The Free Trade Commission held its second official meeting in Toronto on 7 June 1995. At that meeting the trade ministers reached agreement to accelerate tariff reduction on certain products beyond what had been agreed in the NAFTA agreement. In addition, the commission requested that each of its subordinate bodies submit work plans by the next year (ibid.).

The commission did not meet at all during 1996, partly because of the distraction caused by the presidential election in the United States. It held its next official meeting on 20 March 1997 in Washington, D.C. At that meeting it concluded the first round of talks on accelerated tariff reduction, and initiated a second round of these negotiations. It also acted upon recommendations from the advisory committee on private commercial disputes and from the working group on rules of origin. Further, it received reports from more than twenty trilateral committees and working groups dealing with a wide range of issues relating to the implementation of the NAFTA agreement (USTR 1997, 2).

The Free Trade Commission held its 1998 meeting in Paris on 29 April. At that meeting the trade ministers approved another package of accelerated tariff elimination, which they estimated would benefit about U.S. $1 billion of NAFTA trade. They noted, as well, that the negotiations carried out in agreeing on this package had affected the process of communication and consultation among the business communities of the North American countries positively. They took note of the work being done by the subsidiary bodies of NAFTA, and instructed the officials responsible for their activities to conduct an operational review of the work program before the end of the year "on the structure, mandates and priorities of these bodies" (USTR 1998,1).

At its 1999 meeting, which was held in Ottawa, Canada, on 23 April, the Free Trade Commission reviewed the results of the operational review of the NAFTA work program (discussed further below) and expressed satisfaction with the oversight structure that had been put in place. At that meeting the trade ministers received a report from the committee on trade in goods summarizing trade facilitation measures, and directed that further possible improvements in that area be identified. They also established a NAFTA working group on agricultural grading and marketing to supersede existing bilateral working groups in these areas, and established a working group on tariff rate quota administration. Finally, the trade ministers noted the fact that the committee on sanitary and phytosanitary measures had established new technical working groups in eight areas: animal health; plant health; dairy, fruits, vegetables, and processed foods; meat, poultry, and egg inspection; pesticides; food additives and contaminants; fish and fishery products; and veterinary drugs and feeds (USDOC 1999, 1–2).

In addition to their annual meetings, the Free Trade Commission has established other mechanisms for fostering communication and for overseeing the work program of the various NAFTA committees and working groups. At their meeting on 29 April 1998, the Free Trade Commission members directed their deputy ministers to meet regularly twice a year, "to provide high-level, ongoing oversight of the NAFTA work program" (USTR 1998, 1). Furthermore, NAFTA coordinators (chosen from within each of the respective trade ministries) have been designated by the member countries to facilitate the work program. These NAFTA coordinators confer monthly by telephone to discuss the progress of the various committees and working groups and to help keep their work organized (CEC 1997b, 23).

Operational Review of NAFTA Work Program

At its April 1998 meeting, the Free Trade Commission ordered a comprehensive review of the "mandates, achievements, pending implementation issues and recommended future priorities" of the NAFTA committees and working groups. In this operational review the commission received information about each the of the NAFTA subsidiary bodies. The review included an assessment of five committees, four subcommittees, two advisory committees, fifteen working groups, and one subgroup. The review was conducted during the summer and fall of 1998 and was approved in September 1998 by the NAFTA deputy ministers of trade. They in turn forwarded it to the NAFTA trade ministers for their review (CDFAIT 1998).

From this report it is apparent that some of the subsidiary bodies have been more active than others. Some that were considered important at the time they were formed have turned out not to be so. For example, the committee on trade in worn clothing, that was formed to assess the potential benefits and risks arising from elimination of trade restrictions on used clothing, has done nothing more than exchange statistics on trade in used clothing. The committee has no plans for future activities. The working group on emergency action, which was formed to alleviate concerns about import surges resulting from NAFTA, has been totally inactive. While supposedly required to meet at least once a year, it has never met and has no plans to do so (ibid., 1–27).

By way of contrast, the committee on standards-related matters, which deals with the issue of technical barriers to trade, has met an average of three times a year. This committee monitors the activities of four subcommittees dealing with matters such as land transportation and telecommunications standards. The committee on sanitary and phytosanitary measures has also met frequently, and oversees the activities of several working groups that focus on specific issues such as plant health, animal health, inspection of foods, and labeling of foods (ibid.).

A major benefit of having the various NAFTA committees, subcommittees, and working groups in place is that they can address potential problems at low levels as they arise. If issues rise to the level where they become politicized, dealing with them becomes much more problematic. Members of these subsidiary bodies typically are persons with considerable expertise in the issues at hand, who therefore can help to find solutions that might escape those less knowledgeable. In addition, the personal relationships established within the trinational institutions foster cooperation and facilitate the development of solutions to problems that must be addressed.

General Dispute Settlement Provisions

While the existence of the subsidiary bodies of the Free Trade Commission certainly contributes to dispute avoidance, as disagreements are often referred to them for analysis and suggestion, some disputes cannot be avoided and therefore must be resolved. A major function of the commission is to resolve disputes that arise concerning NAFTA's interpretation or application. As mentioned earlier, the commission is assisted in this task by the NAFTA secretariat.

Chapter 20 of NAFTA sets forth provisions dealing with settlement of disputes that arise from interpretation or application of the agreement, except for those relating to investment, financial services, or trade remedies that are all covered elsewhere in the agreement. Dispute settlement procedures regarding investment issues (covered in Chapter 11 of NAFTA) and those dealing with antidumping and countervailing duty cases (covered in Chapter 19 of NAFTA) are discussed in Chapter 8 of this book. Dispute settlement concerning financial issues (covered in Chapter 14 of NAFTA) is similar to Chapter 20 described below, except that the dispute resolution panel is selected from a roster of panelists having particular expertise in financial matters. As of mid-1999, no NAFTA dispute settlement cases dealing specifically with financial issues had arisen.

Under the terms of NAFTA's Chapter 20, private parties do not have direct access to the dispute settlement process. Instead, the government of the aggrieved party must deliver a written request to its own section of the NAFTA secretariat. The dispute settlement process then has three steps. First, the aggrieved party requests formal consultations with the offending party. Sometimes the dispute is settled at that stage. If the dispute is not settled through consultation within thirty days from the time of the request, then either party may request a meeting of the commission.

The Free Trade Commission is to meet within ten days to consider the matter. It can draw upon the advice of experts, and can make recommendations to the parties for the resolution of the dispute. If the dispute is not resolved within thirty days of the time that the commission has convened, either party can request the appointment of an arbitral panel. The panel consists of five persons selected by the disputing parties from a roster of thirty arbitrators who are well-versed in trade policy and trade law. The parties first agree on a chairperson for the panel, and then each country selects from the roster two panelists who are citizens of the other disputing party.

The arbitration panel makes an initial report on the case within ninety days, and after receiving written comments on that report, the panel makes a final report within thirty days of the initial report. The arbitrators' final report is delivered to the disputing parties, who then transmit it to the Free Trade Commission. Strictly speaking, the arbitrators' report is a recommendation to the commission rather than a formal decision. Unless it decides otherwise, the commission makes the report public within fifteen days of its receipt. The parties are then expected to resolve the dispute along the lines recommended by the arbitration panel. Should the offending party refuse to comply, the complaining party is authorized to suspend NAFTA benefits to the offending party roughly equivalent to the harm suffered from the violation of the agreement. An unusual provision of this procedure is that the benefits suspended are to be in the same trade sector (or sectors) originally affected by the dispute.

General dispute resolution cases dealt with under the terms of Chapter 20 of NAFTA have seldom proceeded as far as panel arbitration. A few have been settled through consultations. Most have proceeded to the stage of being considered by the Free Trade Commission. Often they have not been resolved at that stage either. For whatever reasons, the parties have generally decided against taking the matter to panel arbitration. In some cases, such as the complaint against the United States by both Canada and Mexico concerning the Helms-Burton Law's provisions concerning investment in Cuba, political sensitivities have prevented further pursuit of the case. In other cases, the matters continue to be discussed periodically at the ministerial level, but without satisfactory resolution.

As of mid-1999, only two Chapter 20 cases had been taken to arbitral panels, and two more were active. Of those that have been decided, the first involved a U.S. challenge of Canada's imposition of import tariffs on dairy, poultry, and egg products. The arbitration panel ruled unanimously that the NAFTA member countries had intended to exempt these products from the tariff elimination provisions of NAFTA, and, therefore, the tariffs did not violate the terms of the agreement (Lopez 1997, 173).

The other Chapter 20 case decided by an arbitral panel was one that Mexico brought against the United States for imposing tariffs on broomcorn brooms. When consultations failed to resolve this issue, Mexico retaliated with tariffs against U.S. exports, and requested panel arbitration. The panel ruled that the United States had, through imposing the trade restriction, violated the terms of NAFTA, and the panel recommended removal of the tariffs. After having the U.S. International Trade Commission study the actions taken by the broomcorn broom industry to become more efficient, President Clinton removed the tariffs in December 1998, two years after they had been imposed and almost a year after the NAFTA arbitral panel decision (Lucentini 1998, 3A).

The two other requested Chapter 20 arbitral panel proceedings have both been initiated by Mexico to review U.S. measures. Both of these relate to transportation issues, one pertaining to cross-border trucking services and investment, and the other to cross-border bus services. They are the result of the United States's refusal to follow through on what had been agreed in NAFTA with regard to allowing Mexican trucks and buses to operate in U.S. border states. Safety concerns have been given as the reason for failure to abide by the terms of the agreement, although the influence of transportation unions on both sides of the border has also been a factor.

When one considers the breadth of trade relations among the three countries of North America, it is remarkable that during the first five and a half years of the agreement only four arbitral panels have been requested for cases dealing with alleged violation of the agreement's terms. Obviously, most of the disputes are being handled through consultation and are being defused before they become so politically charged that they require adjudication.

Separate provisions are set forth in Chapter 19 of the NAFTA agreement for dealing with disputes arising from the enforcement of antidumping and countervailing duty statutes. Antidumping penalties are imposed in cases where producers of a country sell their product in another country at less than its total cost of production, or at a price lower than the identical product is sold in the producer's domestic market, and domestic producers of the receiving country are harmed. Countervailing duties are imposed to offset the adverse effect of foreign government subsidies. As Chapter 19 cases involve reconsideration of decisions previously made by governmental administrative agencies, no provisions exist for consultations or involvement of the Free Trade Commission before the matter goes to an arbitral panel. Presumably, the proceedings leading up to the administrative agencies' decisions provide opportunities for fact finding and complaint responses. These ordinarily would take place at the trade ministerial level for other matters (Lopez 1997, 174). Since the commission is not directly involved in the resolution of these disputes, they are not analyzed here but are considered in further detail in Chapter 7.

Evaluation of the Free Trade Commission

Assessments of the effectiveness and usefulness of the Free Trade Commission will depend heavily on the standard against which it is assessed. Certainly, in comparison to the European Commission of the European Union, the Free Trade Commission is a minimalist institution. It has no physical location and no staff members of its own. It is staffed by the government employees of the member nations that have been assigned to the respective secretariats, and working groups, subgroups, committees, and subcommittees. The transparency of the institution leaves something to be desired, for it maintains no web site (other than those of the national sections of the NAFTA secretariat that are focused exclusively on dispute settlement) and does not otherwise effectively disseminate information about its activities. The Canadian Department of Foreign Affairs and International Trade has posted on its web site helpful information about the NAFTA committees and working groups, and a copy of the operational review of the NAFTA work program.

As its name indicates, the Free Trade Commission was established to deal primarily with trade facilitation matters as they arise in the context of the NAFTA agreement. It was neither intended nor designed to deal with the broader issues of economic integration such as those that the European commission regularly addresses. The European Union has chosen to pursue a deeper level of regional economic integration than have the countries of North America, and a more elaborate institutional structure is required.

Yet, NAFTA is more than a simple free trade agreement, and certain of its provisions imply deep integration. NAFTA allows member countries to challenge the ways in which partner countries enforce their anti-dumping and countervailing duty laws. The agreement commits the member countries to specific measures to protect intellectual property, and limits the ways in which investment can be regulated. The NAFTA side agreements on labor and the environment provide that member countries can challenge the failure of partner countries to enforce their domestic labor and environmental laws. In many ways the domestic regulations of the member countries have become matters of mutual concern, and when this occurs institutional structures are often needed to facilitate optimal cooperation.

The Free Trade Commission and its related institutions have undoubtedly served a useful purpose through their role in increasing cooperation and communication among the countries of North America, particularly with regard to trade facilitation matters. These institutions are especially important to Canada and Mexico, the smaller countries in the relationship, since they help to keep economic relationships within North America based upon established rules rather than upon economic or political power.

As economic integration in North America deepens further, the Free Trade Commission and the other institutions created by NAFTA can be expected to assume new responsibilities. They will, of necessity, become more robust. However, by design this evolutionary process will be much slower in North America than it has been in Western Europe, and the institutions that evolve in North America will have a character that uniquely reflects the values and preferences of the NAFTA countries.

4

Commission for Labor Cooperation and National Administrative Offices

When the NAFTA agreement was being debated, labor organizations were among its strongest opponents in the United States. Realizing that the NAFTA agreement would significantly lower and eventually eliminate restrictions on trade with Mexico, and would provide a more favorable investment climate there, organized labor feared adverse effects on both wage levels and employment rates in the United States. These fears were magnified by statements of politicians such as Pat Buchanan alleging harmful effects of expanded trade with Mexico, and those of Ross Perot predicting a "giant sucking sound" of capital being drained to Mexico to be combined with low-cost labor there.

President Bill Clinton was elected in 1992 with strong support from organized labor after having promised during the presidential campaign that, if elected, he would require the NAFTA package to have certain protections for labor in the United States. Rather than reopening negotiations on the NAFTA agreement to incorporate such provisions, the NAFTA countries negotiated a supplementary agreement, entitled the North American Agreement on Labor Cooperation (NAALC).

In Article 1 the NAALC sets forth seven basic objectives:

1. Improve working conditions and living standards in each party's territory.
2. Promote, to the maximum extent possible, the labor principles set out in Annex 1(see below).
3. Encourage cooperation to promote innovation and rising levels of productivity and quality.

4. Encourage publication and exchange of information, data development and coordination, and joint studies to enhance mutually beneficial understanding of the laws and institutions governing labor in
   each party's territory.
5. Pursue cooperative labor-related activities on the basis of mutual
   benefit.
6. Promote compliance with, and effective enforcement by each party
   of, its labor law.
7. Foster transparency in the administration of labor law.

As can be seen from this list of objectives, the NAALC emphasizes
cooperation. It makes no attempt to establish a common set of labor
standards or labor regulations. Annex 1 of the NAALC sets forth eleven
guiding principles that the member countries committed themselves to
follow, but states clearly that each of the countries has leeway to promote these principles through its own domestic law in ways of its own
choosing.
   These eleven principles are as follows:

1. Freedom of association and protection of the right to organize
2. The right to bargain collectively
3. The right to strike
4. Prohibition of forced labor
5. Labor protections for children and young persons
6. Minimum employment standards
7. Elimination of employment discrimination
8. Equal pay for women and men
9. Prevention of occupational injuries and illnesses
10. Compensation in cases of occupational injuries and illnesses
11. Protection of migrant workers

   In order to carry out its objectives, the NAALC set up a commission
for labor cooperation with national administrative offices located in the
labor ministry of each of the parties. The commission is composed of a
ministerial council and a secretariat.

The Council of the Commission for Labor Cooperation

The NAALC provides that the council comprises the labor ministers of
the member countries, or their designees. Thus far the labor ministers

have served as the council, and can be expected to continue doing so. The council meets at least once a year in regular session, with special sessions held at the request of any member country. Chairing of the regular sessions of the council rotates among the members. The council generally makes its decisions and recommendations by consensus, although they can be decided otherwise. The council is authorized to establish committees, working groups, or expert groups at its discretion. In contrast to the Free Trade Commission, which has established a large number of such groups, thus far the labor council has established only one working group. This working group on cross-border situations in worker's compensation in Canada, Mexico, and the United States completed a report in mid-1999, but at the time of this writing it had not been released to the public (Lara-Saenz 1999).

The council is the governing body of the Commission for Labor Cooperation (CLC). As such, it oversees the implementation of the NAALC and directs the work of the secretariat, approving for publication the secretariat's reports and studies. It approves the annual work plan and activities of the commission, and establishes priorities for cooperative action among the member countries. In various ways the council fosters the flow of communication and encourages cooperative activities among the member countries.

The council has an annual meeting at which it approves the budget for the secretariat for the coming year, and receives reports from the secretariat and from the senior officials from each country who are responsible for interacting with the secretariat. The labor ministers typically summarize labor conditions in their countries at the annual meeting, and reiterate their countries' commitments to the objectives and principles spelled out in the NAALC. They also approve a program of cooperative activities scheduled for the coming year that has been drawn up by the national administrative offices.

The Secretariat

The secretariat of the CLC has been headquartered in Dallas, Texas, although it recently announced plans to relocate to Washington, D.C. The secretariat has a staff of approximately fifteen people plus three support staff members. It currently operates on an annual budget of about $2 million. It is headed by an executive director, chosen by the council, and appointed to a three-year term that can be renewed for an additional three years. The position of executive director rotates consecutively among the nationals of each member country.

According to Article 12 (5) of the NAALC, "[i]n the performance of their duties, the Executive Director and the staff shall not seek or receive instructions from any government or any other authority external to the council. Each Party shall respect the international character of the responsibilities of the Executive Director and the staff and shall not seek to influence them in the discharge of their responsibilities."

The secretariat prepares studies on labor issues as requested by the council, making use of independent experts as necessary. The secretariat also prepares background reports on labor market conditions in the member countries, on their programs for human resource development, and on their labor laws and administrative procedures relating to the enforcement of these laws. Reports and studies prepared by the secretariat are made public after having been approved by the council.

In addition to periodic bulletins and annual reports, the secretariat's major publications to date include *North American Labor Markets: A Comparative Profile*; *Incomes and Productivity in North America* (which consists of papers from a seminar and comments on them); *Preliminary Report to the Ministerial Council on Labor and Industrial Relations Law in Canada, the United States and Mexico*; *Plant Closings and Labor Rights*; and *The Employment of Women in North America*. These reports have provided information concerning comparative labor market conditions and labor market practices in North America that was not previously available.

The secretariat coordinates with the national administrative offices of the member countries to carry out the cooperative activities of the commission. These activities include workshops, seminars, courses, and conferences on a wide range of labor-related matters. The purpose of these cooperative activities is to affirm the principles on which the NAALC is based, and to promote its objectives. Some cooperative activities are assigned to the secretariat directly by the council, whereas others are carried out either jointly or separately by the national administrative offices.

National Administrative Offices

As part of the institutional structure for dealing with labor issues, the NAALC provided that each of the member countries would create a national administrative office (NAO).

The NAOs are domestic institutions and technically are not a part of the CLC. They are staffed solely by government employees of each of the individual member countries and are located in the labor ministries of the countries.

The purpose of the NAOs is to implement the NAALC with regard to labor law issues, and to serve as contact points between the secretariat, agencies of the national governments, and the other NAOs. They also provide information concerning the NAALC and labor law matters to the public at large.

The NAALC also provides that each country may, at its discretion, establish a national advisory committee (NAC) and a governmental advisory committee (GAC). The NAC, composed of an equal number of representatives from labor, business, and academia, advises its government on implementation of the NAALC. Each of the three NAFTA countries has established such a group. In addition, the agreement provides for the formation of a GAC, which comprises the representatives of federal and state or provincial governments and provides their perspective on the agreement's implementation. Canada and Mexico have each formed a governmental advisory committee, but to date the United States has not (CLC 1998, Annex 1: I, 4).

A major part of the responsibility of the NAOs is to receive and respond to submissions from individuals, unions, nongovernmental organizations, employers, or other private parties alleging that another member government is failing to enforce its labor laws or to abide by the labor principles stated in the agreement. As stated earlier, the member countries, realizing the differences in labor laws and labor practices among them, did not attempt harmonization of labor laws in the NAALC. Instead, they set up procedures that would help to ensure that each of the member countries effectively enforces its own labor laws.

By the time that the NAFTA agreement went into effect on 1 January 1994, each of the NAFTA countries had set up a NAO in its capital city. Each of these offices was given leeway to establish its own procedures for processing submissions. In general, the matters complained of must allege a pattern of nonenforcement of the partner country's labor laws that has resulted in some harm to the submitter or to another party. The matters complained of must also constitute a violation of the member country's obligations under the terms of the NAALC. Further, relief must have been sought unsuccessfully under the domestic laws of the partner country, and the matter must not be pending before an international body.

The preferred methods of dealing with labor disputes clearly were intended to be non-adversarial. Cooperation among the member countries is encouraged in the NAALC through provisions for consultations, exchanges of information, and assistance on technical matters. The council promotes cooperative activities among the member countries, but does so through and with the active assistance of the NAOs. Often the cooperative activities chosen are based upon issues raised in submissions to the NAOs. Numerous conferences, seminars, research projects, and technical assistance measures have been conducted dealing with occupational safety and health issues, employment training issues, child labor and gender initiatives, and industrial relations issues, with a focus on fostering constructive labor-management relations.

When a submission is filed with an NAO alleging that a partner country is failing to enforce its labor laws and that some harm has consequently resulted, the NAO to which the allegation is submitted first decides whether to accept the submission for review or to decline it. Generally, a submission is accepted for review if it is judged to meet the minimum standards for review (as discussed above), and if having a review would further the objectives of the NAALC. If the submission is accepted for review, the next step is consultation with other NAOs on the issue. The NAO may gather information from a wide variety of sources, and, in the case of the U.S.'s NAO, will hold a public hearing on the matter. In the case of Canada, because of the federal system there, decisions are made in consultation with the Canadian Inter-Governmental Committee. A public hearing may be held, but is not required. In Mexico, a public hearing has not been made a part of the process on the grounds that it is adversarial in nature and is contrary to the spirit of the NAALC, which is to settle matters through cooperation and consultation (ibid., III, 2).

After the necessary information has been gathered, a public report of review is issued setting forth the findings. If the matter remains unresolved after the public report is issued, the next step is ministerial level consultations. According to the terms of the NAALC, the labor minister of any of the partner countries may request consultation with the other ministers concerning any labor law matter pertaining to the principles stated in the agreement. Every effort is to be made to resolve the matter through ministerial consultations. Sufficient information to make possible a full assessment of the matter is exchanged and made publicly available.

Evaluation Committee of Experts

Should the matter remain unresolved after ministerial consultations, either party may request the appointment of an Evaluation Committee of Experts (ECE) to analyze the issue. The scope of issues that may be considered at this stage is narrowed somewhat, in that an ECE cannot be appointed to report on freedom of association, right to bargain collectively, or right to strike cases (principles 1, 2, and 3 as listed earlier in this chapter). Furthermore, to be considered at the level of an ECE, the matter at issue must also be trade related and must be covered by mutually recognized labor laws of the NAFTA countries.

The ECE normally will comprise three members who are experts in labor law and who can be objective and independent in their judgment of the matter. The chair is to be chosen from a roster of experts developed in consultation with the International Labor Organization. The other two panel members are chosen from a roster maintained by the NAFTA member countries.

The ECE performs an independent, non-adversarial analysis of the labor law enforcement of all three NAFTA countries with regard to the issue in dispute, and makes recommendations pertaining to all of the member countries. After studying the issue the ECE first presents a draft report for consideration by the council. Each of the member countries has opportunity to comment on the draft report. After having received and considered these comments, the ECE issues a final report. Unless the council decides otherwise, the final report is published. The disputing parties then provide written responses to the final report to each other and to the secretariat. These responses and the final report are then tabled for consideration at the next regularly scheduled meeting of the council of ministers.

If the matter remains unresolved after ministerial consultations at their regular meeting, either member country may request a special session of the council of ministers to deal specifically with this issue. Unless it decides otherwise the council meets within twenty days of the request to focus on the issue. In attempting to resolve the issue, it may make use of technical experts, may establish working groups to consider the issue, and may make use of mediation, conciliation, or other dispute resolution measures. The council may also make its own recommendations as to how the matter might be resolved.

Panel Arbitration

If the matter in dispute deals with child labor, minimum wages, or occupational safety and health (principles 5, 6, and 9 from the list earlier in this chapter), and it still remains unresolved after the steps described above, upon the request of any consulting member country the council can, by a two-thirds vote, convene an arbitral panel. An arbitral panel is composed of five members, chosen according to set procedures from a roster of forty-five labor law experts.

The panel can, with the agreement of the parties to the dispute, seek further information or technical advice from any source that it deems appropriate. After considering all of the information available to it, the panel renders an initial report setting forth the facts of the case and deciding whether there has been a persistent pattern of failure to enforce labor laws in the matter at issue. If it finds that there has been a persistent pattern of failure to enforce labor laws, it makes recommendations for settling the dispute, which normally involve recommending an action plan through which the member country complained against can remedy the nonenforcement.

After receiving written comments on the initial report, the panel transmits to the council a final report that is published within five days of receipt. At this stage an opportunity is provided for the disputing parties to agree upon a mutually acceptable action plan. If they cannot agree, or if it is determined that the party complained against is not fully implementing the action plan to which it has previously agreed, any disputing party may request that the panel be reconvened. Should the panel find that the action plan is not being satisfactorily implemented, it can assess a monetary enforcement assessment of up to .007 percent of the total trade between the disputing parties. The proceeds of such monetary enforcement assessment are to be placed in a fund to be used, at the discretion of the council, to enhance the enforcement of labor laws in the offending country, consistent with its law.

Should the offending country refuse to pay the monetary enforcement assessment, the complaining party is authorized to suspend NAFTA benefits until the amount of the monetary enforcement assessment is collected. This is done by applying the lesser of the pre-NAFTA tariff rate or the most-favored-nation tariff rate to the trade of the offending country. In this case, the tariff revenues accrue to the country imposing the tariffs, rather than accruing to the commission to be used as directed by the council in enhancing the enforcement of labor laws in the offending country.

Submissions

As of mid-1999, twenty-one submissions have been filed under the terms of the NAALC. Of these, thirteen were filed with the U.S. NAO, five with the Mexican NAO, and only three with the Canadian NAO. Twelve of the twenty-one submissions involved allegations against Mexico, seven involved allegations against the United States, and only two involved allegations against Canada.*

Cases Submitted to the U.S. NAO

Of the thirteen cases filed with the U.S. NAO, two involved allegations against Canada and eleven involved allegations against Mexico. Of the two against Canada, one contended that a particular Canadian law failed to extend treatment to rural mail carriers equal to that received by their urban counterparts. The U.S. NAO declined to accept that submission for review, presumably because the submission questioned the law itself, and not the application of the law.

The other submission against Canada alleged antiunion-motivated plant closing, delays in union certification procedure, and other unfair labor practices on the part of a McDonald's restaurant in the province of Quebec. After consultations were held among the U.S. NAO, the Canadian NAO, and the government of Quebec, they reached agreement with the submitting labor organizations to have the issues of the case studied by a provincial council.

Of the eleven cases filed with the U.S. NAO involving allegations against Mexico, nine of these raised freedom of association issues (with two of them adding to this charge issues of safety and health), one alleged illegal child labor, and the remaining one dealt with pregnancy-based gender discrimination.

---

*The summaries of submissions below are extracted from Status of Submissions and Public Reports of Review that are posted on the web site of the U.S. NAO (*http://www.dol.gov/dol/ilab/public/programs/nao/main.htm*), supplemented as indicated in the text from other sources.

In two of the cases, the submitters withdrew their cases before the review process was complete. One of these was a case filed by the United Electrical, Radio, and Machine Workers of America alleging violation of workers' rights of association and rights to organize by General Electric during a union election at a plant in Ciudad Juarez. Before a hearing was held on the matter the union withdrew in disgust, expressing a lack of confidence in the NAO's investigation (CLC 1998, Annex 1, III:5). It also objected to the fact that the hearing was scheduled to take place in San Antonio, Texas, hundreds of miles away from the location of the plant where the intimidation of workers allegedly occurred.

In the other case that was withdrawn by the submitter before a public report was issued, the Communications Workers of America, the Union of Telephone Workers of Mexico, and the Federation of Goods and Services Companies of Mexico had alleged that Maxi-Switch, in various illegal ways, tried to prevent the organization of a production facility in Sonora, Mexico. The unions had appealed to the local conciliation and arbitration board in Mexico, but were told that Maxi-Switch already had a contract with an unidentified union at the plant. The U.S. NAO accepted the case for review, but before a hearing was held the conciliation and arbitration board reversed its position and allowed the union to be registered. The unions then withdrew their submission, saying that their fundamental objectives had been attained.

The U.S. NAO declined to accept a case brought by Mexican flight attendants who had been ordered back to work upon the threat of termination when the Mexican government took over their airline after they went on strike. However, the NAO did agree to conduct a research project concerning the issue of how strikes that are judged to threaten the general welfare are handled in each of the three NAFTA countries.

The U.S. NAO is holding in abeyance a case dealing with the issue of child labor pending the gathering of further information. The Florida Tomato Exchange filed this case, alleging the use of child labor in the production of vegetables and fruits in Mexico.

Hearings have been held on the other seven cases filed with the U.S. NAO. In the first two cases filed the International Brotherhood of Teamsters and the United Electrical, Radio, and Machine Workers of America alleged that Honeywell Corporation and General Electric Corporation had, among other things, dismissed workers for union activities and required them to sign forms waiving their rights to challenge the action in order to collect severance pay. In its public report, the U.S. NAO took the position that by signing the waivers and collecting the severance pay, the workers had preempted a determination by the Mexican government as to whether the action was proper. Therefore, the NAO did not recommend ministerial consultations in these cases.

The remaining five cases submitted to the U.S. NAO have proceeded to the level of ministerial consultations. The first case to be taken to this level was one filed by the International Labor Rights Education and Research Fund and three other workers' rights and human rights organizations. In the submission these organizations alleged that Sony Corporation acted illegally in a number of ways as it sought to prevent representation of workers by an independent union in a Nuevo Laredo, Mexico, plant. The submission further claimed that the government of Mexico failed to protect the workers' rights of freedom of association and right to organize, and that it arbitrarily refused to register the independent union. In its public report the U.S. NAO was very critical of the Mexican government, and recommended ministerial consultations to discuss the union registration process in Mexico (Lopez 1997, 197). As a result of the ministerial consultations, the council scheduled public seminars on union registration and certification, and commissioned a study by independent experts on Mexican labor law dealing with these issues.

The International Labor Rights Fund, Human Rights Watch/Americas, and the Mexican National Association of Democratic Lawyers filed a second case that proceeded to the level of ministerial consultation. This submission "raised issues of freedom of association for federal workers and questioned the impartiality of the labor tribunals reviewing these issues" (USDOL [1999], Status of Submissions, 3). The issue concerned whether two unions could represent workers in a single ministry of the Mexican government. The NAOs organized and held a conference in Baltimore to discuss the relationship between international treaty provisions dealing with labor issues (such as International Labor Organization Conventions) and the constitutional provisions of the United States and Mexico pertaining to labor union organization. The nongovernmental organizations that originally filed the submission asked the U.S. NAO to reconsider the issue because they were dissatisfied with how it had been addressed, but their request was denied.

Two relatively recent cases also involving freedom of association issues have proceeded to the level of ministerial consultations, and negotiations on them are pending. One of them was submitted by the Union of Metal, Steel, Iron, and Allied Workers and three workers' rights groups alleging that the Mexican government failed to enforce various of its laws in connection with union organizational activities and a representation election at the Han Young maquiladora plant in Tijuana. It alleges that union activists were beaten and fired, and that in various ways workers were threatened and intimidated in order to keep them from joining an independent union. The submission also raises certain health and safety issues.

The other case was filed by seven United States and Canadian labor unions, with the support of a large number of Mexican unions and nongovernmental organizations in the United States and Mexico. Much like the previous case, it alleges that the government of Mexico has failed to enforce various laws relating to freedom of association and right to organize in connection with the antiunion activities of Echlin, Inc., at its Ciudad de los Reyes maquiladora plant in the state of Mexico. The submission alleges intimidation, physical abuse, and other harassment by both the company and the existing union of the plant, the Confederation of Mexican Workers. The submission further alleges that governmental authorities in Mexico knew that the illegal activities were occurring and failed to take remedial action.

The remaining case filed with the U.S. NAO alleges gender discrimination. The Human Rights Watch, the International Labor Rights Fund, and the National Association of Democratic Lawyers of Mexico filed this case. It alleges that firms in the maquiladora industry refuse to hire pregnant women, that they require pregnancy testing as a condition of employment, and that in some cases they mistreat or discharge pregnant women to avoid paying maternity benefits. During the course of the investigation questions arose concerning whether Mexican law affords protection against pregnancy discrimination before workers are hired. The Mexican NAO objected to this case on the grounds that it questioned Mexican law rather than the administration and enforcement of the law. As a result of ministerial consultations on the matter a conference entitled, "Protecting the Labor Rights of Working Women," was organized and held in Merida, Mexico. Also, outreach sessions will be held to educate workers in the Mexican border region about these issues.

Cases Submitted to the Mexican NAO

Of the five cases submitted to the Mexican NAO, all but one are relatively recent. The first case submitted to the Mexican NAO, in 1995, charged that Sprint Corporation closed a subsidiary in San Francisco and laid off about 240 workers shortly before a union representation election in order to thwart the unionization attempt. This case moved to the ministerial level. The ministerial consultations led eventually to a public forum being held in San Francisco on the effects of sudden plant closure. In addition, the secretariat published a study in 1997 of the effects of sudden plant closing on freedom of association and the right to organize in each of the North American countries. Simultaneously with this submission, the union involved filed an unfair labor practice case with the National Labor Relations Board (NLRB). The NLRB eventually ordered the workers to be reinstated with back pay, but that decision was subsequently overturned when an appeals court ruled that the plant had legitimately been closed for financial reasons.

A more recent case filed with the Mexican NAO raised issues relating to freedom of association and occupational safety and health at Solec, Inc., a California manufacturer of solar panels. In this case the Mexican NAO requested ministerial consultations to gather further information about both freedom of association issues and working conditions at the plant.

The other three cases filed with the Mexican NAO deal with the treatment of Mexican migrant workers in the United States. One relates to working conditions of migrant workers in Washington state's apple industry. In this case the Mexican NAO has requested ministerial consultations to obtain further information on a wide range of issues concerning migrant agricultural workers, including freedom of association, right to organize, working conditions, and discrimination in the workplace. Another case deals with the alleged maltreatment of migrant workers at Decoster Farms, an egg producer in the state of Maine, and was at the time of this writing still under review. The third case is more general, dealing with whether a memorandum of understanding between the U.S. Department of Labor and the Immigration and Naturalization Service deprives migrant workers of protections they rightfully should receive under U.S. law. It also was still under review.

Cases Submitted to the Canadian NAO

The cases submitted to the Canadian NAO also are of relatively recent vintage. One of these, alleging failure of the United States to enforce a part of the National Labor Relations Act, was not accepted for review by the Canadian NAO. Another, duplicating a case submitted to the U.S. NAO, alleged failure of the United States to enforce its minimum wage and overtime protections in the case of foreign nationals, due to a memorandum of understanding between the U.S. Department of Labor and the Immigration and Naturalization Service. After a new memorandum of understanding between these entities had been signed, the Canadian NAO considered a review inappropriate and closed its file on the matter. The third case submitted to the Canadian NAO, also replicating a case submitted to the U.S. NAO, deals with both freedom of association issues and occupational health and safety issues in a maquiladora firm in Mexico. The Canadian NAO has issued a report on the issues in question, and has formally requested ministerial consultations with Mexico on the issues.

In none of the submissions to the NAOs has a case proceeded beyond the level of ministerial consultation. That is partly because most of the cases have dealt with issues, such as freedom of association, right to organize, and the right to bargain collectively, that are not eligible to go to higher levels of dispute resolution. Additionally, however, it is because the clear intent of the NAALC was to have labor issues in North America dealt with through cooperation and consultation rather than through adversarial proceedings.

While monetary enforcement assessments and trade sanctions exist as possible methods of enforcing the terms of the NAALC for some issues, their use for that purpose is highly unlikely. The road to having a matter considered by an arbitral panel is a long and tortuous one. Multiple opportunities and incentives are provided to settle the dispute before that stage. Even after the dispute reaches the stage of arbitration, opportunities for settling it still exist. Yet, the mere possibility of a matter eventually ending up before an arbitral panel, with the further possibility of monetary enforcement assessment or trade sanctions, no doubt provides some incentive to settle matters through consultation and cooperation.

Four-Year Review of the NAALC

The NAALC provided that within four years of the time that it took effect the council should "review its operation and effectiveness in the light of experience" (NAALC [1993], Article 10(1)(a)). This review process involved a summary by the secretariat of the activities under the agreement, assessments by each of the national advisory committees and the governmental advisory committees, comments from the public at large, and an assessment by a review committee of experts that was appointed by the council.

The review committee of experts was made up of Pierre Verge of Canada, Clyde Summers of the United States, and Luis Medina of Mexico. After providing a rather extensive survey of the various activities carried out as a result of the NAALC, the experts made several observations and recommendations. It is noteworthy that assessment of the operation and effectiveness of the agreement differed sharply on the part of the Canadian and U.S. members on one hand, and the Mexican member on the other. In fact, the Mexican member of the review committee disagreed so strongly with the majority report that he filed a rather lengthy dissenting opinion.

In their majority opinion, the Canadian and U.S. members look favorably upon the trinational consultations that have taken place at the ministerial level, noting that consultations of this type would not have taken place in the absence of the NAALC. They also commend the work of the secretariat, while at the same time raising questions about whether the level of future funding for the secretariat will be sufficient for it to play its intended role in attaining the objectives of the agreement.

The majority opinion urges greater uniformity in the rules of procedure that have been independently adopted by each of the NAOs. They recommend that use be made of ECEs to render independent judgments on labor issues, and suggest that the council of ministers might be proactive in having labor issues investigated rather than merely reacting to issues that are raised by the filing of submissions. The review committee looks favorably upon the many cooperative activities, such as conferences, seminars, and courses that have been conducted, but recommends that the results of these activities be much more widely disseminated. They urgently recommend the publication of a translation of the labor laws and regulations of all three North American countries in English, Spanish, and French.

The majority report favorably regards the cross-border scrutiny of labor law administration that has arisen out of the submission process. However, the report decries the fact that the process involves no remedial action in cases where there have been victims of unlawful actions, or where systems of labor law enforcement have obvious defects. The majority members of the review committee noted that lack of remedial action may over time lead to cynicism and loss of confidence in the process. The majority report also suggests broadening the scope of NAALC provisions. It questions why the principles of freedom of association and the right to organize, the right to bargain collectively, and the right to strike should not be issues eligible for examination by ECEs. These are the labor principles that have overwhelmingly been at issue in the submissions thus far. In addition, the report chides both the U.S. NAO and the council for failing to declare that unfair procedures, even those that may not violate domestic law, nevertheless violate the terms of the NAALC and need to be changed.

The dissenting opinion, filed by the Mexican representative on the review committee of experts, registers several objections. The first objection is that the review committee had exceeded its mandate, in that it was tasked simply to evaluate how effectively the NAALC had operated during its first four years, but had instead made recommendations that would imply changes in the agreement. The minority opinion also objects to the use of submission procedures to resolve specific conflicts, saying they never were intended to be instruments for changing the way in which national laws are enforced or changed. It further asserts that "enforcement or modification of laws is strictly subject to the sovereignty of each of the NAALC countries" (CLC 1998 Annex 1: A Dissenting Opinion, 2).

The dissenting member of the review committee further charges that the U.S. NAO has been biased in its evaluation of submissions. He contends that the U.S. NAO gave undue consideration to information submitted by the petitioners, while giving minimal consideration to information from other sources, including from the Mexican NAO. In his opinion none of the submissions should have been accepted. In support of this position, he points out that in all but one of the cases domestic legal proceedings were still in process, and that the petitioners could hardly argue nonenforcement of domestic laws when their legal recourse had not yet been exhausted domestically. He further contends that the submission process has been politicized, pointing to a correlation between the acceptance of submissions by the U.S. NAO and important election campaigns in the United States.

After receiving input from the various sources in the four-year review, the council agreed, among other things: to conduct ministerial consultations as rapidly as possible; to use evaluation committees of experts in a non-adversarial manner and to discuss their role further at a subsequent council meeting; to have the NAOs develop multiyear work plans, encourage greater public involvement in cooperative activities, and facilitate better dissemination of information about the NAALC; and to have the secretariat better coordinate activities with the NAOs and work to improve public awareness of the CLC.

Significance of the Labor-Related Institutions

The NAALC was pathbreaking in the way that it linked an agreement on labor standards and practices formally to an international trade agreement. Over the past several years, as the real wages of relatively unskilled workers have stagnated in the major developed countries, apprehensions about the effects of globalization on wages have increased. Specifically in the case of North America, organized labor in the United States has worried about the possible adverse impact of lower wages and poor enforcement of labor standards in Mexico on labor conditions in the United States.

The NAALC was a small and tentative step toward addressing these concerns. Very little support existed in North America for truly supranational institutions to deal with labor issues. Consequently, the institutions that have grown out of the NAALC are for the most part domestic institutions rather than supranational institutions. Private parties in the NAFTA countries do not have direct access to North American institutions dealing with labor matters. Instead, complainants must work through the NAOs of each country and then, ultimately, through the labor ministers.

However a supranationalist element does exist in the institutions established by the NAALC. If the government of a NAFTA country is accused of not enforcing its own labor laws or of failing to abide by the labor principles spelled out in the agreement, its actions (or lack thereof) can be investigated and reported on by the NAO of a partner country. Should the matter proceed to the level of ministerial consultation, for most issues it can be referred for further analysis and report to an ECE even over the objection of the labor minister of the accused country. In the case of a narrower range of issues, the matter theoretically could proceed to arbitral panel decision, and monetary enforcement assessment or trade sanctions, over the objection of the accused country. Additionally, the labor secretariat is given some independence and insulation from national authorities, and is staffed by nationals of all of the member countries.

As the name of the NAALC indicates, and as the agreement repeatedly states, the expectation and intention is that disputes among North American countries concerning labor issues will be resolved through cooperation and consultation. The agreement specifies a long list of labor-related subjects regarding which the council is to promote cooperative activities through technical assistance, joint research projects, seminars, conferences, and training sessions. Multiple opportunities exist to settle disputes over labor issues before they proceed (in cases where they meet the specified criteria) to binding arbitration.

As evidenced in the minority opinion of the review committee of experts, and also in the report of the Mexican NAC for the four-year review, Mexico has not been pleased with the functioning of the institutions established by the NAALC during its first four years. The agreement was designed so that, in addition to setting up procedures that would encourage consultation and enhance cooperation among the three countries of North America, labor conditions might be improved through the "sunshine effect" of bringing labor abuses and poor labor conditions into the glare of publicity. During the first few years of the agreement, the sun has shone almost exclusively on Mexico, and the country has begun to feel singled out unfairly.

More recently several cases have been submitted alleging failure to enforce or properly administer labor laws in the United States and Canada. Several of these have focused on alleged maltreatment of Mexican migrant workers in the United States. Cases of this type, in which Mexico can feel that it is benefiting from the terms of the NAALC, are important for maintaining support for the agreement in Mexico.

In the United States, the AFL-CIO opposed both the NAFTA agreement and the NAALC from their inceptions. The functioning of the NAALC thus far has done little to engender organized labor's confidence in, or support for, labor-related regional institutions. Because the agreement is short on remedial action where labor abuses are shown to have occurred, the actions taken have not helped to convince an already skeptical labor movement that the agreement will actually improve working conditions in North America and effectively promote the labor principles articulated in the agreement. The mere organization of a conference or seminar on freedom of association is of little consolation to workers terminated or abused for engaging in union activity. The very limited responses to labor abuses have not inspired much confidence in the efficacy of the NAALC to improve labor conditions.

On the other hand, one must keep in mind the NAFTA agreement attempts to integrate three economies with significantly different histories, distinctive labor movements, and contrasting legal traditions. Each of the three countries of North America jealously guards its national sovereignty. Consequently, when the NAO of one country has to pass judgment on whether a partner country is enforcing or effectively administering its labor laws, cultural differences, sovereignty issues, and foreign policy considerations all enter into the equation to make for a very complicated situation.

At this point in time, the labor-related institutions are at a very early stage in their development. The labor secretariat was not formed until late 1995, and Canada could not fully participate in the NAALC until 1997, after provinces containing more than 55 percent of the Canadian population had ratified the agreement. Only in August 1998 were rules of procedure established for evaluation committees of experts. The number of submissions filed has amounted to only a handful each year, so experience in dealing with them has been limited. No precedent exists for exactly the type of structure established in the NAALC, so the institutions are having to gradually discover how best to function and to work with each other.

Before the Commission on Labor Cooperation and the NAOs were established, almost no trilateral interaction on labor issues took place among the countries of North America. As a result of the institutions established by the NAALC, transparency and public debate on labor issues of interest to the citizens of the NAFTA countries have reached levels previously unknown. No doubt over time the institutions will evolve to broaden their scope and to take on a more supranational character. It is perhaps worth remembering that, even though institutionalized economic integration in Western Europe began more than forty years ago, only recently have labor issues been addressed on a regional basis there.

If the labor institutions are judged according to whether they have greatly enhanced labor conditions, or strongly promoted the labor principles set forth in the NAALC, one would have to conclude that they have not. However, if their success is judged according to whether they have increased cooperation and mutual understanding of labor issues among the countries of North America, they would have to be judged successful according to this criterion. At this stage they are minimalist institutions, but they have laid a foundation on which strengthened institutions can be built over time.

An important and often overlooked effect of the NAALC is that, by institutionalizing the link between labor issues and a major trade agreement, the agenda of future trade talks has been forever altered. Even though in 1996 the Singapore trade ministerial issued a declaration stating that the International Labor Organization is the competent body to deal with labor standards, the issue refuses to go away whenever trade negotiations are being discussed. The United Nations Development Programme in its most recent Human Development Report called for principles of performance on labor standards for multinational corporations (Balls and Peel 1999, 4). Sir Leon Brittan, former director general of the World Trade Organization and outgoing European Union trade commissioner, recently advocated giving the International Labor Organization observer status at the World Trade Organization and called for organizing a high-level conference on trade, globalization, and labor issues (BRIDGES 1999, 1). Every major trade bill submitted to the U.S. Congress since the passage of NAFTA has had provisions dealing with labor issues, and this pattern likely will prevail for the foreseeable future. The precedent set by the NAALC may, in the long run, be much more significant than its specific provisions.

Appendix 4.1
North American Agreement on Labor Cooperation

PREAMBLE

The Government of Canada, the Government of the United Mexican States and the Government of the United States of America:

RECALLING their resolve in the North American Free Trade Agreement (NAFTA) to:

- *create* an expanded and secure market for the goods and services produced in their territories,
- *enhance* the competitiveness of their firms in global markets,
- *create* new employment opportunities and improve working conditions and living standards in their respective territories, and
- *protect*, enhance and enforce basic workers' rights;

AFFIRMING their continuing respect for each Party's constitution and law;

DESIRING to build on their respective international commitments and to strengthen their cooperation on labor matters;

RECOGNIZING that their mutual prosperity depends on the promotion of competition based on innovation and rising levels of productivity and quality;

SEEKING to complement the economic opportunities created by the NAFTA with the human resource development, labor-management cooperation and continuous learning that characterize high-productivity economies;

ACKNOWLEDGING that protecting basic workers' rights will encourage firms to adopt high-productivity competitive strategies;

RESOLVED to promote, in accordance with their respective laws, high-skill, high-productivity economic development in North America by:

- *investing* in continuous human resource development, including for entry into the workforce and during periods of unemployment;
- *promoting* employment security and career opportunities for all workers through referral and other employment services;
- *strengthening* labor-management cooperation to promote greater dialogue between worker organizations and employers and to foster creativity and productivity in the workplace;
- *promoting* higher living standards as productivity increases;
- *encouraging* consultation and dialogue between labor, business and government both in each country and in North America;
- *fostering* investment with due regard for the importance of labor laws and principles;
- *encouraging* employers and employees in each country to comply with labor laws and to work together in maintaining a progressive, fair, safe and healthy working environment;

BUILDING on existing institutions and mechanisms in Canada, Mexico and the United States to achieve the preceding economic and social goals; and

CONVINCED of the benefits to be gained from further cooperation between them on labor matters;

HAVE AGREED as follows:

PART ONE

OBJECTIVES

Article 1:   Objectives

The objectives of this Agreement are to:
- (a)   improve working conditions and living standards in each Party's territory;
- (b)   promote, to the maximum extent possible, the labor principles set out in Annex 1;
- (c)   encourage cooperation to promote innovation and rising levels of productivity and quality;

(d) encourage publication and exchange of information, data development and coordination, and joint studies to enhance mutually beneficial understanding of the laws and institutions governing labor in each Party's territory;

(e) pursue cooperative labor-related activities on the basis of mutual benefit;

(f) promote compliance with, and effective enforcement by each Party of, its labor law; and

(g) foster transparency in the administration of labor law.

PART TWO

OBLIGATIONS

Article 2:   Levels of Protection

Affirming full respect for each Party's constitution, and recognizing the right of each Party to establish its own domestic labor standards, and to adopt or modify accordingly its labor laws and regulations, each Party shall ensure that its labor laws and regulations provide for high labor standards, consistent with high quality and productivity workplaces, and shall continue to strive to improve those standards in that light.

Article 3:   Government Enforcement Action

1.   Each Party shall promote compliance with and effectively enforce its labor law through appropriate government action, subject to Article 42, such as:

(a) appointing and training inspectors;

(b) monitoring compliance and investigating suspected violations, including through on-site inspections;

(c) seeking assurances of voluntary compliance;

(d) requiring record keeping and reporting;

(e) encouraging the establishment of worker-management committees to address labor regulation of the workplace;

(f) providing or encouraging mediation, conciliation and arbitration services; or

(g)   initiating, in a timely manner, proceedings to seek appropriate sanctions or remedies for violations of its labor law.

2.   Each Party shall ensure that its competent authorities give due consideration in accordance with its law to any request by an employer, employee or their representatives, or other interested person, for an investigation of an alleged violation of the Party's labor law.

Article 4:   Private Action

1.   Each Party shall ensure that persons with a legally recognized interest under its law in a particular matter have appropriate access to administrative, quasijudicial, judicial or labor tribunals for the enforcement of the Party's labor law.

2.   Each Party's law shall ensure that such persons may have recourse to, as appropriate, procedures by which rights arising under:

(a)   its labor law, including in respect of occupational safety and health, employment standards, industrial relations and migrant workers; and

(b)   collective agreements, can be enforced.

Article 5:   Procedural Guarantees

1.   Each Party shall ensure that its administrative, quasijudicial, judicial and labor tribunal proceedings for the enforcement of its labor law are fair, equitable and transparent and, to this end, each Party shall provide that:

(a)   such proceedings comply with due process of law;

(b)   any hearings in such proceedings are open to the public, except where the administration of justice otherwise requires;

(c)   the parties to such proceedings are entitled to support or defend their respective positions and to present information or evidence; and

(d)   such proceedings are not unnecessarily complicated and do not entail unreasonable charges or time limits or unwarranted delays.

2.   Each Party shall provide that final decisions on the merits of the case in such proceedings are:

(a) in writing and preferably state the reasons on which the decisions are based;

(b) made available without undue delay to the parties to the proceedings and, consistent with its law, to the public; and

(c) based on information or evidence in respect of which the parties were offered the opportunity to be heard.

3. Each Party shall provide, as appropriate, that parties to such proceedings have the right, in accordance with its law, to seek review and, where warranted, correction of final decisions issued in such proceedings.

4. Each Party shall ensure that tribunals that conduct or review such proceedings are impartial and independent and do not have any substantial interest in the outcome of the matter.

5. Each Party shall provide that the parties to administrative, quasijudicial, judicial or labor tribunal proceedings may seek remedies to ensure the enforcement of their labor rights. Such remedies may include, as appropriate, orders, compliance agreements, fines, penalties, imprisonment, injunctions or emergency workplace closures.

6. Each Party may, as appropriate, adopt or maintain labor defense offices to represent or advise workers or their organizations.

7. Nothing in this Article shall be construed to require a Party to establish, or to prevent a Party from establishing, a judicial system for the enforcement of its labor law distinct from its system for the enforcement of laws in general.

8. For greater certainty, decisions by each Party's administrative, quasijudicial, judicial or labor tribunals, or pending decisions, as well as related proceedings shall not be subject to revision or reopened under the provisions of this Agreement.

Article 6:   Publication

1. Each Party shall ensure that its laws, regulations, procedures and administrative rulings of general application respecting any matter covered by this Agreement are promptly published or otherwise made available in such a manner as to enable interested persons and Parties to become acquainted with them.

2. When so established by its law, each Party shall:

(a)   publish in advance any such measure that it proposes to adopt; and

(b)   provide interested persons a reasonable opportunity to comment on such proposed measures.

Article 7: Public Information and Awareness

Each Party shall promote public awareness of its labor law, including by:

(a)   ensuring that public information is available related to its labor law and enforcement and compliance procedures; and

(b)   promoting public education regarding its labor law.

PART THREE

COMMISSION FOR LABOR COOPERATION

Article 8:   The Commission

1.   The Parties hereby establish the Commission for Labor Cooperation.

2.   The Commission shall comprise a ministerial Council and a Secretariat. The Commission shall be assisted by the National Administrative Office of each Party.

Section A: The Council

Article 9:   Council Structure and Procedures

1.   The Council shall comprise labor ministers of the Parties or their designees.

2.   The Council shall establish its rules and procedures.

3.   The Council shall convene:

(a)   at least once a year in regular session; and

(b)   in special session at the request of any Party. Regular sessions shall be chaired successively by each Party.

4.   The Council may hold public sessions to report on appropriate matters.

5.   The Council may:

      (a)   establish, and assign responsibilities to, committees, working groups or expert groups; and

      (b)   seek the advice of independent experts.

6.   All decisions and recommendations of the Council shall be taken by consensus, except as the Council may otherwise decide or as otherwise provided in this Agreement.

Article 10:   Council Functions

1.   The Council shall be the governing body of the Commission and shall:

      (a)   oversee the implementation and develop recommendations on the further elaboration of this Agreement and, to this end, the Council shall, within four years after the date of entry into force of this Agreement, review its operation and effectiveness in the light of experience;

      (b)   direct the work and activities of the Secretariat and of any committees or working groups convened by the Council;

      (c)   establish priorities for cooperative action and, as appropriate, develop technical assistance programs on the matters set out in Article 11;

      (d)   approve the annual plan of activities and budget of the Commission;

      (e)   approve for publication, subject to such terms or conditions as it may impose, reports and studies prepared by the Secretariat, independent experts or working groups;

      (f)   facilitate Party-to-Party consultations, including through the exchange of information;

      (g)   address questions and differences that may arise between the Parties regarding the interpretation or application of this Agreement; and

      (h)   promote the collection and publication of comparable data on enforcement, labor standards and labor market indicators.

2.   The Council may consider any other matter within the scope of

this Agreement and take such other action in the exercise of its functions as the Parties may agree.

Article 11:   Cooperative Activities

1.   The Council shall promote cooperative activities between the Parties, as appropriate, regarding:
- (a)   occupational safety and health;
- (b)   child labor;
- (c)   migrant workers of the Parties;
- (d)   human resource development;
- (e)   labor statistics;
- (f)   work benefits;
- (g)   social programs for workers and their families;
- (h)   programs, methodologies and experiences regarding productivity improvement;
- (i)   labor-management relations and collective bargaining procedures;
- (j)   employment standards and their implementation;
- (k)   compensation for work-related injury or illness;
- (l)   legislation relating to the formation and operation of unions, collective bargaining and the resolution of labor disputes, and its implementation;
- (m)   the equality of women and men in the workplace;
- (n)   forms of cooperation among workers, management and government;
- (o)   the provision of technical assistance, at the request of a Party, for the development of its labor standards; and
- (p)   such other matters as the Parties may agree.

2.   In carrying out the activities referred to in paragraph 1, the Parties may, commensurate with the availability of resources in each Party, cooperate through:
- (a)   seminars, training sessions, working groups and conferences;
- (b)   joint research projects, including sectoral studies;
- (c)   technical assistance; and
- (d)   such other means as the Parties may agree.

3.   The Parties shall carry out the cooperative activities referred to in paragraph 1 with due regard for the economic, social, cultural and legislative differences between them.

Section B: *The Secretariat*

Article 12:   **Secretariat Structure and Procedures**

1.   The Secretariat shall be headed by an Executive Director, who shall be chosen by the Council for a three-year term, which may be renewed by the Council for one additional three-year term. The position of Executive Director shall rotate consecutively between nationals of each Party. The Council may remove the Executive Director solely for cause.

2.   The Executive Director shall appoint and supervise the staff of the Secretariat, regulate their powers and duties and fix their remuneration in accordance with general standards to be established by the Council. The general standards shall provide that:

(a)   staff shall be appointed and retained, and their conditions of employment shall be determined, strictly on the basis of efficiency, competence and integrity;

(b)   in appointing staff, the Executive Director shall take into account lists of candidates prepared by the Parties;

(c)   due regard shall be paid to the importance of recruiting an equitable proportion of the professional staff from among the nationals of each Party; and

(d)   the Executive Director shall inform the Council of all appointments.

3.   The number of staff positions shall initially be set at 15 and may be changed thereafter by the Council.

4.   The Council may decide, by a two-thirds vote, to reject any appointment that does not meet the general standards. Any such decision shall be made and held in confidence.

5.   In the performance of their duties, the Executive Director and the staff shall not seek or receive instructions from any government or any other authority external to the Council. Each Party shall respect the international character of the responsibilities of the Executive Director and the staff and shall not seek to influence them in the discharge of their responsibilities.

6.   The Secretariat shall safeguard:

(a)   from disclosure information it receives that could identify an organization or person if the person or organization so requests or the Secretariat otherwise considers it appropriate; and

(b)   from public disclosure any information it receives from any organization or person where the information is designated by that organization or person as confidential or proprietary.

7.   The Secretariat shall act under the direction of the Council in accordance with Article 10(1)(b).

Article 13:   Secretariat Functions

1.   The Secretariat shall assist the Council in exercising its functions and shall provide such other support as the Council may direct.

2.   The Executive Director shall submit for the approval of the Council the annual plan of activities and budget for the Commission, including provision for contingencies and proposed cooperative activities.

3.   The Secretariat shall report to the Council annually on its activities and expenditures.

4.   The Secretariat shall periodically publish a list of matters resolved under Part Four or referred to Evaluation Committees of Experts.

Article 14:   Secretariat Reports and Studies

1.   The Secretariat shall periodically prepare background reports setting out publicly available information supplied by each Party on:

(a)   labor law and administrative procedures;

(b)   trends and administrative strategies related to the implementation and enforcement of labor law;

(c)   labor market conditions such as employment rates, average wages and labor productivity; and

(d)   human resource development issues such as training and adjustment programs.

2.   The Secretariat shall prepare a study on any matter as the Council may request. The Secretariat shall prepare any such study in accordance with terms of reference established by the Council, and may

(a)   consider any relevant information;

(b)   where it does not have specific expertise in the matter, engage one or more independent experts of recognized experience; and

(c)   include proposals on the matter.

3.   The Secretariat shall submit a draft of any report or study that it

prepares pursuant to paragraph 1 or 2 to the Council. If the Council considers that a report or study is materially inaccurate or otherwise deficient, the Council may remand it to the Secretariat for reconsideration or other disposition.

4.   Secretariat reports and studies shall be made public 45 days after their approval by the Council, unless the Council otherwise decides.

Section C: National Administrative Offices

Article 15:   National Administrative Office Structure

1.   Each Party shall establish a National Administrative Office (NAO) at the federal government level and notify the Secretariat and the other Parties of its location.

2.   Each Party shall designate a Secretary for its NAO, who shall be responsible for its administration and management.

3.   Each Party shall be responsible for the operation and costs of its NAO.

Article 16:   NAO Functions

1.   Each NAO shall serve as a point of contact with:
   (a)   governmental agencies of that Party;
   (b)   NAOs of the other Parties; and
   (c)   the Secretariat.

2.   Each NAO shall promptly provide publicly available information requested by:
   (a)   the Secretariat for reports under Article 14(1);
   (b)   the Secretariat for studies under Article 14(2);
   (c)   a NAO of another Party; and
   (d)   an ECE.

3.   Each NAO shall provide for the submission and receipt, and periodically publish a list, of public communications on labor law matters arising in the territory of another Party. Each NAO shall review such matters, as appropriate, in accordance with domestic procedures.

Section D: National Committees

Article 17:   National Advisory Committee

Each Party may convene a national advisory committee, comprising members of its public, including representatives of its labor and business organizations and other persons, to advise it on the implementation and further elaboration of this Agreement.

Article 18: Governmental Committee

Each Party may convene a governmental committee, which may comprise or include representatives of federal and state or provincial governments, to advise it on the implementation and further elaboration of this Agreement.

Section E: Official Languages

Article 19: Official Languages

The official languages of the Commission shall be English, French and Spanish. The Council shall establish rules and procedures regarding interpretation and translation.

PART FOUR

COOPERATIVE CONSULTATIONS AND EVALUATIONS

Article 20: Cooperation

The Parties shall at all times endeavor to agree on the interpretation and application of this Agreement, and shall make every attempt through cooperation and consultations to resolve any matter that might affect its operation.

Section A: Cooperative Consultations

Article 21: Consultations between NAOs

1.   A NAO may request consultations, to be conducted in accor-

dance with the procedures set out in paragraph 2, with another NAO in relation to the other Party's labor law, its administration, or labor market conditions in its territory. The requesting NAO shall notify the NAOs of the other Parties and the Secretariat of its request.

2.   In such consultations, the requested NAO shall promptly provide such publicly available data or information, including:

    (a)   descriptions of its laws, regulations, procedures, policies or practices;

    (b)   proposed changes to such procedures, policies or practices; and

    (c)   such clarifications and explanations related to such matters, as may assist the consulting NAOs to better understand and respond to the issues raised.

3.   Any other NAO shall be entitled to participate in the consultations on notice to the other NAOs and the Secretariat.

Article 22:   Ministerial Consultations

1.   Any Party may request in writing consultations with another Party at the ministerial level regarding any matter within the scope of this Agreement. The requesting Party shall provide specific and sufficient information to allow the requested Party to respond.

2.   The requesting Party shall promptly notify the other Parties of the request. A third Party that considers it has a substantial interest in the matter shall be entitled to participate in the consultations on notice to the other Parties.

3.   The consulting Parties shall make every attempt to resolve the matter through consultations under this Article, including through the exchange of sufficient publicly available information to enable a full examination of the matter.

Section B: Evaluations

Article 23:   Evaluation Committee of Experts

1.   If a matter has not been resolved after ministerial consultations pursuant to Article 22, any consulting Party may request in writing the establishment of an Evaluation Committee of Experts (ECE). The requesting Party shall deliver the request to the other Parties and to the

Secretariat. Subject to paragraphs 3 and 4, the Council shall establish an ECE on delivery of the request.

2.   The ECE shall analyze, in the light of the objectives of this Agreement and in a non-adversarial manner, patterns of practice by each Party in the enforcement of its occupational safety and health or other technical labor standards as they apply to the particular matter considered by the Parties under Article 22.

3.   No ECE may be convened if a Party obtains a ruling under Annex 23 that the matter:

    (a)   is not trade-related; or

    (b)   is not covered by mutually recognized labor laws.

4.   No ECE may be convened regarding any matter that was previously the subject of an ECE report in the absence of such new information as would warrant a further report.

Article 24:   Rules of Procedure

1.   The Council shall establish rules of procedure for ECEs, which shall apply unless the Council otherwise decides. The rules of procedure shall provide that:

    (a)   an ECE shall normally comprise three members;

    (b)   the chair shall be selected by the Council from a roster of experts developed in consultation with the ILO pursuant to Article 45 and, where possible, other members shall be selected from a roster developed by the Parties;

    (c)   ECE members shall:

        (i)   have expertise or experience in labor matters or other appropriate disciplines,

        (ii)   be chosen strictly on the basis of objectivity, reliability and sound judgment,

        (iii)   be independent of, and not be affiliated with or take instructions from, any Party or the Secretariat, and

        (iv)   comply with a code of conduct to be established by the Council;

    (d)   an ECE may invite written submissions from the Parties and the public;

    (e)   an ECE may consider, in preparing its report, any information provided by:

(i)   the Secretariat,

(ii)   the NAO of each Party,

(iii)   organizations, institutions and persons with relevant expertise, and

(iv)   the public; and

(f)   each Party shall have a reasonable opportunity to review and comment on information that the ECE receives and to make written submissions to the ECE.

2.   The Secretariat and the NAOs shall provide appropriate administrative assistance to an ECE, in accordance with the rules of procedure established by the Council under paragraph 1.

Article 25:   Draft Evaluation Reports

1.   Within 120 days after it is established, or such other period as the Council may decide, the ECE shall present a draft report for consideration by the Council, which shall contain:

(a)   a comparative assessment of the matter under consideration;

(b)   its conclusions; and

(c)   where appropriate, practical recommendations that may assist the Parties in respect of the matter.

2.   Each Party may submit written views to the ECE on its draft report. The ECE shall take such views into account in preparing its final report.

Article 26:   Final Evaluation Reports

1.   The ECE shall present a final report to the Council within 60 days after presentation of the draft report, unless the Council otherwise decides.

2.   The final report shall be published within 30 days after its presentation to the Council, unless the Council otherwise decides.

3.   The Parties shall provide to each other and the Secretariat written responses to the recommendations contained in the ECE report within 90 days of its publication.

4.   The final report and such written responses shall be tabled for consideration at the next regular session of the Council. The Council may keep the matter under review.

PART FIVE

RESOLUTION OF DISPUTES

Article 27:   Consultations

1.   Following presentation to the Council under Article 26(1) of an ECE final report that addresses the enforcement of a Party's occupational safety and health, child labor or minimum wage technical labor standards, any Party may request in writing consultations with any other Party regarding whether there has been a persistent pattern of failure by that other Party to effectively enforce such standards in respect of the general subject matter addressed in the report.

2.   The requesting Party shall deliver the request to the other Parties and to the Secretariat.

3.   Unless the Council otherwise provides in its rules and procedures established under Article 9(2), a third Party that considers it has a substantial interest in the matter shall be entitled to participate in the consultations on delivery of written notice to the other Parties and to the Secretariat.

4.   The consulting Parties shall make every attempt to arrive at a mutually satisfactory resolution of the matter through consultations under this Article.

Article 28:   Initiation of Procedures

1.   If the consulting Parties fail to resolve the matter pursuant to Article 27 within 60 days of delivery of a request for consultations, or such other period as the consulting Parties may agree, any such Party may request in writing a special session of the Council.

2.   The requesting Party shall state in the request the matter complained of and shall deliver the request to the other Parties and to the Secretariat.

3.   Unless it decides otherwise, the Council shall convene within 20 days of delivery of the request and shall endeavor to resolve the dispute promptly.

4.   The Council may:

(a)   call on such technical advisers or create such working groups or expert groups as it deems necessary;

(b) have recourse to good offices, conciliation, mediation or such other dispute resolution procedures; or

(c) make recommendations, as may assist the consulting Parties to reach a mutually satisfactory resolution of the dispute. Any such recommendations shall be made public if the Council, by a two-thirds vote, so decides.

5. Where the Council decides that a matter is more properly covered by another agreement or arrangement to which the consulting Parties are party, it shall refer the matter to those Parties for appropriate action in accordance with such other agreement or arrangement.

Article 29: Request for an Arbitral Panel

1. If the matter has not been resolved within 60 days after the Council has convened pursuant to Article 28, the Council shall, on the written request of any consulting Party and by a two-thirds vote, convene an arbitral panel to consider the matter where the alleged persistent pattern of failure by the Party complained against to effectively enforce its occupational safety and health, child labor or minimum wage technical labor standards is:

(a) trade-related; and

(b) covered by mutually recognized labor laws.

2. A third Party that considers it has a substantial interest in the matter shall be entitled to join as a complaining Party on delivery of written notice of its intention to participate to the disputing Parties and the Secretariat. The notice shall be delivered at the earliest possible time, and in any event no later than seven days after the date of the vote of the Council to convene a panel.

3. Unless otherwise agreed by the disputing Parties, the panel shall be established and perform its functions in a manner consistent with the provisions of this Part.

Article 30: Roster

1. The Council shall establish and maintain a roster of up to 45 individuals who are willing and able to serve as panelists. The roster members shall be appointed by consensus for terms of three years, and may be reappointed.

2. Roster members shall:

    (a)   have expertise or experience in labor law or its enforcement, or in the resolution of disputes arising under international agreements, or other relevant scientific, technical or professional expertise or experience;

    (b)   be chosen strictly on the basis of objectivity, reliability and sound judgment;

    (c)   be independent of, and not be affiliated with or take instructions from, any Party or the Secretariat; and

    (d)   comply with a code of conduct to be established by the Council.

Article 31:   Qualifications of Panelists

1.   All panelists shall meet the qualifications set out in Article 30.

2.   Individuals may not serve as panelists for a dispute where:

    (a)   they have participated pursuant to Article 28(4) or participated as members of an ECE that addressed the matter; or

    (b)   they have, or a person or organization with which they are affiliated has, an interest in the matter, as set out in the code of conduct established under Article 30(2)(d).

Article 32:   Panel Selection

1.   Where there are two disputing Parties, the following procedures shall apply:

    (a)   The panel shall comprise five members.

    (b)   The disputing Parties shall endeavor to agree on the chair of the panel within 15 days after the Council votes to convene the panel. If the disputing Parties are unable to agree on the chair within this period, the disputing Party chosen by lot shall select within five days a chair who is not a citizen of that Party.

    (c)   Within 15 days of selection of the chair, each disputing Party shall select two panelists who are citizens of the other disputing Party.

    (d)   If a disputing Party fails to select its panelists within such period, such panelists shall be selected by lot from among the roster members who are citizens of the other disputing Party.

2.　　Where there are more than two disputing Parties, the following procedures shall apply:

(a)　　The panel shall comprise five members.

(b)　　The disputing Parties shall endeavor to agree on the chair of the panel within 15 days after the Council votes to convene the panel. If the disputing Parties are unable to agree on the chair within this period, the Party or Parties on the side of the dispute chosen by lot shall select within 10 days a chair who is not a citizen of such Party or Parties.

(c)　　Within 30 days of selection of the chair, the Party complained against shall select two panelists, one of whom is a citizen of a complaining Party, and the other of whom is a citizen of another complaining Party. The complaining Parties shall select two panelists who are citizens of the Party complained against.

(d)　　If any disputing Party fails to select a panelist within such period, such panelist shall be selected by lot in accordance with the citizenship criteria of subparagraph (c).

3.　　Panelists shall normally be selected from the roster. Any disputing Party may exercise a peremptory challenge against any individual not on the roster who is proposed as a panelist by a disputing Party within 30 days after the individual has been proposed.

4.　　If a disputing Party believes that a panelist is in violation of the code of conduct, the disputing Parties shall consult and, if they agree, the panelist shall be removed and a new panelist shall be selected in accordance with this Article.

Article 33:　　Rules of Procedure

1.　　The Council shall establish Model Rules of Procedure. The procedures shall provide:

(a)　　a right to at least one hearing before the panel;

(b)　　the opportunity to make initial and rebuttal written submissions; and

(c)　　that no panel may disclose which panelists are

associated with majority or minority opinions.

2.   Unless the disputing Parties otherwise agree, panels convened under this Part shall be established and conduct their proceedings in accordance with the Model Rules of Procedure.

3.   Unless the disputing Parties otherwise agree within 20 days after the Council votes to convene the panel, the terms of reference shall be:

> To examine, in light of the relevant provisions of the Agreement, including those contained in Part Five, whether there has been a persistent pattern of failure by the Party complained against to effectively enforce its occupational safety and health, child labor or minimum wage technical labor standards, and to make findings, determinations and recommendations in accordance with Article 36(2).

Article 34:   Third Party Participation

A Party that is not a disputing Party, on delivery of a written notice to the disputing Parties and the Secretariat, shall be entitled to attend all hearings, to make written and oral submissions to the panel and to receive written submissions of the disputing Parties.

Article 35:   Role of Experts

On request of a disputing Party, or on its own initiative, the panel may seek information and technical advice from any person or body that it deems appropriate, provided that the disputing Parties so agree and subject to such terms and conditions as such Parties may agree.

Article 36:   Initial Report

1.   Unless the disputing Parties otherwise agree, the panel shall base its report on the submissions and arguments of the disputing Parties and on any information before it pursuant to Article 35.

2.   Unless the disputing Parties otherwise agree, the panel shall, within 180 days after the last panelist is selected, present to the disputing Parties an initial report containing:

(a)   findings of fact;

(b)   its determination as to whether there has been a persistent pattern of failure by the Party complained against to effectively enforce its occupational safety and health, child labor or minimum wage technical labor standards in a matter that is trade-related and covered by mutually recognized labor laws, or any other determination requested in the terms of reference; and

(c)   in the event the panel makes an affirmative determination under subparagraph (b), its recommendations, if any, for the resolution of the dispute, which normally shall be that the Party complained against adopt and implement an action plan sufficient to remedy the pattern of non-enforcement.

3.   Panelists may furnish separate opinions on matters not unanimously agreed.

4.   A disputing Party may submit written comments to the panel on its initial report within 30 days of presentation of the report.

5.   In such an event, and after considering such written comments, the panel, on its own initiative or on the request of any disputing Party, may:

(a)   request the views of any participating Party;

(b)   reconsider its report; and

(c)   make any further examination that it considers appropriate.

Article 37:   Final Report

1.   The panel shall present to the disputing Parties a final report, including any separate opinions on matters not unanimously agreed, within 60 days of presentation of the initial report, unless the disputing Parties otherwise agree.

2.   The disputing Parties shall transmit to the Council the final report of the panel, as well as any written views that a disputing Party desires to be appended, on a confidential basis within 15 days after it is presented to them.

3.   The final report of the panel shall be published five days after it is transmitted to the Council.

Article 38:   Implementation of Final Report

If, in its final report, a panel determines that there has been a persistent pattern of failure by the Party complained against to effectively enforce its occupational safety and health, child labor or minimum wage technical labor standards, the disputing Parties may agree on a mutually satisfactory action plan, which normally shall conform with the determinations and recommendations of the panel. The disputing Parties shall promptly notify the Secretariat and the Council of any agreed resolution of the dispute.

Article 39:   Review of Implementation

1.   If, in its final report, a panel determines that there has been a persistent pattern of failure by the Party complained against to effectively enforce its occupational safety and health, child labor or minimum wage technical labor standards, and:

      (a)   the disputing Parties have not agreed on an action plan under Article 38 within 60 days of the date of the final report; or

      (b)   the disputing Parties cannot agree on whether the Party complained against is fully implementing:

           (i)   an action plan agreed under Article 38,

           (ii)   an action plan deemed to have been established by a panel under paragraph 2, or

           (iii)   an action plan approved or established by a panel under paragraph 4, any disputing Party may request that the panel be reconvened. The requesting Party shall deliver the request in writing to the other Parties and to the Secretariat. The Council shall reconvene the panel on delivery of the request to the Secretariat.

2.   No Party may make a request under paragraph 1(a) earlier than 60 days, or later than 120 days, after the date of the final report. If the disputing Parties have not agreed to an action plan and if no request was made under paragraph 1(a), the last action plan, if any, submitted by the Party complained against to the complaining Party or Parties within 60 days of the date of the final report, or such other period as the disputing Parties may agree, shall be deemed to have been established by the panel 120 days after the date of the final report.

3.   A request under paragraph l(b) may be made no earlier than 180 days after an action plan has been:

(a)   agreed under Article 38;

(b)   deemed to have been established by a panel under paragraph 2; or

(c)   approved or established by a panel under paragraph 4, and only during the term of any such action plan.

4.   Where a panel has been reconvened under paragraph l(a), it:

(a)   shall determine whether any action plan proposed by the Party complained against is sufficient to remedy the pattern of non-enforcement and:

(i)   if so, shall approve the plan, or

(ii)   if not, shall establish such a plan consistent with the law of the Party complained against, and

(b)   may, where warranted, impose a monetary enforcement assessment in accordance with Annex 39, within 90 days after the panel has been reconvened or such other period as the disputing Parties may agree.

5.   Where a panel has been reconvened under paragraph l(b), it shall determine either that:

(a)   the Party complained against is fully implementing the action plan, in which case the panel may not impose a monetary enforcement assessment; or

(b)   the Party complained against is not fully implementing the action plan, in which case the panel shall impose a monetary enforcement assessment in accordance with Annex 39, within 60 days after it has been reconvened or such other period as the disputing Parties may agree.

6.   A panel reconvened under this Article shall provide that the Party complained against shall fully implement any action plan referred to in paragraph 4(a)(ii) or 5(b), and pay any monetary enforcement assessment imposed under paragraph 4(b) or 5(b), and any such provision shall be final.

Article 40:   Farther Proceeding

A complaining Party may, at any time beginning 180 days after a panel determination under Article 39(5)(b), request in writing that a panel be reconvened to determine whether the Party complained against is fully implementing the action plan. On delivery of the request to the other Parties and the Secretariat, the Council shall reconvene the panel. The panel shall make the determination within 60 days after it has been reconvened or such other period as the disputing Parties may agree.

Article 41:   Suspension of Benefits

1.   Subject to Annex 41A, where a Party fails to pay a monetary enforcement assessment within 180 days after it is imposed by a panel:

      (a)   under Article 39(4)(b); or

      (b)   under Article 39(5)(b), except where benefits may be suspended under paragraph 2(a), any complaining Party or Parties may suspend, in accordance with Annex 41B, the application to the Party complained against of NAFTA benefits in an amount no greater than that sufficient to collect the monetary enforcement assessment.

2.   Subject to Annex 41A, where a panel has made a determination under Article 39(5)(b) and the panel:

      (a)   has previously imposed a monetary enforcement assessment under Article 39 4(b) or established an action plan under Article 39(4)(a)(ii); or

      (b)   has subsequently determined under Article 40 that a Party is not fully implementing an action plan, the complaining Party or Parties may, in accordance with Annex 41B, suspend annually the application to the Party complained against of NAFTA benefits in an amount no greater than the monetary enforcement assessment imposed by the panel under Article 39(5)(b).

3.   Where more than one complaining Party suspends benefits under paragraph 1 or 2, the combined suspension shall be no greater than the amount of the monetary enforcement assessment.

4.   Where a Party has suspended benefits under paragraph 1 or 2, the Council shall, on the delivery of a written request by the Party complained against to the other Parties and the Secretariat, reconvene the panel to determine whether the monetary enforcement assessment has been paid or collected, or whether the Party complained against is fully implementing the action plan, as the case may be. The panel shall submit its report within 45 days after it has been reconvened. If the panel

determines that the assessment has been paid or collected, or that the Party complained against is fully implementing the action plan, the suspension of benefits under paragraph 1 or 2, as the case may be, shall be terminated.

5.	On the written request of the Party complained against, delivered to the other Parties and the Secretariat, the Council shall reconvene the panel to determine whether the suspension of benefits by the complaining Party or Parties pursuant to paragraph 1 or 2 is manifestly excessive. Within 45 days of the request, the panel shall present a report to the disputing Parties containing its determination.

PART SIX

GENERAL PROVISIONS

Article 42:	**Enforcement Principle**

Nothing in this Agreement shall be construed to empower a Party's authorities to undertake labor law enforcement activities in the territory of another Party.

Article 43:	**Private Rights**

No Party may provide for a right of action under its domestic law against any other Party on the ground that another Party has acted in a manner inconsistent with this Agreement.

Article 44:	**Protection of Information**

1.	If a Party provides confidential or proprietary information to another Party, including its NAO, the Council or the Secretariat, the recipient shall treat the information on the same basis as the Party providing the information.

2.	Confidential or proprietary information provided by a Party to an ECE or a panel under this Agreement shall be treated in accordance with the rules of procedure established under Articles 24 and 33.

Article 45:	**Cooperation with the ILO**

The Parties shall seek to establish cooperative arrangements with the ILO to enable the Council and Parties to draw on the expertise and experience of the ILO for purposes of implementing Article 24(1).

Article 46:   Extent of Obligations

Annex 46 applies to the Parties specified in that Annex.

Article 47:   Funding of the Commission

Each Party shall contribute an equal share of the annual budget of the Commission, subject to the availability of appropriated funds in accordance with the Party's legal procedures. No Party shall be obligated to pay more than any other Party in respect of an annual budget.

Article 48:   Privileges and Immunities

The Executive Director and staff of the Secretariat shall enjoy in the territory of each of the Parties such privileges and immunities as are necessary for the exercise of their functions.

Article 49:   Definitions

1.   For purposes of this Agreement:

A Party has not failed to "effectively enforce its occupational safety and health, child labor or minimum wage technical labor standards" or comply with Article 3(1) in a particular case where the action or inaction by agencies or officials of that Party:

     (a)   reflects a reasonable exercise of the agency's or the official's discretion with respect to investigatory, prosecutorial, regulatory or compliance matters; or

     (b)   results from *bona fide* decisions to allocate resources to enforcement in respect of other labor matters determined to have higher priorities;

"**labor law**" means laws and regulations, or provisions thereof, that are directly related to:

(a) freedom of association and protection of the right to organize;

(b) the right to bargain collectively;

(c) the right to strike;

(d) prohibition of forced labor;

(e) labor protections for children and young persons;

(f) minimum employment standards, such as minimum wages and overtime pay, covering wage earners, including those not covered by collective agreements;

(g) elimination of employment discrimination on the basis of grounds such as race, religion, age, sex, or other grounds as determined by each Party's domestic laws;

(h) equal pay for men and women;

(i) prevention of occupational injuries and illnesses;

(j) compensation in cases of occupational injuries and illnesses;

(k) protection of migrant workers;

"**mutually recognized labor laws**" means laws of both a requesting Party and the Party whose laws were the subject of ministerial consultations under Article 22 that address the same general subject matter in a manner that provides enforceable rights, protections or standards;

"**pattern of practice**" means a course of action or inaction beginning after the date of entry into force of the Agreement, and does not include a single instance or case;

"**persistent pattern**" means a sustained or recurring pattern of practice;

"**province**" means a province of Canada, and includes the Yukon Territory and the Northwest Territories and their successors;

"**publicly available information**" means information to which the public has a legal right under the statutory laws of the Party;

"**technical labor standards**" means laws and regulations, or specific provisions thereof, that are directly related to subparagraphs (d) through (k) of the definition of labor law. For greater certainty and consistent with the provisions of this Agreement, the setting of all standards and levels in respect of minimum wages and labor protections for children and young persons by each Party shall not be subject to obligations under this Agreement. Each Party's obligations under this Agreement pertain to enforcing the level of the general minimum wage and child labor age limits established by that Party;

"territory" means for a Party the territory of that Party as set out in Annex 49; and

"trade-related" means related to a situation involving workplaces, firms, companies or sectors that produce goods or provide services:

    (a)   traded between the territories of the Parties; or

    (b)   that compete, in the territory of the Party whose labor law was the subject of ministerial consultations under Article 22, with goods or services produced or provided by persons of another Party.

PART SEVEN

FINAL PROVISIONS

Article 50:   **Annexes**

The Annexes to this Agreement constitute an integral part of the Agreement.

Article 51:   **Entry into Force**

This Agreement shall enter into force on January 1, 1994, immediately after entry into force of the NAFTA, on an exchange of written notifications certifying the completion of necessary legal procedures.

Article 52:   **Amendments**

1.   The Parties may agree on any modification of or addition to this Agreement.

2.   When so agreed, and approved in accordance with the applicable legal procedures of each Party, a modification or addition shall constitute an integral part of this Agreement.

Article 53:   Accession

Any country or group of countries may accede to this Agreement subject to such terms and conditions as may be agreed between such country or countries and the Council and following approval in accordance with the applicable legal procedures of each country.

Article 54:   Withdrawal

A Party may withdraw from this Agreement six months after it provides written notice of withdrawal to the other Parties. If a Party withdraws, the Agreement shall remain in force for the remaining Parties.

Article 55:   Authentic Texts

The English, French and Spanish texts of this Agreement are equally authentic.

IN WITNESS WHEREOF, the undersigned, being duly authorized by the respective Governments, have signed this Agreement.

ANNEX 1

LABOR PRINCIPLES

The foll wing are guiding principles that the Parties are committed to promote, subject to each Party's domestic law, but do not establish common minimum standards for their domestic law. They indicate broad areas of concern where the Parties have developed, each in its own way, laws, regulations, procedures and practices that protect the rights and interests of their respective workforces.

1.   Freedom of association and protection of the right to organize

The right of workers exercised freely and without impediment to establish and join organizations of their own choosing to further and defend their interests.

2.   The right to bargain collectively

The protection of the right of organized workers to freely engage in collective bargaining on matters concerning the terms and conditions of employment.

3.   The right to strike

The protection of the right of workers to strike in order to defend their collective interests.

4.   Prohibition of forced labor

The prohibition and suppression of all forms of forced or compulsory labor, except for types of compulsory work generally considered acceptable by the Parties, such as compulsory military service, certain civic obligations, prison labor not for private purposes and work exacted in cases of emergency.

5.   Labor protections for children and young persons

The establishment of restrictions on the employment of children and young persons that may vary taking into consideration relevant factors likely to jeopardize the full physical, mental and moral development of young persons, including schooling and safety requirements.

6.   Minimum employment standards

The establishment of minimum employment standards, such as minimum wages and overtime pay, for wage earners, including those not covered by collective agreements.

7.   Elimination of employment discrimination

Elimination of employment discrimination on such grounds as race, religion, age, sex or other grounds, subject to certain reasonable exceptions, such as, where applicable, *bona fide* occupational requirements or qualifications and established practices or rules governing retirement ages, and special measures of protection or assistance for particular groups designed to take into account the effects of discrimination.

8. Equal pay for women and men

Equal wages for women and men by applying the principle of equal pay for equal work in the same establishment.

9. Prevention of occupational injuries and illnesses

Prescribing and implementing standards to minimize the causes of occupational injuries and illnesses.

10. Compensation in cases of occupational injuries and illnesses

The establishment of a system providing benefits and compensation to workers or their dependents in cases of occupational injuries, accidents or fatalities arising out of, linked with or occurring in the course of employment.

11. Protection of migrant workers

Providing migrant workers in a Party's territory with the same legal protection as the Party's nationals in respect of working conditions.

ANNEX 23

INTERPRETIVE RULING

1.   Where a Party has requested the Council to convene an ECE, the Council shall, on the written request of any other Party, select an independent expert to make a ruling concerning whether the matter is:

      (a)   trade-related; or

      (b)   covered by mutually recognized labor laws.

2.   The Council shall establish rules of procedure for the selection of the expert and for submissions by the Parties. Unless the Council decides otherwise, the expert shall present a ruling within I5 days after the expert is selected.

ANNEX 39

MONETARY ENFORCEMENT ASSESSMENTS

1.   For the first year after the date of entry into force of this Agreement, any monetary enforcement assessment shall be no greater than 20 million dollars (U.S.) or its equivalent in the currency of the Party complained against. Thereafter, any monetary enforcement assessment shall be no greater than .007 percent of total trade in goods between the Parties during the most recent year for which data are available.

2.   In determining the amount of the assessment, the panel shall take into account:

   (a)   the pervasiveness and duration of the Party's persistent pattern of failure to effectively enforce its occupational safety and health, child labor or minimum wage technical labor standards;

   (b)   the level of enforcement that could reasonably be expected of a Party given its resource constraints;

   (c)   the reasons, if any, provided by the Party for not fully implementing an action plan;

   (d)   efforts made by the Party to begin remedying the pattern of non-enforcement after the final report of the panel; and

   (e)   any other relevant factors.

3.   All monetary enforcement assessments shall be paid in the currency of the Party complained against into a fund established in the name of the Commission by the Council and shall be expended at the direction of the Council to improve or enhance the labor law enforcement in the Party complained against, consistent with its law.

ANNEX 41A

CANADIAN DOMESTIC ENFORCEMENT AND COLLECTION

1.   For the purposes of this Annex, "panel determination" means:

   (a)   a determination by a panel under Article 39(4)(b) or 5(b) that provides that Canada shall pay a monetary enforcement assessment; and

(b)   a determination by a panel under Article 39(5)(b) that provides that Canada shall fully implement an action plan where the panel:

    (i)   has previously established an action plan under Article 39(4)(a)(ii) or imposed a monetary enforcement assessment under Article 39(4)(b), or

    (ii)   has subsequently determined under Article 40 that Canada is not fully implementing an action plan.

2.   Canada shall adopt and maintain procedures that provide that:

(a)   subject to subparagraph (b), the Commission, at the request of a complaining Party, may in its own name file in a court of competent jurisdiction a certified copy of a panel determination;

(b)   the Commission may file in court a panel determination that is a panel determination described in paragraph l(a) only if Canada has failed to comply with the determination within 180 days of when the determination was made;

(c)   when filed, the panel determination, for purposes of enforcement, shall become an order of the court;

(d)   the Commission may take proceedings for enforcement of a panel determination that is made an order of the court, in that court, against the person against whom the panel determination is addressed in accordance with paragraph 6 of Annex 46;

(e)   proceedings to enforce a panel determination that has been made an order of the court shall be conducted by way of summary proceedings;

(f)   in proceedings to enforce a panel determination that is a panel determination described in paragraph l(b) and that has been made an order of the court, the court shall promptly refer any question of fact or any question of interpretation of the panel determination to the panel that made the panel determination, and the decision of the panel shall be binding on the court;

(g)   a panel determination that has been made an order of

the court shall not be subject to domestic review or
appeal; and

(h)   an order made by the court in proceedings to enforce a
panel determination that has been made an order of the
court shall not be subject to review or appeal.

3.   Where Canada is the Party complained against, the procedures
adopted and maintained by Canada under this Annex shall apply and the
procedures set out in Article 41 shall not apply.

4.   Any change by Canada to the procedures adopted and maintained
by Canada under this Annex that have the effect of undermining the provisions of this Annex shall be considered a breach of this Agreement.

ANNEX 41B

SUSPENSION OF BENEFITS

1.   Where a complaining Party suspends NAFTA tariff benefits in
accordance with this Agreement, the Party may increase the rates of
duty on originating goods of the Party complained against to levels not
to exceed the lesser of:

(a)   the rate that was applicable to those goods immediately
prior to the date of entry into force of the NAFTA; and

(b)   the Most-Favored-Nation rate applicable to those goods
on the date the Party suspends such benefits, and such
increase may be applied only for such time as is
necessary to collect, through such increase, the
monetary enforcement assessment.

2.   In considering what tariff or other benefits to suspend pursuant
to Article 41(1) or (2):

(a)   a complaining Party shall first seek to suspend benefits
in the same sector or sectors as that in respect of which
there has been a persistent pattern of failure by the Party
complained against to effectively enforce its
occupational safety and health, child labor or minimum
wage technical labor standards; and

(b)   a complaining Party that considers it is not practicable
or effective to suspend benefits in the same sector or
sectors may suspend benefits in other sectors.

ANNEX 46

EXTENT OF OBLIGATIONS

1.　　On the date of signature of this Agreement, or of the exchange of written notifications under Article 51, Canada shall set out in a declaration a list of any provinces for which Canada is to be bound in respect of matters within their jurisdiction. The declaration shall be effective on delivery to the other Parties, and shall carry no implication as to the internal distribution of powers within Canada. Canada shall notify the other Parties six months in advance of any modification to its declaration.

2.　　Unless a communication relates to a matter that would be under federal jurisdiction if it were to arise within the territory of Canada, the Canadian NAO shall identify the province of residence or establishment of the author of any communication regarding the labor law of another Party that it forwards to the NAO of another Party. That NAO may choose not to respond if that province is not included in the declaration made under paragraph 1.

3.　　Canada may not request consultations under Article 22, the establishment of an Evaluation Committee of Experts under Article 23, consultations under Article 27, the initiation of procedures under Article 28 or the establishment of a panel or join as a complaining Party under Article 29 at the instance, or primarily for the benefit, of the government of a province not included in the declaration made under paragraph 1.

4.　　Canada may not request consultations under Article 22, the establishment of an Evaluation Committee of Experts under Article 23, consultations under Article 27, the initiation of procedures under Article 28 or the establishment of a panel or join as a complaining Party under Article 29, unless Canada states in writing that the matter would be under federal jurisdiction if it were to arise within the territory of Canada, or:

　　　　(a)　　Canada states in writing that the matter would be under provincial jurisdiction if it were to arise within the territory of Canada; and

　　　　(b)　　the federal government and the provinces included in the declaration account for at least 35 percent of Canada's labor force for the most recent year in which data are available; and

(c)   where the matter concerns a specific industry or sector, at least 55 percent of the workers concerned are employed in provinces included in Canada's declaration under paragraph 1.

5.   No other Party may request consultations under Article 22, the establishment of an Evaluation Committee of Experts under Article 23, consultations under Article 27, the initiation of procedures under Article 28 or the establishment of a panel or join as a complaining Party under Article 29, concerning a matter related to a labor law of a province unless that province is included in the declaration made under paragraph 1 and the requirements of subparagraphs 4(b) and (c) have been met.

6.   Canada shall, no later than the date on which an arbitral panel is convened pursuant to Article 29 respecting a matter within the scope of paragraph 5 of this Annex, notify in writing the complaining Parties and the Secretariat of whether any monetary enforcement assessment or action plan imposed by a panel under Article 39(4) or (5) against Canada shall be addressed to Her Majesty in right of Canada or Her Majesty in right of the province concerned.

7.   Canada shall use its best efforts to make the Agreement applicable to as many of its provinces as possible.

8.   Two years after the date of entry into force of this Agreement, the Council shall review the operation of this Annex and, in particular, shall consider whether the Parties should amend the thresholds established in paragraph 4.

ANNEX 49

COUNTRY-SPECIFIC DEFINITIONS

For purposes of this Agreement:

"territory" means:

(a)   with respect to Canada, the territory to which its customs laws apply, including any areas beyond the territorial seas of Canada within which, in accordance with international law and its domestic law, Canada may exercise rights with respect to the seabed and subsoil and their natural resources;

(b)   with respect to Mexico,

    (i)   the states of the Federation and the Federal District,

    (ii)   the islands, including the reefs and keys, in adjacent seas,

    (iii)   the islands of Guadalupe and Revillagigedo situated in the Pacific Ocean,

    (iv)   the continental shelf and the submarine shelf of such islands, keys and reefs,

    (v)   the waters of the territorial seas, in accordance with international law, and its interior maritime waters,

    (vi)   the space located above the national territory, in accordance with international law, and

    (vii)   any areas beyond the territorial seas of Mexico within which, in accordance with international law, including the *United Nations Convention on the Law of the Sea*, and its domestic law, Mexico may exercise rights with respect to the seabed and subsoil and their natural resources; and

(c)   with respect to the United States,

    (i)   the customs territory of the United States, which includes the 50 states, the District of Columbia and Puerto Rico,

    (ii)   the foreign trade zones located in the United States and Puerto Rico, and

    (iii)   any areas beyond the territorial seas of the United States within which, in accordance with international law and its domestic law, the United States may exercise rights with respect to the seabed and subsoil and their natural resources.

5

North American Commission for Environmental Cooperation

Introduction

The North American Free Trade Agreement (NAFTA) is unique among trade agreements in the disparity of economic development among its member countries, with Mexico being much less developed than the other two partners. Because of its lower level of economic development, Mexico has had significantly less stringent environmental protection than either the United States or Canada. Air pollution problems in Mexico City are legendary, and pollution along the Mexican border with the United States has reached deplorable levels by almost any standard.

Because of this disparity, environmental groups in the United States had great concerns about NAFTA. They feared that polluting industries might migrate to Mexico, causing further deterioration of the environment there and long-term damage to the global commons. They also wondered whether, if this migration of industries to minimize their pollution control costs did occur, that would not make it more difficult to raise environmental standards in the United States. Some even talked of a "race to the bottom" implying competitive erosion of environmental standards as countries attempted to attract or retain capital. Labor unions worried about the possible effects of capital migration to "pollution havens" on employment and wage rates in the United States.

Because of opposition of environmental nongovernmental organizations (NGOs), it eventually became apparent that NAFTA would not gain the necessary approval from the U.S. Congress without some measures to deal with environmental concerns. During the presidential campaign of 1992, candidate Clinton stated that he would support the NAFTA agreement only if there were supplemental agreements on environmental and labor issues. Negotiations began soon after the election, which ultimately resulted in the North American Agreement on Environmental Cooperation (NAAEC).

These were sensitive negotiations because both Canada and Mexico have historically gone to some lengths to protect their national sovereignty against encroachment by the superpower next door. The fact that Mexico would consider entering into a free trade agreement of any sort with the United States was virtually unthinkable a mere ten years earlier. Negotiations that would address the concerns of environmentalists in the United States and at the same time not offend the sensibilities of the other two partners, particularly Mexico, were indeed a challenge. The NAAEC that resulted from these negotiations definitely reflects in its provisions the tensions inherent in trying to balance these two objectives.

For many years environmentalists have worried about the effects of increasing globalization on the environment. The trade policy establishment has been leery of linking environmental issues with trade issues, fearing that environmental regulations could easily be used as nontariff barriers to trade. A clash of cultures has occurred between the environmental and trade policy communities. Trade negotiations have traditionally been carried out, if not in secret, at least with a low degree of transparency. The environmental community has been politically active and at times confrontational in pursuit of its goals. A high level of mistrust has characterized relations between the two communities. A trade and environment committee was established within the General Agreement on Tariffs and Trade (GATT) as early as 1990, but for several years it did not meet. Only recently have steps been taken to seriously consider some of the issues of greatest concern to environmentalists.

Within the context of the NAFTA negotiations, the environmental NGOs would have preferred harmonization of environmental policies among the countries of North America, with trade sanctions available as an enforcement mechanism. This would, of course, have implied upward harmonization of the environmental policies and practices of Mexico to match those of the United States and Canada. Economists generally contend that economically efficient environmental policies must differ according to the economic conditions of the countries involved and the preferences of their citizens. Nevertheless, pressures for harmonization of both environmental and social policies arise whenever the level of economic integration is deepened, as it undoubtedly has been because of the NAFTA agreement.

Actually, the concerns of environmentalists regarding Mexico related more to their poor enforcement of environmental regulations than to deficiencies in the regulations themselves. In many instances the environmental standards of Mexico did not differ greatly from those in the United States and Canada. However, enforcement of the regulations has been hampered by a lack of resources for inspection, and by limitations of the technical and scientific expertise required for adequate monitoring of environmental conditions. In some cases corruption of government officials has allowed businesses to escape the burden of pollution control costs.

Because of this concern over poor enforcement of environmental regulations in Mexico, the NAAEC focuses on measures that would improve enforcement and make some additional resources available for monitoring environmental conditions and for remedying deficiencies in them. Several trilateral institutions were established for this purpose, along with bilateral institutions focused specifically on the U.S.-Mexico border region. Chief among the trilateral institutions is the North American Commission for Environmental Cooperation (CEC).

Commission for Environmental Cooperation

The CEC is composed of three parts: a council, a secretariat, and a joint public advisory committee.

The Council

The council is composed of cabinet-level representatives of the member countries (or those whom they designate) who have responsibility for environmental issues. To date, cabinet-level officials have served as the council, a practice that is likely to continue. In addition, each country has designated alternate representatives to represent council members as necessary, and a general standing committee consisting of a government employee of each member country to act as liaison with the secretariat on most routine matters.

The council meets at least once a year, and more frequently on request, with the chairmanship rotating among the members. The council generally makes decisions by consensus, with some important exceptions discussed below. It holds public meetings at each of its regular sessions, and may hold other public meetings at its own discretion.

The council serves as the governing body of the commission, approving its annual budget and program, and overseeing the secretariat. The council fosters cooperation among the member countries, deals with disputes concerning the implementation or application of the NAAEC, and in general oversees implementation of the agreement. The council may develop recommendations concerning a wide variety of stated environmental issues. It is also to work toward the strengthening of environmental laws and regulations through fostering the exchange of information about how domestic environmental policies are established, and to encourage the upward harmonization of environmental standards and regulations.

The council is supposed to work with the NAFTA Free Trade Commission toward the attainment of the environmental goals and objectives implicit in NAFTA. This task is to be accomplished in a number of ways: by receiving input from NGOs and others concerning the environmental goals and objectives of NAFTA; by helping to deal with cases of suspected weakening of environmental standards to attract investment; by regularly assessing the environmental effects of NAFTA; and by seeking in various other ways to help the member countries avoid or resolve disputes over environmental issues.

The Secretariat

The secretariat is the administrative organ of the North American CEC, and is located in Montreal, Canada. An executive director, who is appointed by the council for a renewable three-year term, heads the secretariat. The position of executive director rotates among nationals of the three members of the agreement. The staff members of the secretariat are chosen based on their qualifications and with a genuine attempt to ensure that the professional staff members are equitably proportioned among nationals of the three member countries.

The secretariat is directed to act independently, neither seeking nor receiving instructions from any of the member governments, and the governments are instructed to respect this independence. Also, the secretariat provides technical advice and expertise on environmental issues to the council, to the committees and working groups that it establishes, and to the public as appropriate.

Each year the secretariat publishes an annual report of the CEC that summarizes the activities of the commission, accounts for its expenses during the previous year, and presents its budget for the next. It also provides information about to what extent each of the member countries is living up to the terms of the NAAEC, including data on how each is enforcing environmental regulations.

The secretariat periodically assesses environmental conditions in each of the member countries. The NAAEC makes specific provision for the inclusion of information submitted by NGOs, this reflecting the insistence by those responsible for the NAFTA supplemental agreements that the views of civil society find expression through the institutions created by the agreements.

The secretariat prepares and publishes reports in connection with the CEC's work program. Examples of such reports are the annual publication, *Taking Stock: North American Pollutant Releases and Transfers*, and specialized reports such as *Status of Pollution Prevention in North America.* Also, through the secretariat the CEC issues research studies in support of the annual work program. These are not intended for publication and general dissemination, but are available upon request from the CEC. Examples of these studies are: "Analysis of the Potential for a Greenhouse Gas Trading System for North America," and "North American Cooperation on Voluntary Energy Efficiency Programs: A Case Study."

Article 13 Reports

Article 13 of the NAAEC provides that the secretariat can, at its own initiative or at the request of a private party, carry out in-depth investigations of environmental issues that have significant importance to the North American region. Article 13 investigations are limited to "nonenforcement" matters. That is, the secretariat cannot conduct an Article 13 investigation into whether a member country is enforcing its environmental laws. Other parts of the agreement provide for that type of investigation. If the matter to be investigated is within the scope of the annual work program of the CEC, the secretariat can initiate an investigation on its own. If it wishes to investigate other environmental matters it must notify the council of its intent, and unless the council by a two-thirds vote objects to the study within thirty days, the secretariat may proceed with the plan. During the first five years of the CEC's existence, only three issues have been studied by the secretariat under Article 13 authorization.

First Article 13 Investigation

The first Article 13 investigation was in response to a petition filed in mid-1995 by the National Audubon Society of the United States and the Centro Mexicano de Derecho Ambiental and the Grupo de los Cien International[e] of Mexico. These organizations requested investigation into why so many migratory birds were dying at the Silva Reservoir in Guanajuato, Mexico. In December of the previous year an estimated 20,000 to 40,000 birds had perished at the reservoir.

The Silva reservoir was constructed in 1884 to provide water for irrigation of surrounding farmland. Rivers feeding the reservoir carry untreated wastewater from cities, farms, and numerous industries. Mexico had tried previously, without much success, to deal with the problem. After the mass bird mortality in late 1994, the following February Mexico launched a new effort, called the Turbio Basin Initiative to try to clean up the wastewater being generated by surrounding municipalities and industries.

The secretariat, noting that migratory birds are a shared North American resource protected by agreements signed by each of the countries, responded to the petition by commissioning a trinational panel of nine scientists to look into the matter and determine the causes of the waterbird mortality. The panel was asked to assess other instances of mass mortality of waterbirds in the member countries. It was also charged to consider what could be done to deal with pollution in the Turbio River Basin, particularly through international cooperative efforts. The results of its investigation were published as *CEC Secretariat Report on the Death of Migratory Birds at the Silva Reservoir (1994–95)* (CEC 1995).

The panel noted that many instances of mass mortality of migratory birds had occurred in North America during this century, with the worst episodes occurring in the United States and Canada. In the summer of 1995 an estimated 60,000 birds died in an incident in Alberta, Canada. After studying the evidence in the Silva Reservoir case, the panel concluded that the deaths were primarily attributable to botulism. This botulism could have been caused by untreated sewage in the water. On the other hand, the scientists found concentrations of chromium, lead, and mercury in the water. The many tanneries located in the region use chromium in the tanning process. If birds were killed by the concentrations of heavy metals, their carcasses could then have served as the protein source for the botulism.

The panel of experts suggested several possible options for management of the Silva Reservoir, and recommended that Mexico develop a program of surveillance of wildlife health and strategies for responding to disease outbreaks among wildlife. They also recommended a partnership among Mexico, Canada, and the United States to address this issue and others relating to the welfare of wildlife in North America. The council moved in 1996 to establish a team of experts on migratory waterfowl to serve as a rapid response team in case other instances such as the one at the Silva Reservoir were detected.

Second Article 13 Investigation

The second Article 13 investigation was initiated by the secretariat in 1996 to study air quality conditions in North America. As in the case of migratory birds, air pollutants are of concern to all three NAFTA countries. Because the ecosystems of North America are shared and transcend national boundaries, control of air quality is beyond the capability of any of the countries acting alone. In recognition of the threats posed to human health and to the environment by various air pollutants, the secretariat launched this study of the long-range transport of air pollutants in North America.

The final report, entitled *Continental Pollutant Pathways: An Agenda for Cooperation to Address Long Range Transport of Air Pollutants in North America* (CEC 1997a) drew upon several sources of expertise. The secretariat appointed an expert advisory panel on continental pollutant pathways, consisting of more than thirty scientists from the NAFTA countries, to study the issue. A consultative group on continental pollutant pathways consisting of approximately fifty representatives of various interest groups advised the panel. Also involved were a policy group of twenty persons experienced in formulating and implementing policies related to air pollution, and an advisory group of the CEC Air Monitoring and Modeling Project consisting of fifteen government and academic experts who regularly advise the CEC on air quality issues.

The report studied acid rain, mercury, ozone, particulate matter, and airborne persistent organic pollutants. It concluded that significant spillovers of pollutants occur among the countries of North America, and that while bilateral and international efforts at pollution control existed, a continental perspective was lacking.

The study identified major sources of continental pollutants and noted that the risks arising from continental pollutants could be significantly reduced by focusing on a relatively small number of common source categories. The report recommended greater coordination and more frequent updating of emission inventories, and more collaboration of the scientists involved in monitoring and researching air pollution problems. It noted that resources devoted to researching and monitoring continental pollutant pathways had declined in recent years, and recommended a reversal of that trend. In general, the report called for making control of continental air pollution a matter of high trinational priority.

Third Article 13 Investigation

The third Article 13 investigation was initiated in May 1997 to assess problems of water quality and quantity in the San Pedro River Basin that crosses the border between Mexico and Arizona. The complaint that initiated the investigation was filed by the Southwest Center for Biological Diversity and Dr. Robin Silver. It was prompted, at least in part, by expansion of the Fort Huachuca army base and the potential impact of that expansion on the region's water supply.

The San Pedro River Basin is one of unusual ecological richness and diversity. It is the habitat of a large number of mammals, some of which are endangered. More than 390 different bird species have been documented as being present in the area, several of which are listed as endangered species. The riparian forest in the area is populated at certain times of the year by 1 million to 4 million migratory birds as they make their way between wintering sites in Mexico and Central America to breeding grounds in the United States and Canada.

The major concern with regard to the San Pedro River Basin is that, at current rates of water extraction from the underlying aquifer, the ecological integrity of the area cannot be sustained over the long term. Withdrawals from the aquifer presently exceed recharges by an estimated 7,000 acre-feet per year. Without major changes that deficit is likely to grow as population and industrialization in the areas that draw upon the aquifer increase.

The secretariat first commissioned a six-member expert study team to conduct a scientific investigation of the physical and biological requirements to preserve and enhance the riparian resources of the San Pedro River Basin. After the report of the study team was released in June 1998, a process of public review and comment was launched to gather reactions from a large number of interested parties. Next, the secretariat convened a thirteen-member Upper San Pedro Advisory Panel that included members from all three NAFTA countries. This task of this panel was to formulate policy recommendations to help attain the goals identified in the previous two steps.

Based upon the work of the groups previously mentioned, the secretariat in June 1999 issued a report titled *Ribbon of Life: An Agenda for Preserving Transboundary Migratory Bird Habitat on the Upper San Pedro River*. In this report, the secretariat concluded that binational resource management would be essential to preserving the riparian habitat of the Upper San Pedro Basin. Although this area lies entirely within the United States, the water flow into the area is influenced by actions in Mexico where the San Pedro River originates. One outcome of the study was a suggestion that the area of riparian forest could possibly be extended southward into Mexico. The report recommends more information gathering and research on the ecological problems of the area. It also recommends various measures to encourage water conservation, including voluntary retirement of irrigated fields. International agencies, such as the CEC, the International Boundary and Water Commission, and the Border Environment Cooperation Commission were encouraged to facilitate the efforts of local governments and to help obtain financing to implement projects suggested in the advisory panel report.

The Article 13 investigations have looked into matters that are of much environmental concern to all of the countries of North America. The sensitivity of environmental issues is apparent from the fact that two of these investigations were carried out over the objections of member governments. The Mexican government objected to the Silva Reservoir report, probably because it feared embarrassment over the high levels of pollution that existed there. The U.S. government objected to the Upper San Pedro River Basin study because one of the main users of water in the area is Fort Huachuca, a U.S. army base. The existence of the NAAEC made possible the study of environmental issues in each of these cases, and full consideration of them, in ways that likely would not have been possible without the agreement.

Article 14 Submissions*

Article 14 of the NAAEC provides that the secretariat may consider submissions from persons or organizations in any member country alleging that one of the member countries is failing to effectively enforce its environmental regulations. Such submissions must allege harm to the person or organization making the charge, and first must have been submitted to the relevant authorities in the country accused and must include their response. Also, the person or organization submitting the allegation must have exhausted any possible private remedies.

The secretariat decides whether a submission merits a response from the accused country, such decision being based primarily on whether further study of the issues raised by the submission would advance the purposes of the NAAEC. When the secretariat so decides, the response by the accused country is to be made within thirty days (or sixty days in exceptional circumstances). After receiving the response, the secretariat decides whether or not a factual record on the issue should be developed. The factual record sets forth the facts of the case, including the secretariat's assessment concerning to what degree, and in what ways, the accused country is failing to enforce its own environmental regulations.

Article 15 of the agreement provides that when the secretariat decides that a factual record should be developed, it makes this recommendation to the council, providing reasons for its recommendation. If two of the three council members agree, a factual record is prepared, drawing upon information from a variety of sources. Specific mention is made in the NAAEC of possible input from both NGOs and the Joint Public Advisory Committee (JPAC), again emphasizing the desire for participation by civil society in the process.

After a draft of the factual record has been prepared, it is submitted to the member country governments for comments on its accuracy within forty-five days. After taking account of such comments, the factual record is made public (normally within sixty days) upon the approval of two of the three council members. This is where the matter ends for submissions from individuals and NGOs. No provision exists for an arbitral panel or for trade sanctions as a result of such submissions.

_____

*Information on the citizen submissions discussed in this section is extracted from the Registry of Submissions on Enforcement Matters as found on the web page of the CEC.

1995 Submissions

The first two submissions under Article 14 were made in 1995, and both alleged that the United States was failing to enforce its environmental laws. The first of these was filed by the Biodiversity Legal Foundation, et al., contending that enactment of the Recissions Act of 1995 prevented the enforcement of certain provisions of the Endangered Species Act. The secretariat terminated this submission, rationalizing that by passing the Recissions Act the U.S. Congress had implemented laws that superceded the provisions of the Endangered Species Act. Therefore, since a new legal regime had been established, the United States could not be accused of failing to enforce its laws.

The second submission in 1995 was filed by the Sierra Club of the United States, and Mexican and Canadian environmental groups. This submission also contended that a rider to the Recissions Act of 1995 suspended the enforcement of environmental laws, in this case laws related to a logging program on public lands. This submission was terminated for the same reason as the previous one, and also because the alleged failure to effectively enforce environmental laws lacked a factual basis.

That these two submissions were terminated should surprise no one. Certainly the lawmakers of a country retain the right to modify or to change the application of existing laws by passing new legislation. Because these cases dealt with specific instances rather than alleging a "persistent failure" to apply environmental laws, they could not be filed under Part V of the NAAEC and therefore could not proceed to arbitration. Article 14 submissions can lead only to the publication of a factual record. In any event, had the secretariat pursued these submissions to the level of a factual record the political fallout would have been severe.

1996 Submissions

During 1996, four submissions were filed, one against Mexico, two against Canada, and one against the United States. The submission against Mexico, filed by several NGOs, contended that the government of Mexico failed to enforce its environmental laws by allowing the construction of a cruise ship terminal on the island of Cozumel without the required environmental impact statement. The terminal and related works were built in a protected area and allegedly endangered the Paradise Reef and the Caribbean Barrier Reef. The secretariat judged this submission to have sufficient merit to proceed to the development of a factual record. After receiving requisite approval by the council, the CEC proceeded to conduct an investigation of the matter and to prepare a factual record that was published and released to the public in late 1997.

The submission in 1996 charging the United States with failure to enforce its environmental laws was filed by the Southwest Center for Biological Diversity and Dr. Robin Silver. The submission contended that the United States failed to enforce environmental laws pertaining to the expansion of a U.S. Army base that would have an adverse impact on the water supplies of the Upper San Pedro River Basin. The submitters withdrew their petition after receiving the response of the U.S. government. Figuring into the decision to withdraw the petition was the knowledge that the secretariat would study the matter under the provisions of Article 13, as described earlier in this chapter.

Of the two submissions against Canada during 1996, one charged the Canadian government with failure to enforce environmental laws that would have prevented pollution of wetlands, thereby adversely affecting both fish and migratory bird habitats. The other submission charged failure to enforce habitat protection sections of the Canadian Fisheries Act and the Canadian Environmental Assessment Act. The secretariat ruled in both cases that the submissions did not merit requesting a response from the Canadian government because the matters were pending before Canadian courts of law. The secretariat noted that if the plaintiffs prevailed in the legal cases, the concerns expressed in the submissions would have been remedied by domestic court actions. The secretariat invited the submitters to refile the submissions at a later time if the Canadian court decisions were not sufficient to satisfy the stated concerns.

1997 Submissions

In 1997, seven submissions were filed under Article 14, two against Mexico and five against Canada. In one of the submissions against Mexico, the government was charged with failure to enforce Mexican environmental legislation concerning the disposal of wastewater. Specifically, the submission charged that three municipalities in the Mexican state of Sonora were discharging untreated wastewater into the Magdalena River. In its response the Mexican government pointed to economic limitations on its ability to completely fulfill its obligations under existing laws. As of mid-1999 the secretariat was still reviewing the submission in the light of the Mexican government's response of 29 July 1998.

The second submission against Mexico in 1997 charged that proper administrative procedures had not been followed in the response to a citizen's complaint seeking to declare a state of emergency in the Lake Chapala ecosystem. The Mexican government's response contended that: the complainant had not exhausted domestic legal remedies; the delay in responding to the citizen's complaint was caused by the need to obtain a technical analysis from the National Water Commission in order to decide if there was a state of emergency; and, an ecological emergency did not exist. As of mid-1999, the secretariat was reviewing this submission in light of the response provided by the Mexican government on 16 December 1998.

Of the five submissions against Canada during 1997, two were terminated by the secretariat. One of these charged that the Canadian government had failed to conduct an environmental impact assessment of the Atlantic groundfish strategy, thereby jeopardizing the future of Canada's east coast fisheries. The secretariat rejected this submission on the grounds that Article 14 requires a contention that a government "is failing" to enforce its environmental laws. Since the failure to conduct the environmental impact assessment had occurred three years earlier, and no apparent reason existed for the complainant not filing the submission at that time, the secretariat ruled that the submission did not meet the requisite criteria.

In the other 1997 submission against Canada that was terminated by the secretariat, several NGOs contended that the Canadian government was not living up to the terms of the Convention on Biological Diversity signed at the Rio Earth Summit in 1992. The treaty requires the signatory countries to maintain endangered species lists, which Canada was not doing. The NGOs contended that, by ratifying the Convention on Biological Diversity, the ratifying instrument had become a legally binding document, and had thereby become an environmental regulation that Canada was obligated to enforce under the terms of the NAAEC. After studying the issue, the secretariat concluded that, "In Canada there is a fundamental and long-standing constitutional principle, derived from Canada's legal heritage, that the ratification process does not import international obligations into domestic law. Until international obligations are implemented by way of statute or regulation pursuant to a statute, those obligations do not constitute the domestic law of Canada" (CEC 1998b). Therefore, the secretariat ruled that the submission did not legitimately assert a failure by Canada to effectively enforce its environmental law, and the secretariat terminated the case.

Two of the 1997 submissions against Canada alleged a failure to protect fish habitat as required by Canadian law. One of these concerned the building of hydroelectric dams on British Columbian rivers and the resultant adverse impact on fish habitat. In this case the council has instructed the secretariat to develop a factual record on the matter. The other submission is a refiling of one of the 1996 submissions terminated because, at the time, the issue was a matter of domestic litigation in Canada. It contends that prosecutions for damage to fish habitat under the Fisheries Act are too few and are unevenly distributed across the country. In mid-1999 the secretariat was still reviewing the Canadian government's response to the submission.

The final submission against Canada in 1997 was filed by a large number of NGOs in Quebec alleging that the government there was failing to enforce environmental protection standards concerning pollution originating in animal production facilities, particularly hog farms. In mid-1999 the secretariat was still evaluating the submission to determine whether it warranted development of a factual record.

1998 Submissions

Of the seven submissions filed during 1998, one was against the United States, one against Canada, and five against Mexico. The submission against the United States charged that the U.S. Environmental Protection Agency had failed to enforce domestic laws of the United States, and U.S.–Canada treaties, concerning regulations controlling airborne emissions of mercury and other toxic substances. The submitters contended that U.S. regulations for solid waste and medical waste incinerators were not as stringent as agreed in the Great Lakes Water Quality Agreement. The secretariat terminated the case, arguing that the dispute dealt with the setting of standards, not with whether standards were being effectively enforced. Since Article 14 submissions can be filed only to contend that a country is not enforcing its own environmental regulations, not to challenge whether the appropriate regulations were established, the secretariat ruled that the submission did not qualify for further consideration.

The one submission against Canada in 1998 dealt again with alleged failure to protect fish habitat. In this case the concern was with acid-generating mines in British Columbia that allegedly are depositing toxic substances into the water. The submitters contend that staff reductions and other cutbacks at Environment Canada were responsible for Canada's not enforcing its Fisheries Act against the mining companies. In mid-1999 the secretariat had requested a response from the government of Canada on this issue.

Of the five submissions against Mexico during 1998, one was terminated and the others were awaiting review from the secretariat as of mid-1999. In the case that was terminated, the submitter alleged improper administrative procedures in connection with a lumbering operation in the state of Jalisco. After reviewing the matter the secretariat referred to it as a "private commercial dispute." In any event, the case dealt with the exploitation of a natural resource, a subject area for which disputes are off limits for NAAEC submissions under Article 14.

Of the four submissions against Mexico that are currently under review by the secretariat, one alleges that failure to enforce environmental laws led to the explosion in gasoline-tainted sewers in Guadalajara on 22 April 1992 that killed more than 200 people and injured more than 1,400. The Mexican government has not yet responded to the allegation.

Another contends that the Mexican government authorized operation of a hazardous waste landfill less than six kilometers from the city of Hermosillo, Sonora, when according to regulations it should have been at least twenty-five miles away. The Mexican government responded that the submitter did not exhaust all available domestic remedies, and that, in any case, the landfill was authorized before the regulation in question existed.

Of the remaining two submissions against Mexico in 1998, one alleged failure to enforce numerous environmental laws in connection with the establishment and operation of a shrimp farm in Isla del Conde. The Mexican government acknowledged environmental problems in connection with this shrimp farm, but contended that, under the terms of the NAAEC, the submitters should have exhausted all available domestic legal remedies before filing the submission, which they did not do.

The final submission against Mexico alleged that the government of Mexico has failed to enforce its environmental law in connection with an abandoned lead smelter in Tijuana, Baja California. The submission alleges that a U.S. firm closed the Mexican operation and abandoned the facility without returning the hazardous waste that it generated to the United States, as required by Mexican law and the La Paz Agreement. The waste included 6,000 metric tons of lead slag, sulfuric acid, and various heavy metals and other debris left over from a battery recycling operation. In addition to filing the submission requesting a factual record, the complainant also has requested that the matter be investigated and a report published under Article 13 of the NAAEC.

Summary of the Submissions

Of the twenty submissions filed during the first five and a half years of the NAAEC, eight have been against Mexico, eight against Canada, and four against the United States. Nine of the cases have been terminated by the secretariat as either not having merit or not having been valid submissions under the criteria set forth in the NAAEC. Nine of the cases were, as of mid-1999, still under various stages of review by the secretariat. In only one case, that dealing with the construction of a cruise ship terminal in Cozumel, Mexico, had a factual record been developed and published. In only one other case, that dealing with the impact of hydroelectric dam construction on fish habitat in British Columbia, Canada, had the council instructed the secretariat to develop a factual record. The council will need to act again on the matter before the factual record is released to the public.

It is perhaps worthy of note that during the first seven months of 1999 no Article 14 submissions had been filed. The low likelihood that a submission will lead to a factual record (based upon experience thus far) and the delays involved in the process seem to be having an inhibiting effect on the filing of submissions. An alternative explanation could be that the member governments, fearing the exposure that an Article 14 submission brings, are being more careful about the enforcement of their laws.

Advisory Committees

In addition to giving individuals and NGOs access to the secretariat through the Article 14 submissions process, the NAAEC makes provision for further public input into the work of the CEC through the establishment of a joint public advisory committee (JPAC). The JPAC is a trinational committee composed of fifteen members, with an equal number chosen by each of the member countries. It meets at least once a year at the time of the regular session of the council. The JPAC can advise the council on any matters within the scope of the agreement. It receives reports and other information developed by the secretariat, and with the approval of two of the three council members may receive a factual record (even if the factual record is not being released to the public).

At its option, each member country may convene a national advisory committee (NAC) to provide further input from civil society concerning the implementation of the NAAEC. Both the United States and Canada have formed such committees and they have been quite active. To date, Mexico has chosen not to establish a NAC. In addition, each country may form a governmental advisory committee (GAC) to provide input from federal and state, or provincial, government agencies. Both the United States and Canada have formed such committees, although in Canada participation in the GAC is limited to representatives of those provinces that have approved the NAAEC through the federal-provincial agreement. Mexico has not yet established a GAC.

Consultation and Dispute Resolution Under Part V of the NAAEC

If one of the NAFTA member countries has a complaint about a *persistent pattern* of failure by a partner country to enforce its environmental law, and if the enforcement failure is trade related, Part V of the NAAEC provides that the case can be taken before an arbitral panel. Trade sanctions can possibly be employed as an enforcement mechanism.

However, the NAAEC places a strong emphasis on settling environmental disputes among the NAFTA members in a cooperative fashion. Accordingly, whenever a question is raised concerning whether one of the member countries has a persistent pattern of failure to enforce its environmental law, the mandated first step is to request in writing consultations with the accused country on the matter. Every effort is to be made to achieve a mutually satisfactory solution through consultations.

Should consultations fail to provide a satisfactory resolution of the matter within sixty days, the complaining party may request a special session of the council that, unless it decides otherwise, is to meet within twenty days to try to resolve the dispute. The council may draw upon the expertise of technical advisers, employ various dispute resolution procedures such as mediation and conciliation, or make its own recommendations concerning how the dispute should be resolved.

If the matter cannot be resolved within sixty days of the convening of the council, the complaining party may request an arbitral panel to resolve the dispute. If two of the three council members agree, a panel will be convened, drawn from a roster of up to forty-five panelists maintained by the council. The panelists are persons who are knowledgeable about environmental law and its enforcement, who are experienced in international dispute resolution, or who have particular technical or other expertise suitable for dealing with environmental issues. They should have no conflict of interest regarding the dispute. The panelists are to act independently of any of the member governments.

The dispute settlement panels consist of five members. The disputing parties ideally agree, within fifteen days, on a chair of the panel from the roster of panelists. Should they not be able to agree, one of the countries is selected by lot to choose as chair a panelist who is a citizen of the other country. Within fifteen days after the chair of the panel is selected, each country then chooses two panelists from the roster who are citizens of the other country. In the case where there are more than two disputing parties, each of the complaining parties chooses one panelist from the country complained against.

The dispute settlement panel receives submissions from each of the parties to the dispute, and also rebuttal submissions. The panel may consider information from technical experts or other sources of information as agreed by the disputing parties. Normally, the panel will make an initial report to the disputing parties within 180 days from the time that the last panelist is chosen. This report includes the facts of the case as the panel sees them, and a judgment concerning whether or not the accused member country is failing to effectively enforce its environmental law. Upon an affirmative finding of failure to enforce, the panel makes recommendations concerning how the dispute can be resolved. Minority opinions can be expressed, but the panel is not to disclose which panelists are associated with majority and minority opinions.

After the disputing parties have received the initial report, they have thirty days to react to it in the form of written comments. After receiving these comments, the panel may then request further information, may reconsider its decision, or may conduct further investigation. The panel issues a final report within sixty days of the initial report, unless the disputing parties agree otherwise. The disputing parties, within fifteen days of receiving the final report, forward it to the council, appending any information on a confidential basis that they would like the council to consider. The final report is then published five days after it has been transmitted to the council.

After the final report is published, if the panel has found a persistent pattern of failure to enforce environmental law the disputing parties may agree on a mutually satisfactory action plan. If they cannot agree on such a plan within sixty days after the date of the final report, within the next sixty days the complaining party can request the reconvening of the dispute settlement panel. The reconvened panel makes an assessment concerning whether the action plan proposed by the party complained against is sufficient to remedy the nonenforcement of environmental law. If it decides that the proposed action plan is a sufficient remedy, then it approves the plan. If it decides that the proposed action plan is not a sufficient remedy, the panel devises an action plan consistent with the law of the party complained against, and may also impose a monetary enforcement assessment. This assessment may be up to .007 percent of the total trade in goods between the disputing parties during the most recent year for which data are available. The funds generated by such an assessment are deposited into an account in the name of the CEC, and are spent at the direction of the council to improve environmental conditions or the enforcement of environmental law in the country against which the assessment was made.

Conceivably, the parties might not agree on a mutually acceptable action plan. Or, if the panel imposes an action plan, the disputing parties could disagree concerning whether the action plan is being fully implemented. In either of these cases, after 180 days from the time that the action plan was established, the complaining party can request that the panel be reconvened to consider the matter. The panel renders its judgment on whether the action plan is being fully implemented within sixty days after it has been reconvened, unless the parties agree otherwise. Should the panel decide that the action plan is not being fully implemented, it imposes a monetary enforcement assessment as described above.

In the unlikely event that the party assessed a fine under the terms of the dispute resolution procedure fails to pay the fine, then the complaining party is authorized to suspend NAFTA benefits sufficient to collect the monetary enforcement assessment. (This provision actually applies only to the United States and Mexico, as Canada has agreed that fines assessed against it will become "an order of the court" and therefore collected through the court system). This suspension of benefits involves raising the tariff rate on goods from the party complained against to the lesser of the rate imposed on goods just before NAFTA entered into force, or the most-favored-nation rate currently in force. To the degree practicable, the benefits suspended are to be in that sector (or sectors) in which there has been a persistent failure to enforce environmental law.

The party which has had its NAFTA benefits suspended can request a reconvening of the panel to render a judgment as to whether the monetary enforcement assessment has been collected, or whether it is presently fully implementing the recommended action plan. The panel renders a judgment on the matter within forty-five days. The suspension of benefits is terminated if the panel determines either that the monetary enforcement assessment has been collected or that the action plan is being fully implemented.

An interesting feature of this enforcement mechanism concerns the ways in which revenues accrue to the countries involved. When trade sanctions are imposed, the tariff revenue accrues to the country that suspends the NAFTA benefits. In contrast, money that is collected from the party complained against through a monetary enforcement assessment goes back to that country to be used for improving environmental conditions or enforcing environmental law. Even in this latter case, however, environmental externalities are not internalized by collecting the assessment from the polluting industry. Furthermore, the funds collected do not necessarily go toward remedying the specific lack of enforcement that was complained against.

As is apparent from the foregoing description, the process involved in sanctioning countries for a persistent failure to apply their environmental laws is by design highly convoluted, with multiple opportunities for the accused country to escape the sanctions. The clear intent is for environmental disputes among the member countries to be settled through consultation and cooperation. No disputes have yet been filed under Part V, and the likelihood that they will be seems remote. No private party access exists under Part V of the NAAEC, that is, consultations that begin the dispute settlement process under Part V of the agreement must be initiated by a NAFTA member government. Informal consultations among the member governments will likely preclude the more formal proceedings of the Part V dispute settlement process.

Work Program of the Commission for Environmental Cooperation

Much of the impact of the CEC will result from its tripartite work program established for the purpose of improving environmental conditions in North America. In 1998 this work program was organized under five headings: environment, economy, and trade; biodiversity and ecosystems; pollutants and health; capacity building; and law and enforcement cooperation.

In 1998, 19.2 percent of the direct program costs were designated for initiatives under the heading of environment, economy, and trade. Some of the projects under this heading dealt with linkages between trade and the environment, linkages between trade and species conservation, sustainable tourism in natural areas, and NAFTA environmental effects.

A very important aspect of this part of the CEC work program has been a project designed to assess the degree to which there is a relationship between trade-induced changes brought about by NAFTA and changes in environmental conditions in North America. As mentioned earlier, a major motivation for the development and adoption of the NAAEC was concern among environmental groups that, in a variety of ways, increased trade due to NAFTA would contribute to environmental degradation. Establishing accurately the relationship between trade and environmental conditions is a daunting task, and the secretariat has devoted a great deal of time and effort to determining an appropriate analytical approach to this problem.

In 1999 the CEC issued a publication as part of the NAFTA effects work program titled: *Assessing Environmental Effects of the North American Free Trade Agreement (NAFTA): An Analytic Framework (Phase II) and Issue Studies* (CEC 1999b). This publication sets forth a methodology for assessing the relationship between international trade and the environment, with particular reference to NAFTA. It suggests, first, putting the issue or sector being studied fully into context by looking at its environmental context, its economic context, its social context, and its geographic context. Next, the NAFTA connection of the issue is examined by taking into account the resulting rule changes, institutional changes, effects on trade and investment flows, and concurrent changes in macroeconomic variables that have resulted from NAFTA. Then the methodology identifies four main ways in which trade and investment changes are linked to the environment: through production, management, and technology; through physical infrastructure; through social organization; and through government policy. Finally, an effort is made to take account of the effect of all of these changes on specific environmental conditions (ibid., 7).

This methodology has been applied to three case studies: feedlot production of cattle in the United States and Canada; maize in Mexico; and electricity in North America.

In the case of feedlot production of cattle, the study found that NAFTA will likely reinforce existing patterns of production and trade, with the United States and Canada expanding their feedlot operations and supplying meat to Mexico, and with Mexico supplying feeder cattle to the United States. The concentration of feedlot operations has several ramifications for the environment. These range from the runoff of fertilizers and pesticides used in grain production, to additional demands on water supply, to potential effects of manure disposal on both air and water quality. However, the study concludes that "the environmental issues surrounding beef production in North America, while potentially serious, are all capable of remediation and prevention if adequate attention and resources are devoted to them" (ibid., Annex 2, 1). The study further notes that having the feedlot operations concentrated in the United States and Canada should allow better regulatory oversight and optimal use of environmental technologies to reduce the adverse environmental effects.

In its study of electricity in North America, the CEC notes that the electricity industry is in a state of rapid change. Some of this change can be attributed to NAFTA trade, but much of it is the result of policy changes that were independent of NAFTA, such as deregulation of electricity markets. If the increased competition arising both from policy changes and NAFTA trade leads to accelerated capital turnover, with older and much more highly polluting plants being replaced more rapidly, the environmental effects of these changes will be strongly positive.

Many of the older and highly polluting electricity plants in the United States are currently operating with much excess capacity, however. If they are allowed to continue operation with lower environmental standards, and if as a result they maintain a cost advantage that allows them to expand output, the environmental impact would be negative. The study concludes that, "Because the electricity sector is experiencing dramatic change, and will continue to do so in each of the three countries, it is premature to qualify the environmental impacts as positive, negative, or a combination of the two" (ibid., Annex 3, 7).

In its study of maize in Mexico, the CEC examined a sector that accounts for approximately two-thirds of total agricultural output in Mexico, and for which up to 18 million people depend for their livelihood (ibid., Annex 3, iii). Corn production in Mexico is commonly recognized as relatively inefficient. Therefore, liberalization of trade in this product has the potential for significant dislocation in Mexico, with resultant environmental effects. The study notes that the effects on the environment will differ according to whether corn production in Mexico is modernized, whether other crops are substituted for corn, or whether corn continues to be produced through traditional methods for self-consumption. Various ecological implications of each scenario are hypothesized, ranging from possible soil depletion to loss of genetic diversity through widespread use of high yield corn varieties.

A second category of the work program, which in 1998 accounted for 14 percent of the project budget, was titled biodiversity and ecosystems. The major project in this category is one aimed at enhancing regional cooperation in the conservation of birds in North America. Another project is the establishment of a North American Biodiversity Information Network that would establish linkages among the providers and users of biodiversity information in North America.

The largest category of the 1998 work program in terms of expenditure, accounting for 37.3 percent of the project budget, was that of pollutants and health. Under this category programs have been implemented dealing with the sound management of pollutant chemicals, such as mercury, chlordane, DDT, and PCBs. North American pollutant release inventories have been prepared using compatible methods of reporting on pollutant emissions from each of the three countries. These inventories are providing for the first time information about the nature and extent of pollutants entering the North American environment. Other programs under this general category have dealt with such issues as the monitoring of air quality, cooperating on a North American system for trading emissions credits as a method of controlling the release of greenhouse gases, and programs for helping small and medium enterprises prevent pollution.

A fourth category of the work program falls under the heading of capacity building. In 1998 it accounted for 19.1 percent of the project budget. Projects under this heading include a binational program between the United States and Mexico to protect the marine and coastal area ecosystems in the Bight of the Californias, and a similar program between the United States and Canada pertaining to the Gulf of Maine.

Also included under this heading are such projects as technical assistance in the phasing out of harmful chemicals such as chlordane and DDT in Mexico, and help for small and medium enterprises in Mexico to obtain financing for pollution prevention.

A fifth category of the work program, which accounted for 10.1 percent of the 1998 budget, falls under the heading of law and enforcement cooperation. Work within this category aims to facilitate cooperation within North America on the enforcement of environmental laws and compliance with environmental regulations. This work is conducted in cooperation with the North American working group on environmental enforcement and compliance that was created by the council in 1996. The program focuses on the sharing of information about enforcement strategies or practices that would be helpful to the other parties in their enforcement efforts. It also works to encourage trinational enforcement cooperation programs and initiatives where they are feasible. A report on environmental enforcement is included as part of the annual report of the CEC. Through work in this area the member countries look for new ways to improve environmental performance, focusing on best practices that exceed minimum levels of compliance with existing regulations.

Participation with the Broader Environmental Community

The CEC leverages its program activities through providing grants to NGOs in support of projects that reinforce CEC priorities. As of mid-October 1999, through its North American Fund for Environmental Cooperation, the CEC had made 125 grants totaling almost $5 million (CEC 1999a). These grants funded projects such as development of a conservation plan for the San Pedro River in Mexico, an awareness-raising campaign among citizens in Canadian communities living in the vicinity of mercury disposal sites, strengthening local producers' cooperatives in the environmentally sound shade coffee industry in Mexico, and programs in Canada to encourage the consumption of shade coffee. This involvement of civil society in the work of the CEC helps to broaden both its scope and depth, and to build support for the institution within the environmental community.

Four-Year Review of the NAAEC

As was the case with the North American Agreement on Labor Cooperation, the NAAEC provided for an independent assessment of the functioning of the agreement after it had been in effect for four years. Accordingly, the CEC appointed a three-person team of external reviewers. The review committee consisted of León Bendesky, director of ERI Economic Consultants in Mexico City; Barbara J. Bramble, senior director of international affairs, National Wildlife Federation in Washington, D.C.; and Stephen Owen, Lam Professor of Law and Public Policy and director of the Institute for Dispute Resolution at the University of Victoria in British Columbia. The review committee did a thorough assessment of the NAAEC and provided a detailed report. (CEC 1998a) They also presented a lengthy list of recommendations. (See Appendix 5.1 of this chapter)

The review committee took note of some of the challenges facing the CEC as an organization. Having only three member countries presents some difficulties, for differences among the countries tend to be magnified. The CEC's task is further complicated by the economic and social differences among the member countries, as well as by the breadth of the subjects with which the institution has to deal. In addition, because the institution was born amidst some conflict, this has caused problems in attaining the ideal level of cooperation.

The review committee expressed the view that the NAAEC should be considered as a free-standing agreement in its own right, and not just a side agreement to NAFTA. The committee criticized the CEC for initially having a work program that was too broad and unfocused. It also noted that the work of the CEC will take on additional significance as the negotiations for the Free Trade Area for the Americas proceed, for environmental issues will be part and parcel of those negotiations. How these issues have been dealt with in the North American context will provide an important model for how they will be addressed in the broader framework of hemispheric free trade, assuming that it materializes.

The review committee sees some problems arising from the fact that Mexico perceives the NAAEC as having been forced upon it as a condition for approval of NAFTA. Partly because of this history, Mexico apparently considers itself a target of CEC actions. While there have been as many citizen submissions under Article 14 against Canada as against Mexico, the first case to proceed to a factual record was against Mexico. Also, the first investigation under Article 13 involved a situation in Mexico. The principle of equal participation in the CEC budget has placed some strain on Mexico's environmental budget, and the return on the investment is not immediately apparent to Mexico.

Another matter of some concern is that the work of the CEC is sometimes hampered by interagency disagreements within the national governments. An attempt should be made to have more interagency cooperation and involvement in CEC matters. Also, in Canada full participation in the agreement is hampered by the fact that only three of the Canadian provinces (Alberta, Quebec, and Manitoba) have signed the Canadian Intergovernmental Agreement to participate with the federal government in implementing the NAAEC. Since much of environmental regulation in Canada is carried out at the provincial level, having less than full participation by the provinces is a definite drawback.

In general, the review committee looked favorably upon the functioning of the CEC thus far. They recommended a more focused work program, more careful evaluation of projects, and the development of a three-year rolling work program. The three-year program, while reassessed each year, would give a longer planning cycle and more stability to the work programs. The committee also recommended more interaction between the CEC and the NAFTA Free Trade Commission. While the review committee considered current funding levels for the CEC to be adequate, they suggested that funding links with donors and major development banks be developed so that more resources would be available for the implementation of agreed projects.

Conclusion

The CEC was the first of the NAFTA-related institutions to establish a secretariat and to get its work program organized and operational. By virtue of its charter the commission is a supranational institution (as is the Commission for Labor Cooperation), in that a significant number of its decisions can be made by a two-thirds vote of the member countries. This is something new in North American relations, and is quite remarkable in view of the reluctance of the United States to cede authority to international or regional institutions, and the caution with which both Canada and Mexico have generally approached their relations with the United States.

For those who expected the NAAEC to greatly improve environmental conditions in North America or to cause much more stringent enforcement of environmental laws, the functioning of the CEC must be a disappointment. In more than five years only three Article 13 investigations have been carried to completion. Of twenty submissions under

Article 14, half of them have been terminated by the secretariat. Eight others are still under review. In only two cases have factual records been developed, and in only one of those has the factual record been made public. Even in the case in which the factual record was made public, it contained not a single recommendation, and did nothing to alleviate the threat to the Paradise Reef from the Cozumel port. No "persistent pattern" of failure to enforce environmental laws has been detected, so the enforcement mechanisms of Part V remain untested, and are likely to remain so, at least in the near term.

Yet, in the long run the NAAEC may well turn out to be a much more significant agreement than is commonly recognized. It does have some successes to point to, such as the phasing out of the hazardous pesticides chlordane and DDT in Mexico, and the voluntary closing of the only plant producing chlordane in the United States. The Silva Reservoir in Mexico is cleaner than it was, and the attention brought to the problems there by the Article 13 study and the resultant cooperation to deal with those problems no doubt owe much to the existence of the CEC. More is understood than before about pollutant pathways in North America, and great strides have been made toward the systematic collection of data on environmental conditions in North America.

On the face of it, the commitment made by countries in the NAAEC to enforce their own environmental laws and regulations does not seem to be very significant. However, the fact that governments can be challenged on their enforcement record, with a mechanism in place to possibly refute their claims of compliance, will over time have a subtle but important effect on attitudes and practices.

The CEC is the first of a new generation of environmental institutions that have a link to international trade. In the words of Neomi Gal-Or, "[T]he formation of NAAEC itself must be considered a victory for the environmental cause. An international trade agreement is providing for an environmental enforcement institution, and whether it is embryonic or fully developed is immaterial at this stage" (Gal-Or 1997, 92). In a real sense, the CEC is serving as a model for the rest of the world in defining the relationship between institutions concerned with environmental issues and those focused on trade issues. Before the NAAEC, very little trinational environmental cooperation existed in North America (although there was considerable bilateral cooperation) and the linkage between international economic interchanges and environmental impacts received minimal consideration. Through the various activities of the

CEC a relatively high level of cooperation on environmental matters now exists within North America. And through the work program of the CEC, pathbreaking work is being carried out to analyze the environmental effects of a regional trade agreement.

The CEC is a very young institution, and has suffered some growing pains. The strategic vision of the institution has been slow to develop, and its early work has been somewhat unfocused. The institution experienced considerable strain when the first executive director of the secretariat, a Mexican national, was forced to resign the day after having fired the top U.S. official at the agency. However, the institution has survived these early challenges and is stronger today than before. In contrast to some of the other NAFTA-related institutions, the CEC is sufficiently funded to carry out its mandate. Its importance as a key regional institution is likely to grow, and over time it will make a significant contribution to improved environmental conditions in North America.

Appendix 5.1
Recommendations of the Independent Review Committee

Recommendation 1: The NAAEC and the CEC should be seen not as just a side deal for trade, but as a complete and vital agreement in its own right.

Recommendation 2: The Parties should pay specific attention to the needs of the others, with a view to ensuring that CEC activities are not used "against" any one of them, or to pursue the interests of any one Party.

Recommendation 3: Political support for the CEC within the three Parties should be built through stronger interagency involvement and internal communications. Relevant agencies of the Parties might also play a constructive role directly in CEC discussions, within their areas of responsibility, so as to broaden the education and communication between governmental and nongovernmental agencies concerned with environment and trade linkages. The environment ministries, however, remain the lead government agencies in the CEC.

Recommendation 4: The Parties should maintain the current level of funding of the CEC, subject to revisiting this issue if the Council's agreed upon program so justifies.

Recommendation 5: The Government of Canada, as one of the three Parties to this Agreement, should redouble its efforts to engage all the provinces in the NAAEC. This could, for example, be linked to further progress in the development of all or part of the Harmonization Agreement on the Environment between the two levels of government.

Recommendation 6: The Council of the CEC should undertake a careful process to articulate both a strategic vision of its contribution to sustainable development in North America and its process for achieving this vision. The vision should be coherent and comprehensive, and set a platform for the annual work program.

Recommendation 7: The strategic vision must be a shared one, based on the consensus of the Council. This flows directly from the first, second, and third recommendations, above.

Recommendation 8: The Alternate Representatives and the General Standing Committee should continue to assist the Council in its oversight of the CEC operations, but this should be done in an efficient manner that avoids duplication and displays internally consistent direction.

Recommendation 9: It should be recognized that the Secretariat acts independently of any one of the Parties, but that it also acts as an integral part of the CEC as a whole. In its traditional functions, the Secretariat serves to assist, advise and inform the Council.

Recommendation 10: The Secretariat, in developing its proposed annual work program and budget, should be mindful of the strategic vision to be established by the Council and work within its spirit and its constraints.

Recommendation 11: The citizen submission process should continue as presently designed, based on a scrupulous application of the Agreement and the Guidelines, respecting the limits of actions they contain as well as the discretion provided to the respective decision-makers at the different points in the process. The existing review of the operation of this process should be completed after more submissions have been processed, including factual records when appropriate, in order to provide a greater body of experience to draw upon. The Secretariat should be expeditious in dealing with the public submissions.

Recommendation 12: Clear divisions should be developed between the staff responsible for the submissions process and those responsible for other work. When some dual functions are required, they should be minimized, using the concept of "Chinese walls"—maintaining strict working divisions between these functions.

Recommendation 13: The practice of having two "national" director positions should be ended as soon as possible after the new Executive Director is selected, in favor of a more broadly based approach to equitable representation of senior-level functional staff.

Recommendation 14: The JPAC should refocus its efforts on its original mandate: to provide trilateral independent advice to the Council. This advice should concentrate on what the Council requires to do its work effectively. Achieving this goal should be facilitated by the establishment of a strategic vision and three-year work program by the Council, which should provide a substantive focus for any JPAC public consultations.

Recommendation 15: Considering the quality of the contributions from the existing NACs and GACs that the Committee has seen, the IRC recommends that Mexico advance its development of these bodies, perhaps working through the Mexican Sustainable Development Council for its NAC. Without restricting the discretion of the NACs, the IRC hopes that a longer planning cycle for the CEC will help their assessments of the CEC work program and of other matters on the Council's agenda.

Recommendation 16: The resources and energy devoted to public consultation should be efficiently used and productive. This requires focused and well prepared consultation processes, on concrete matters. If a three-year work program is adopted, public consultations can be better timed to provide the most support to informed decision-making.

Recommendation 17: NAFEC should continue to be a source of community funding, but with a mandate more related to the programs of the CEC. Building on the three-year program cycle, NAFEC should seek to fund projects so as to develop a critical mass of community-based experience on key topics in the CEC work program, in order to help inform the Secretariat and Council in their respective program and decision-making functions.

Recommendation 18: The CEC should deal with the relationship between environment and trade in an open and constructive manner. Existing projects confirm the ability of the CEC to address practical aspects of this relationship in a manner that demonstrates the positive links between them. This should be creatively built upon, when possible, in other projects.

Recommendation 19: The CEC should continue to pursue its NAFTA effects work. This should be done in an inclusive manner, bringing in experts from environmental and trade backgrounds, and looking at both the positive contributions of trade liberalization to environmental protection and potential negative impacts. This will be an evolving process as the ability to assess these impacts is developed and mutual trust is gained.

Recommendation 20: The CEC should immediately initiate contacts with the NAFTA Free Trade Commission and its subsidiary bodies, with a view to establishing routine contacts for information purposes. Where a NAFTA body is undertaking work with an environmental dimension or impact, appropriate Secretariat liaison should be developed as a conduit to the Council. The goal should be to facilitate a full consideration of the potential impacts in a coordinated and effective manner. In addition, senior environment and trade officials should plan a meeting of the environment and trade ministers as early as possible in order to confirm this relationship.

Recommendation 21: The CEC should adopt a rolling three-year program and budget cycle, updated each year and revised as necessary. The overall program should focus upon a smaller number of clear and meaningful deliverables rather than a large number of less significant ones. Project quality, not coverage of project categories, should be the key factor in program development.

Recommendation 22: The IRC recommends that a process be put in place, in time for the end of the first year of the longer program period, to provide systematic measurement and evaluation of the annual results of each project. This should include a "lessons learned" analysis for both successes and failures in the project. A similar review process following the conclusion of a project should be undertaken.

Recommendation 23: The program contents should reflect the key priorities of the Parties, based on the three-year rolling program already recommended. This will be facilitated through discussions between the Secretariat and the Council prior to drafting the budget, a summer meeting of the Parties and the Secretariat to consider the Parties' priorities, and a clear timetable established by the Council for completion of the process.

Recommendation 24: Program decisions should be based on criteria that reflect the strategic vision and purpose of the CEC. The range of criteria include: the regional nature of the issue being addressed; the ability of projects to build on elements of other projects; the incorporation of key features of sustainable development in the project (e.g., capacity building, scientific information and public participation); the ability to make environment and trade part of the living program; the comparative advantage of the CEC to address the issue; and the need to ensure adequate resources for the CEC's mandatory program items.

Recommendation 25: The CEC should seek to develop funding links with donors as well as the major development banks, such as the World Bank and Inter-American Development Bank, in order to better develop the capacity building elements of its projects.

Recommendation 26: The development of the substantive elements of the work program (outside of the special responsibilities of the Secretariat) are subject to the general oversight of the Council as a whole. At the same time, the Secretariat must act independently of the control of any one Party. This requires a two-way commitment to the neutral position of the Secretariat in its role of supporting, advising and informing the Council. It should also be understood that the reports of the Secretariat or the CEC do not necessarily represent the views of any individual Party.

Source: Commission for Environmental Cooperation. 1998. Four-year review of the North American Agreement on Environmental Cooperation: Report of the Independent Review Committee. Montreal, Canada.

Appendix 5.2
North American Agreement on Environmental Cooperation

PREAMBLE

The Government of Canada, the Government of the United Mexican States and the Government of the United States of America:

CONVINCED of the importance of the conservation, protection and enhancement of the environment in their territories and the essential role of cooperation in these areas in achieving sustainable development for the well-being of present and future generations;

REAFFIRMING the sovereign right of States to exploit their own resources pursuant to their own environmental and development policies and their responsibility to ensure that activities within their jurisdiction or control do not cause damage to the environment of other States or of areas beyond the limits of national jurisdiction;

RECOGNIZING the interrelationship of their environments;

ACKNOWLEDGING the growing economic and social links between them, including the North American Free Trade Agreement (NAFTA);

RECONFIRMING the importance of the environmental goals and objectives of the NAFTA, including enhanced levels of environmental protection;

EMPHASIZING the importance of public participation in conserving, protecting and enhancing the environment;

NOTING the existence of differences in their respective natural endowments, climatic and geographical conditions, and economic, technological and infrastructural capabilities;

REAFFIRMING the Stockholm Declaration on the Human Environment of 1972 and the Rio Declaration on Environment and Development of 1992;

RECALLING their tradition of environmental cooperation and expressing their desire to support and build on international environmental agreements and existing policies and laws, in order to promote cooperation between them; and

CONVINCED of the benefits to be derived from a framework, including a Commission, to facilitate effective cooperation on the conservation, protection and enhancement of the environment in their territories;

HAVE AGREED as follows:

PART ONE

OBJECTIVES

Article 1:   **Objectives**

The objectives of this Agreement are to:

(a)   foster the protection and improvement of the environment in the territories of the Parties for the well-being of present and future generations;

(b)   promote sustainable development based on cooperation and mutually supportive environmental and economic policies;

(c)   increase cooperation between the Parties to better conserve, protect, and enhance the environment, including wild flora and fauna;

(d)   support the environmental goals and objectives of the NAFTA;

(e)   avoid creating trade distortions or new trade barriers;

(f)   strengthen cooperation on the development and improvement of environmental laws, regulations, procedures, policies and practices;

(g)   enhance compliance with, and enforcement of, environmental laws and regulations;

(h)   promote transparency and public participation in the development of environmental laws, regulations and policies;

(i)   promote economically efficient and effective environmental measures; and

(j)   promote pollution prevention policies and practices.

PART TWO

OBLIGATIONS

Article 2:   General Commitments

1.   Each Party shall, with respect to its territory:
   (a)   periodically prepare and make publicly available reports on the state of the environment;
   (b)   develop and review environmental emergency preparedness measures;
   (c)   promote education in environmental matters, including environmental law;
   (d)   further scientific research and technology development in respect of environmental matters;
   (e)   assess, as appropriate, environmental impacts; and
   (f)   promote the use of economic instruments for the efficient achievement of environmental goals.

2.   Each Party shall consider implementing in its law any recommendation developed by the Council under Article 10(5)(b).

3.   Each Party shall consider prohibiting the export to the territories of the other Parties of a pesticide or toxic substance whose use is prohibited within the Party's territory. When a Party adopts a measure prohibiting or severely restricting the use of a pesticide or toxic substance in its territory, it shall notify the other Parties of the measure, either directly or through an appropriate international organization.

Article 3:   Levels of Protection

Recognizing the right of each Party to establish its own levels of domestic environmental protection and environmental development policies and priorities, and to adopt or modify accordingly its environmental laws and regulations, each Party shall ensure that its laws and regulations provide for high levels of environmental protection and shall strive to continue to improve those laws and regulations.

Article 4:   Publication

1.   Each Party shall ensure that its laws, regulations, procedures and administrative rulings of general application respecting any matter covered by this Agreement are promptly published or otherwise made available in such a manner as to enable interested persons and Parties to become acquainted with them.

2.   To the extent possible, each Party shall:
  (a)   publish in advance any such measure that it proposes to adopt; and
  (b)   provide interested persons and Parties a reasonable opportunity to comment on such proposed Measures.

Article 5:   Government Enforcement Action

1.   With the aim of achieving high levels of environmental protection and compliance with its environmental laws and regulations, each Party shall effectively enforce its environmental laws and regulations through appropriate governmental action, subject to Article 37, such as:
  (a)   appointing and training inspectors;
  (b)   monitoring compliance and investigating suspected violations, including through on-site inspections;
  (c)   seeking assurances of voluntary compliance and compliance agreements;
  (d)   publicly releasing non-compliance information;
  (e)   issuing bulletins or other periodic statements on enforcement procedures;
  (f)   promoting environmental audits;
  (g)   requiring record keeping and reporting;
  (h)   providing or encouraging mediation and arbitration services;
  (i)   using licenses, permits or authorizations;
  (j)   initiating, in a timely manner, judicial, quasi-judicial or administrative proceedings to seek appropriate sanctions or remedies for violations of its environmental laws and regulations;

(k)   providing for search, seizure or detention; or

(1)   issuing administrative orders, including orders of a preventative, curative or emergency nature.

2.   Each Party shall ensure that judicial, quasi-judicial or administrative enforcement proceedings are available under its law to sanction or remedy violations of its environmental laws and regulations.

3.   Sanctions and remedies provided for a violation of a Party's environmental laws and regulations shall, as appropriate:

(a)   take into consideration the nature and gravity of the violation, any economic benefit derived from the violation by the violator, the economic condition of the violator, and other relevant factors; and

(b)   include compliance agreements, fines, imprisonment, injunctions, the closure of facilities, and the cost of containing or cleaning up pollution.

Article 6:   Private Access to Remedies

1.   Each Party shall ensure that interested persons may request the Party's competent authorities to investigate alleged violations of its environmental laws and regulations and shall give such requests due consideration in accordance with law.

2.   Each Party shall ensure that persons with a legally recognized interest under its law in a particular matter have appropriate access to administrative, quasi-judicial or judicial proceedings for the enforcement of the Party's environmental laws and regulations.

3.   Private access to remedies shall include rights, in accordance with the Party's law, such as:

(a)   to sue another person under that Party's jurisdiction for damages;

(b)   to seek sanctions or remedies such as monetary penalties, emergency closures or orders to mitigate the consequences of violations of its environmental laws and regulations;

(c)   to request the competent authorities to take appropriate action to enforce that Party's environmental laws and regulations in order to protect the environment or to avoid environmental harm; or

(d)   to seek injunctions where a person suffers, or may

suffer, loss, damage or injury as a result of conduct by another person under that Parity's jurisdiction contrary to that Party's environmental laws and regulations or from tortuous conduct.

Article 7:   **Procedural Guarantees**

1.   Each Party shall ensure that its administrative, quasi-judicial and judicial proceedings referred to in Articles 5(2) and 6(2) are fair, open and equitable, and to this end shall provide that such proceedings:

(a)   comply with due process of law;

(b)   are open to the public, except where the administration of justice otherwise requires;

(c)   entitle the parties to the proceedings to support or defend their respective positions and to present information or evidence; and

(d)   are not unnecessarily complicated and do not entail unreasonable charges or time limits or unwarranted delays.

2.   Each Party shall provide that final decisions on the merits of the case in such proceedings are:

(a)   in writing and preferably state the reasons on which the decisions are based;

(b)   made available without undue delay to the parties to the proceedings and, consistent with its law, to the public; and

(c)   based on information or evidence in respect of which the parties were offered the opportunity to be heard.

3.   Each Party shall provide, as appropriate, that parties to such proceedings have the right, in accordance with its law, to seek review and, where warranted, correction of final decisions issued in such proceedings.

4.   Each Party shall ensure that tribunals that conduct or review such proceedings are impartial and independent and do not have any substantial interest in the outcome of the matter.

PART THREE

COMMISSION FOR ENVIRONMENTAL COOPERATION

Article 8:   The Commission

1.   The Parties hereby establish the Commission for Environmental Cooperation.
2.   The Commission shall comprise a Council, a Secretariat and a Joint Public Advisory Committee.

Section A: The Council

Article 9:   Council Structure and Procedures

1.   The Council shall comprise cabinet-level or equivalent representatives of the Parties, or their designees.
2.   The Council shall establish its rules and procedures.
3.   The Council shall convene:
    (a)   at least once a year in regular session; and
    (b)   in special session at the request of any Party. Regular sessions shall be chaired successively by each Party.
4.   The Council shall hold public meetings in the course of all regular sessions. Other meetings held in the course of regular or special sessions shall be public where the Council so decides.
5.   The Council may:
    (a)   establish, and assign responsibilities to, ad hoc or standing committees, working groups or expert groups;
    (b)   seek the advice of non-governmental organizations or persons, including independent experts; and
    (c)   take such other action in the exercise of its functions as the Parties may agree.
6.   All decisions and recommendations of the Council shall be taken by consensus, except as the Council may otherwise decide or as otherwise provided in this Agreement.
7.   All decisions and recommendations of the Council shall be made public, except as the Council may otherwise decide or as otherwise provided in this Agreement.

Article 10:   Council Functions

1.   The Council shall be the governing body of the Commission and shall:

(a)   serve as a forum for the discussion of environmental matters within the scope of this Agreement;

(b)   oversee the implementation and develop recommendations on the further elaboration of this Agreement and, to this end, the Council shall, within four years after the date of entry into force of this Agreement, review its operation and effectiveness in the light of experience;

(c)   oversee the Secretariat;

(d)   address questions and differences that may arise between the Parties regarding the interpretation or application of this Agreement;

(e)   approve the annual program and budget of the Commission; and

(f)   promote and facilitate cooperation between the Parties with respect to environmental matters.

2.   The Council may consider, and develop recommendations regarding:

(a)   comparability of techniques and methodologies for data gathering and analysis, data management and electronic data communications on matters covered by this Agreement;

(b)   pollution prevention techniques and strategies;

(c)   approaches and common indicators for reporting on the state of the environment;

(d)   the use of economic instruments for the pursuit of domestic and internationally agreed environmental objectives;

(e)   scientific research and technology development in respect of environmental matters;

(f)   promotion of public awareness regarding the environment;

(g)   transboundary and border environmental issues, such as the long-range transport of air and marine pollutants;

(h)   exotic species that may be harmful;

(i)   the conservation and protection of wild flora and fauna and their habitat, and specially protected natural areas;

(j)   the protection of endangered and threatened species;

(k)   environmental emergency preparedness and response activities;

(l)   environmental matters as they relate to economic development;

(m)   the environmental implications of goods throughout their life cycles;

(n)   human resource training and development in the environmental field;

(o)   the exchange of environmental scientists and officials;

(p)   approaches to environmental compliance and enforcement;

(q)   ecologically sensitive national accounts;

(r)   eco-labeling; and

(s)   other matters as it may decide.

3.   The Council shall strengthen cooperation on the development and continuing improvement of environmental laws and regulations, including by:

(a)   promoting the exchange of information on criteria and methodologies used in establishing domestic environmental standards; and

(b)   without reducing levels of environmental protection, establishing a process for developing recommendations on greater compatibility of environmental technical regulations, standards and conformity assessment procedures in a manner consistent with the NAFTA.

4.   The Council shall encourage:

(a)   effective enforcement by each Party of its environmental laws and regulations;

(b)   compliance with those laws and regulations; and

(c)   technical cooperation between the Parties.

5.   The Council shall promote and, as appropriate, develop recommendations regarding:

(a)   public access to information concerning the environment that is held by public authorities of each Party, including information on hazardous materials and activities in its communities, and opportunity to participate in decision-making processes related to such public access; and

(b)   appropriate limits for specific pollutants, taking into account differences in ecosystems.

6.   The Council shall cooperate with the NAFTA Free Trade Commission to achieve the environmental goals and objectives of the NAFTA by:

(a)   acting as a point of inquiry and receipt for comments from non-governmental organizations and persons concerning those goals and objectives;

(b)   providing assistance in consultations under Article 1114 of the NAFTA where a Party considers that another Party is waiving or derogating from, or offering to waive or otherwise derogate from, an environmental measure as an encouragement to establish, acquire, expand or retain an investment of an investor, with a view to avoiding any such encouragement;

(c)   contributing to the prevention or resolution of environment-related trade disputes by:

(i)   seeking to avoid disputes between the Parties,

(ii)   making recommendations to the Free Trade Commission with respect to the avoidance of such disputes, and

(iii)   identifying experts able to provide information or technical advice to NAFTA committees, working groups and other NAFTA bodies;

(d)   considering on an ongoing basis the environmental effects of the NAFTA; and

(e)   otherwise assisting the Free Trade Commission in environment-related matters.

7.   Recognizing the significant bilateral nature of many transboundary environmental issues, the Council shall, with a view to agreement between the Parties pursuant to this Article within three years on obligations, consider and develop recommendations with respect to:

(a)   assessing the environmental impact of proposed projects subject to decisions by a competent government authority and likely to cause significant adverse transboundary effects, including a full evaluation of comments provided by other Parties and persons of other Parties;

(b)   notification, provision of relevant information and consultation between Parties with respect to such projects; and

(c)   mitigation of the potential adverse effects of such projects.

8.   The Council shall encourage the establishment by each Party of appropriate administrative procedures pursuant to its environmental laws to permit another Party to seek the reduction, elimination or mitigation of transboundary pollution on a reciprocal basis.

9.   The Council shall consider and, as appropriate, develop recommendations on the provision by a Party, on a reciprocal basis, of access to and rights and remedies before its courts and administrative agencies for persons in another Party's territory who have suffered or are likely to suffer damage or injury caused by pollution originating in its territory as if the damage or injury were suffered in its territory.

Section B: The Secretariat

Article 11:   Secretariat Structure and Procedures

1.   The Secretariat shall be headed by an Executive Director, who shall be chosen by the Council for a three-year term, which may be renewed by the Council for one additional three-year term. The position of Executive Director shall rotate consecutively between nationals of each Party. The Council may remove the Executive Director solely for cause.

2.   The Executive Director shall appoint and supervise the staff of the Secretariat, regulate their powers and duties and fix their remuneration in accordance with general standards to be established by the Council. The general standards shall provide that:

(a)   staff shall be appointed and retained, and their conditions of employment shall be determined, strictly on the basis of efficiency, competence and integrity;

(b)   in appointing staff, the Executive Director shall take into account lists of candidates prepared by the Parties and by the Joint Public Advisory Committee;

(c)   due regard shall be paid to the importance of recruiting

> an equitable proportion of the professional staff from among the nationals of each Party; and
>
> (d)   the Executive Director shall inform the Council of all appointments.

3.   The Council may decide, by a two-thirds vote, to reject any appointment that does not meet the general standards. Any such decision shall be made and held in confidence.

4.   In the performance of their duties, the Executive Director and the staff shall not seek or receive instructions from any government or any other authority external to the Council. Each Party shall respect the international character of the responsibilities of the Executive Director and the staff and shall not seek to influence them in the discharge of their responsibilities.

5.   The Secretariat shall provide technical, administrative and operational support to the Council and to committees and groups established by the Council, and such other support as the Council may direct.

6.   The Executive Director shall submit for the approval of the Council the annual program and budget of the Commission, including provision for proposed cooperative activities and for the Secretariat to respond to contingencies.

7.   The Secretariat shall, as appropriate, provide the Parties and the public information on where they may receive technical advice and expertise with respect to environmental matters.

8.   The Secretariat shall safeguard:

> (a)   from disclosure information it receives that could identify a non-governmental organization or person making a submission if the person or organization so requests or the Secretariat otherwise considers it appropriate; and
>
> (b)   from public disclosure any information it receives from any non-governmental organization or person where the information is designated by that non-governmental organization or person as confidential or proprietary.

Article 12:   Annual Report of the Commission

1.   The Secretariat shall prepare an annual report of the Commission in accordance with instructions from the Council. The Secretariat shall submit a draft of the report for review by the Council. The final report shall be released publicly.

2.   The report shall cover:

   (a)   activities and expenses of the Commission during the
         previous year;

   (b)   the approved program and budget of the Commission
         for the subsequent year;

   (c)   the actions taken by each Party in connection with its
         obligations under this Agreement, including data on the
         Party's environmental enforcement activities;

   (d)   relevant views and information submitted by non-
         governmental organizations and persons, including
         summary data regarding submissions, and any other
         relevant information the Council deems appropriate;

   (e)   recommendations made on any matter within the scope
         of this Agreement; and

   (f)   any other matter that the Council instructs the
         Secretariat to include.

3.   The report shall periodically address the state of the environment in the territories of the Parties.

Article 13:   Secretariat Reports

1.   The Secretariat may prepare a report for the Council on any
matter within the scope of the annual program. Should the Secretariat
wish to prepare a report on any other environmental matter related to
the cooperative functions of this Agreement, it shall notify the Council
and may proceed unless, within 30 days of such notification, the Council objects by a two-thirds vote to the preparation of the report. Such
other environmental matters shall not include issues related to whether
a Party has failed to enforce its environmental laws and regulations.
Where the Secretariat does not have specific expertise in the matter under review, it shall obtain the assistance of one or more independent
experts of recognized experience in the matter to assist in the preparation of the report.

2.   In preparing such a report, the Secretariat may draw upon
any relevant technical, scientific or other information, including information:

   (a)   that is publicly available;

   (b)   submitted by interested non-governmental organizations
         and persons;

(c)   submitted by the Joint Public Advisory Committee;

(d)   furnished by a Party;

(e)   gathered through public consultations, such as conferences, seminars and symposia; or

(f)   developed by the Secretariat, or by independent experts engaged pursuant to paragraph 1.

3.   The Secretariat shall submit its report to the Council, which shall make it publicly available, normally within 60 days following its submission, unless the Council otherwise decides.

Article 14:   Submissions on Enforcement Matters

1.   The Secretariat may consider a submission from any non-governmental organization or person asserting that a Party is failing to effectively enforce its environmental law, if the Secretariat finds that the submission:

(a)   is in writing in a language designated by that Party in a notification to the Secretariat;

(b)   clearly identifies the person or organization making the submission;

(c)   provides sufficient information to allow the Secretariat to review the submission, including any documentary evidence on which the submission may be based;

(d)   appears to be aimed at promoting enforcement rather than at harassing industry;

(e)   indicates that the matter has been communicated in writing to the relevant authorities of the Party and indicates the Party's response, if any; and

(f)   is filed by a person or organization residing or established in the territory of a Party.

2.   Where the Secretariat determines that a submission meets the criteria set out in paragraph 1, the Secretariat shall determine whether the submission merits requesting a response from the Party. In deciding whether to request a response, the Secretariat shall be guided by whether:

(a)   the submission alleges harm to the person or organization making the submission;

(b)   the submission, alone or in combination with other submissions, raises matters whose further study in this process would advance the goals of this Agreement;

(c)   private remedies available under the Party's law have been pursued; and

(d)   the submission is drawn exclusively from mass media reports.

Where the Secretariat makes such a request, it shall forward to the Party a copy of the submission and any supporting information provided with the submission.

3.   The Party shall advise the Secretariat within 30 days or, in exceptional circumstances and on notification to the Secretariat, within 60 days of delivery of the request:

      (a)   whether the matter is the subject of a pending judicial or administrative proceeding, in which case the Secretariat shall proceed no further; and

      (b)   of any other information that the Party wishes to submit, such as

            (i)   whether the matter was previously the subject of a judicial or administrative proceeding, and

            (ii)   whether private remedies in connection with the matter are available to the person or organization making the submission and whether they have been pursued.

Article 15:   Factual Record

1.   If the Secretariat considers that the submission, in the light of any response provided by the Party, warrants developing a factual record, the Secretariat shall so inform the Council and provide its reasons.

2.   The Secretariat shall prepare a factual record if the Council, by a two-thirds vote, instructs it to do so.

3.   The preparation of a factual record by the Secretariat pursuant to this Article shall be without prejudice to any further steps that may be taken with respect to any submission.

4.   In preparing a factual record, the Secretariat shall consider any information furnished by a Party and may consider any relevant technical, scientific or other information:

      (a)   that is publicly available;

      (b)   submitted by interested non-governmental organizations or persons;

      (c)   submitted by the Joint Public Advisory Committee; or

(d)   developed by the Secretariat or by independent experts.

5.   The Secretariat shall submit a draft factual record to the Council. Any Party may provide comments on the accuracy of the draft within 45 days thereafter.

6.   The Secretariat shall incorporate, as appropriate, any such comments in the final factual record and submit it to the Council.

7.   The Council may, by a two-thirds vote, make the final factual record publicly available, normally within 60 days following its submission.

Section C: *Advisory Committees*

Article 16:   Joint Public Advisory Committee

1.   The Joint Public Advisory Committee shall comprise 15 members, unless the Council otherwise decides. Each Party or, if the Party so decides, its National Advisory Committee convened under Article 17, shall appoint an equal number of members.

2.   The Council shall establish the rules of procedure for the Joint Public Advisory Committee, which shall choose its own chair.

3.   The Joint Public Advisory Committee shall convene at least once a year at the time of the regular session of the Council and at such other times as the Council, or the Committee's chair with the consent of a majority of its members, may decide.

4.   The Joint Public Advisory Committee may provide advice to the Council on any matter within the scope of this Agreement, including on any documents provided to it under paragraph 6, and on the implementation and further elaboration of this Agreement, and may perform such other functions as the Council may direct.

5.   The Joint Public Advisory Committee may provide relevant technical, scientific or other information to the Secretariat, including for purposes of developing a factual record under Article 15. The Secretariat shall forward to the Council copies of any such information.

6.   The Secretariat shall provide to the Joint Public Advisory Committee at the time they are submitted to the Council copies of the proposed annual program and budget of the Commission, the draft annual report, and any report the Secretariat prepares pursuant to Article 13.

7.   The Council may, by a two-thirds vote, make a factual record available to the Joint Public Advisory Committee.

Article 17:   National Advisory Committees

Each Party may convene a national advisory committee, comprising members of its public, including representatives of non-governmental organizations and persons, to advise it on the implementation and further elaboration of this Agreement.

Article 18:   Governmental Committees

Each Party may convene a governmental committee, which may comprise or include representatives of federal and state or provincial governments, to advise it on the implementation and further elaboration of this Agreement.

Section D: Official Languages

Article 19:   Official Languages

The official languages of the Commission shall be English, French and Spanish. All annual reports under Article 12, reports submitted to the Council under Article 13, factual records submitted to the Council under Article 15(6) and panel reports under Part Five shall be available in each official language at the time they are made public. The Council shall establish rules and procedures regarding interpretation and translation.

PART FOUR

COOPERATION AND PROVISION OF INFORMATION

Article 20:   Cooperation

1.   The Parties shall at all times endeavor to agree on the interpretation and application of this Agreement, and shall make every attempt through cooperation and consultations to resolve any matter that might affect its operation.

2.   To the maximum extent possible, each Party shall notify any

other Party with an interest in the matter of any proposed or actual environmental measure that the Party considers might materially affect the operation of this Agreement or otherwise substantially affect that other Party's interests under this Agreement.

3.	On request of any other Party, a Party shall promptly provide information and respond to questions pertaining to any such actual or proposed environmental measure, whether or not that other Party has been previously notified of that measure.

4.	Any Party may notify any other Party of, and provide to that Party, any credible information regarding possible violations of its environmental law, specific and sufficient to allow the other Party to inquire into the matter. The notified Party shall take appropriate steps in accordance with its law to so inquire and to respond to the other Party.

**Article 21:	Provision of Information**

1.	On request of the Council or the Secretariat, each Party shall, in accordance with its law, provide such information as the Council or the Secretariat may require, including:

    (a)	promptly making available any information in its possession required for the preparation of a report or factual record, including compliance and enforcement data; and

    (b)	taking all reasonable steps to make available any other such information requested.

2.	If a Party considers that a request for information from the Secretariat is excessive or otherwise unduly burdensome, it may so notify the Council. The Secretariat shall revise the scope of its request to comply with any limitations established by the Council by a two-thirds vote.

3.	If a Party does not make available information requested by the Secretariat, as may be limited pursuant to paragraph 2, it shall promptly advise the Secretariat of its reasons in writing.

PART FIVE

CONSULTATION AND RESOLUTION OF DISPUTES

Article 22: Consultations

1.   Any Party may request in writing consultations with any other Party regarding whether there has been a persistent pattern of failure by that other Party to effectively enforce its environmental law.

2.   The requesting Party shall deliver the request to the other Parties and to the Secretariat.

3.   Unless the Council otherwise provides in its rules and procedures established under Article 9(2), a third Party that considers it has a substantial interest in the matter shall be entitled to participate in the consultations on delivery of written notice to the other Parties and to the Secretariat.

4.   The consulting Parties shall make every attempt to arrive at a mutually satisfactory resolution of the matter through consultations under this Article.

Article 23:   Initiation of Procedures

1.   If the consulting Parties fail to resolve the matter pursuant to Article 22 within 60 days of delivery of a request for consultations, or such other period as the consulting Parties may agree, any such Party may request in writing a special session of the Council.

2.   The requesting Party shall state in the request the matter complained of and shall deliver the request to the other Parties and to the Secretariat.

3.   Unless it decides otherwise, the Council shall convene within 20 days of delivery of the request and shall endeavor to resolve the dispute promptly.

4.   The Council may:

(a)   call on such technical advisers or create such working groups or expert groups as it deems necessary,

(b)   have recourse to good offices, conciliation, mediation or such other dispute resolution procedures, or

(c)   make recommendations,

as may assist the consulting Parties to reach a mutually satisfactory resolution of the dispute. Any such recommendations shall be made public if the Council, by a two-thirds vote, so decides.

5.   Where the Council decides that a matter is more properly covered by another agreement or arrangement to which the consulting Parties are party, it shall refer the matter to those Parties for appropriate action in accordance with such other agreement or arrangement.

Article 24: Request for an Arbitral Panel

1.   If the matter has not been resolved within 60 days after the Council has convened pursuant to Article 23, the Council shall, on the written request of any consulting Party and by a two-thirds vote, convene an arbitral panel to consider the matter where the alleged persistent pattern of failure by the Party complained against to effectively enforce its environmental law relates to a situation involving workplaces, firms, companies or sectors that produce goods or provide services:

(a)   traded between the territories of the Parties; or

(b)   that compete, in the territory of the Party complained against, with goods or services produced or provided by persons of another Party.

2.   A third Party that considers it has a substantial interest in the matter shall be entitled to join as a complaining Party on delivery of written notice of its intention to participate to the disputing Parties and the Secretariat. The notice shall be delivered at the earliest possible time, and in any event no later than seven days after the date of the vote of the Council to convene a panel.

3.   Unless otherwise agreed by the disputing Parties, the panel shall be established and perform its functions in a manner consistent with the provisions of this Part.

Article 25:   Roster

1.   The Council shall establish and maintain a roster of up to 45 individuals who are willing and able to serve as panelists. The roster members shall be appointed by consensus for terms of three years, and may be reappointed.

2.   Roster members shall:

(a)   have expertise or experience in environmental law or

its enforcement, or in the resolution of disputes arising
under international agreements, or other relevant
scientific, technical or professional expertise or
experience;

(b)   be chosen strictly on the basis of objectivity, reliability
and sound judgment;

(c)   be independent of, and not be affiliated with or take
instructions from, any Party, the Secretariat or the Joint
Public Advisory Committee; and

(d)   comply with a code of conduct to be established by the
Council.

Article 26:   Qualifications of Panelists

1.   All panelists shall meet the qualifications set out in Article 25(2).
2.   Individuals may not serve as panelists for a dispute in which:

(a)   they have participated pursuant to Article 23(4); or

(b)   they have, or a person or organization with which they
are affiliated has, an interest, as set out in the code of
conduct established under Article 25(2)(d).

Article 27:   Panel Selection

1.   Where there are two disputing Parties, the following procedures
shall apply:

(a)   The panel shall comprise five members.

(b)   The disputing Parties shall endeavor to agree on the chair
of the panel within 15 days after the Council votes to
convene the panel. If the disputing Parties are unable to
agree on the chair within this period, the disputing Party
chosen by lot shall select within five days a chair who
is not a citizen of that Party.

(c)   Within 15 days of selection of the chair, each disputing
Party shall select two panelists who are citizens of the
other disputing Party.

(d)   If a disputing Party fails to select its panelists within
such period, such panelists shall be selected by lot from
among the roster members who are citizens of the other
disputing Party.

2.   Where there are more than two disputing Parties, the following procedures shall apply:

(a)   The panel shall comprise five members.

(b)   The disputing Parties shall endeavor to agree on the chair of the panel within 15 days after the Council votes to convene the panel. If the disputing Parties are unable to agree on the chair within this period, the Party or Parties on the side of the dispute chosen by lot shall select within 10 days a chair who is not a citizen of such Party or Parties.

(c)   Within 30 days of selection of the chair, the Party complained against shall select two panelists, one of whom is a citizen of a complaining Party, and the other of whom is a citizen of another complaining Party. The complaining Parties shall select two panelists who are citizens of the Party complained against.

(d)   If any disputing Party fails to select a panelist within such period, such panelist shall be selected by lot in accordance with the citizenship criteria of subparagraph (c).

3.   Panelists shall normally be selected from the roster. Any disputing Party may exercise a peremptory challenge against any individual not on the roster who is proposed as a panelist by a disputing Party within 30 days after the individual has been proposed.

4.   If a disputing Party believes that a panelist is in violation of the code of conduct, the disputing Parties shall consult and, if they agree, the panelist shall be removed and a new panelist shall be selected in accordance with this Article.

Article 28:   Rules of Procedure

1.   The Council shall establish Model Rules of Procedure. The procedures shall provide:

(a)   a right to at least one hearing before the panel;

(b)   the opportunity to make initial and rebuttal written submissions; and

(c)   that no panel may disclose which panelists are associated with majority or minority opinions.

2.   Unless the disputing Parties otherwise agree, panels convened

under this Part shall be established and conduct their proceedings in accordance with the Model Rules of Procedure.

3.   Unless the disputing Parties otherwise agree within 20 days after the Council votes to convene the panel, the terms of reference shall be:

> To examine, in light of the relevant provisions of the Agreement, including those contained in Part Five, whether there has been a persistent pattern of failure by the Party complained against to effectively enforce its environmental law, and to make findings, determinations and recommendations in accordance with Article 31(2).

Article 29:   Third Party Participation

A Party that is not a disputing Party, on delivery of a written notice to the disputing Parties and to the Secretariat, shall be entitled to attend all hearings, to make written and oral submissions to the panel and to receive written submissions of the disputing Parties.

Article 30:   Role of Experts

On request of a disputing Party, or on its own initiative, the panel may seek information and technical advice from any person or body that it deems appropriate, provided that the disputing Parties so agree and subject to such terms and conditions as such Parties may agree.

Article 31: Initial Report

1.   Unless the disputing Parties otherwise agree, the panel shall base its report on the submissions and arguments of the Parties and on any information before it pursuant to Article 30.

2.   Unless the disputing Parties otherwise agree, the panel shall, within 180 days after the last panelist is selected, present to the disputing Parties an initial report containing:

   (a)   findings of fact;
   (b)   its determination as to whether there has been a persistent pattern of failure by the Party complained against to effectively enforce its environmental law, or any other determination requested in the terms of reference; and

     (c)   in the event the panel makes an affirmative determination under subparagraph (b) its recommendations, if any, for the resolution of the dispute, which normally shall be that the Party complained against adopt and implement an action plan sufficient to remedy the pattern of non-enforcement.

3.   Panelists may furnish separate opinions on matters not unanimously agreed.

4.   A disputing Party may submit written comments to the panel on its initial report within 30 days of presentation of the report.

5.   In such an event, and after considering such written comments, the panel, on its own initiative or on the request of any disputing Party, may:

     (a)   request the views of any participating Party;

     (b)   reconsider its report; and

     (c)   make any further examination that it considers appropriate.

Article 32:   Final Report

1.   The panel shall present to the disputing Parties a final report, including any separate opinions on matters not unanimously agreed, within 60 days of presentation of the initial report, unless the disputing Parties otherwise agree.

2.   The disputing Parties shall transmit to the Council the final report of the panel, as well as any written views that a disputing Party desires to be appended, on a confidential basis within 15 days after it is presented to them.

3.   The final report of the panel shall be published five days after it is transmitted to the Council.

Article 33:   Implementation of Final Report

If, in its final report, a panel determines that there has been a persistent pattern of failure by the Party complained against to effectively enforce its environmental law, the disputing Parties may agree on a mutually satisfactory action plan, which normally shall conform with the determinations and recommendations of the panel. The disputing Parties shall promptly notify the Secretariat and the Council of any agreed resolution of the dispute.

Article 34:   Review of Implementation

1.   If, in its final report, a panel determines that there has been a persistent pattern of failure by the Party complained against to effectively enforce its environmental law, and:

    (a)   the disputing Parties have not agreed on an action plan under Article 33 within 60 days of the date of the final report, or

    (b)   the disputing Parties cannot agree on whether the Party complained against is fully implementing:

        (i)   an action plan agreed under Article 33,

        (ii)   an action plan deemed to have been established by a panel under paragraph 2, or

        (iii)   an action plan approved or established by a panel under paragraph 4,

any disputing Party may request that the panel be reconvened. The requesting Party shall deliver the request in writing to the other Parties and to the Secretariat. The Council shall reconvene the panel on delivery of the request to the Secretariat.

2.   No Party may make a request under paragraph l(a) earlier than 60 days, or later than 120 days, after the date of the final report. If the disputing Parties have not agreed to an action plan and if no request was made under paragraph l(a), the last action plan, if any, submitted by the Party complained against to the complaining Party or Parties within 60 days of the date of the final report, or such other period as the disputing Parties may agree, shall be deemed to have been established by the panel 120 days after the date of the final report.

3.   A request under paragraph l(b) may be made no earlier than 180 days after an action plan has been:

    (a)   agreed under Article 33;

    (b)   deemed to have been established by a panel under paragraph 2; or

    (c)   approved or established by a panel under paragraph 4;

and only during the term of any such action plan.

4.   Where a panel has been reconvened under paragraph l(a), it:

    (a)   shall determine whether any action plan proposed by the Party complained against is sufficient to remedy the pattern of non-enforcement and:

        (i)   if so, shall approve the plan, or

(ii)   if not, shall establish such a plan consistent with the law of the Party complained against, and

(b)   may, where warranted, impose a monetary enforcement assessment in accordance with Annex 34,

within 90 days after the panel has been reconvened or such other period as the disputing Parties may agree.

5.   Where a panel has been reconvened under paragraph l(b), it shall determine either that:

(a)   the Party complained against is fully implementing the action plan, in which case the panel may not impose a monetary enforcement assessment; or

(b)   the Party complained against is not fully implementing the action plan, in which case the panel shall impose a monetary enforcement assessment in accordance with Annex 34;

within 60 days after it has been reconvened or such other period as the disputing Parties may agree.

6.   A panel reconvened under this Article shall provide that the Party complained against shall fully implement any action plan referred to in paragraph 4(a)(ii) or 5(b), and pay any monetary enforcement assessment imposed under paragraph 4(b) or 5(b), and any such provision shall be final.

Article 35:   Further Proceeding

A complaining Party may, at any time beginning 180 days after a panel determination under Article 34(5)(b), request in writing that a panel be reconvened to determine whether the Party complained against is fully implementing the action plan. On delivery of the request to the other Parties and the Secretariat, the Council shall reconvene the panel. The panel shall make the determination within 60 days after it has been reconvened or such other period as the disputing Parties may agree.

Article 36:   Suspension of Benefits

1.   Subject to Annex 36A, where a Party fails to pay a monetary enforcement assessment within 180 days after it is imposed by a panel:

(a)   under Article 34(4)(b); or

(b)   under Article 34(5)(b), except where benefits may be suspended under paragraph 2(a);

any complaining Party or Parties may suspend, in accordance with Annex 36B, the application to the Party complained against of NAFTA benefits in an amount no greater than that sufficient to collect the monetary enforcement assessment.

2.   Subject to Annex 36A, where a panel has made a determination under Article 34(5)(b) and the panel:

     (a)   has previously imposed a monetary enforcement assessment under Article 34(4)(b) or established an action plan under Article 34(4)(a)(ii); or

     (b)   has subsequently determined under Article 35 that a Party is not fully implementing an action plan;

the complaining Party or Parties may, in accordance with Annex 36B, suspend annually the application to the Party complained against of NAFTA benefits in an amount no greater than the monetary enforcement assessment imposed by the panel under Article 34 (5)(b).

3.   Where more than one complaining Party suspends benefits under paragraph 1 or 2, the combined suspension shall be no greater than the amount of the monetary enforcement assessment.

4.   Where a Party has suspended benefits under paragraph 1 or 2, the Council shall, on the delivery of a written request by the Party complained against to the other Parties and the Secretariat, reconvene the panel to determine whether the monetary enforcement assessment has been paid or collected, or whether the Party complained against is fully implementing the action plan, as the case may be. The panel shall submit its report within 45 days after it has been reconvened. If the panel determines that the assessment has been paid or collected, or that the Party complained against is fully implementing the action plan, the suspension of benefits under paragraph 1 or 2, as the case may be, shall be terminated.

5.   On the written request of the Party complained against, delivered to the other Parties and the Secretariat, the Council shall reconvene the panel to determine whether the suspension of benefits by the complaining Party or Parties pursuant to paragraph 1 or 2 is manifestly excessive. Within 45 days of the request, the panel shall present a report to the disputing Parties containing its determination.

PART SIX

GENERAL PROVISIONS

Article 37:   Enforcement Principle

Nothing in this Agreement shall be construed to empower a Party's authorities to undertake environmental law enforcement activities in the territory of another Party.

Article 38:   Private Rights

No Party may provide for a right of action under its law against any other Party on the ground that another Party has acted in a manner inconsistent with this Agreement.

Article 39:   Protection of Information

1.   Nothing in this Agreement shall be construed to require a Party to make available or allow access to information:
      (a)   the disclosure of which would impede its environmental law enforcement; or
      (b)   that is protected from disclosure by its law governing business or proprietary information, personal privacy or the confidentiality of governmental decision making.

2.   If a Party provides confidential or proprietary information to another Party, the Council, the Secretariat or the Joint Public Advisory Committee, the recipient shall treat the information on the same basis as the Party providing the information.

3.   Confidential or proprietary information provided by a Party to a panel under this Agreement shall be treated in accordance with the rules of procedure established under Article 28.

Article 40:   Relation to Other Environmental Agreements

Nothing in this Agreement shall be construed to affect the existing rights and obligations of the Parties under other international environmental agreements, including conservation agreements, to which such Parties are party.

Article 41:   Extent of Obligations

Annex 41 applies to the Parties specified in that Annex.

Article 42:   National Security

Nothing in this Agreement shall be construed:

(a)   to require any Party to make available or provide access to information the disclosure of which it determines to be contrary to its essential security interests; or

(b)   to prevent any Party from taking any actions that it considers necessary for the protection of its essential security interests relating to:

(i)   arms, ammunition and implements of war, or

(ii)   the implementation of national policies or international agreements respecting the non-proliferation of nuclear weapons or other nuclear explosive devices.

Article 43:   Funding of the Commission

Each Party shall contribute an equal share of the annual budget of the Commission, subject to the availability of appropriated funds in accordance with the Party's legal procedures. No Party shall be obligated to pay more than any other Party in respect of an annual budget.

Article 44:   Privileges and Immunities

The Executive Director and staff of the Secretariat shall enjoy in the territory of each Party such privileges and immunities as are necessary for the exercise of their functions.

Article 45:   Definitions

1.   For purposes of this Agreement:

A Party has not failed to **"effectively enforce its environmental law"** or to comply with Article 5(1) in a particular case where the action or inaction in question by agencies or officials of that Party:

   (a)   reflects a reasonable exercise of their discretion in respect of investigatory, prosecutorial, regulatory or compliance matters; or

   (b)   results from *bona fide* decisions to allocate resources to enforcement in respect of other environmental matters determined to have higher priorities;

"non-governmental organization" means any scientific, professional, business, non-profit, or public interest organization or association which is neither affiliated with, nor under the direction of, a government;

"persistent pattern" means a sustained or recurring course of action or inaction beginning after the date of entry into force of this Agreement;

"province" means a province of Canada, and includes the Yukon Territory and the Northwest Territories and their successors; and

"territory" means for a Party the territory of that Party as set out in Annex 45.

2.   For purposes of Article 14(1) and Part Five:

   (a)   **"environmental law"** means any statute or regulation of a Party, or provision thereof, the primary purpose of which is the protection of the environment, or the prevention of a danger to human life or health, through:

      (i)   the prevention, abatement or control of the release, discharge, or emission of pollutants or environmental contaminants,

      (ii)   the control of environmentally hazardous or toxic chemicals, substances, materials and wastes, and the dissemination of information related thereto, or

      (iii)   the protection of wild flora or fauna, including endangered species, their habitat and specially protected natural areas in the Party's territory, but does not include any statute or regulation, or provision thereof, directly related to worker safety or health.

(b)   For greater certainty, the term **"environmental law"** does not include any statute or regulation, or provision thereof, the primary purpose of which is managing the commercial harvest or exploitation, or subsistence or aboriginal harvesting, of natural resources.

(c)   The primary purpose of a particular statutory or regulatory provision for purposes of subparagraphs (a) and (b) shall be determined by reference to its primary purpose, rather than to the primary purpose of the statute or regulation of which it is part.

3.   For purposes of Article 14(3), **"judicial or administrative proceeding"** means:

(a)   a domestic judicial, quasi-judicial or administrative action pursued by the Party in a timely fashion and in accordance with its law. Such actions comprise: mediation; arbitration; the process of issuing a license, permit, or authorization; seeking an assurance of voluntary compliance or a compliance agreement; seeking sanctions or remedies in an administrative or judicial forum; and the process of issuing an administrative order; and

(b)   an international dispute resolution proceeding to which the Party is party.

PART SEVEN

FINAL PROVISIONS

Article 46:   **Annexes**

The Annexes to this Agreement constitute an integral part of the Agreement.

Article 47:   **Entry into Force**

This Agreement shall enter into force on January 1, 1994, immediately after entry into force of the NAFTA, on an exchange of written notifications certifying the completion of necessary legal procedures.

Article 48:   **Amendments**

1.   The Parties may agree on any modification of or addition to this Agreement.
2.   When so agreed, and approved in accordance with the applicable legal procedures of each Party, a modification or addition shall constitute an integral part of this Agreement.

Article 49:   **Accession**

Any country or group of countries may accede to this Agreement subject to such terms and conditions as may be agreed between such country or countries and the Council and following approval in accordance with the applicable legal procedures of each country.

Article 50:   **Withdrawal**

A Party may withdraw from this Agreement six months after it provides written notice of withdrawal to the other Parties. If a Party withdraws, the Agreement shall remain in force for the remaining Parties.

Article 51:   **Authentic Texts**

The English, French, and Spanish texts of this Agreement are equally authentic.

IN WITNESS WHEREOF, the undersigned, being duly authorized by the respective Governments, have signed this Agreement.

ANNEX 34

MONETARY ENFORCEMENT ASSESSMENTS

1.   For the first year after the date of entry into force of this Agreement, any monetary enforcement assessment shall be no greater than 20 million dollars (U.S.) or its equivalent in the currency of the Party complained against. Thereafter, any monetary enforcement assessment shall be no greater than .007 percent of total trade in goods between the Parties during the most recent year for which data are available.

2.   In determining the amount of the assessment, the panel shall take into account:

    (a)   the pervasiveness and duration of the Party's persistent pattern of failure to effectively enforce its environmental law;

    (b)   the level of enforcement that could reasonably be expected of a Party given its resource constraints;

    (c)   the reasons, if any, provided by the Party for not fully implementing an action plan;

    (d)   efforts made by the Party to begin remedying the pattern of non-enforcement after the final report of the panel; and

    (e)   any other relevant factors.

3.   All monetary enforcement assessments shall be paid in the currency of the Party complained against into a fund established in the name of the Commission by the Council and shall be expended at the direction of the Council to improve or enhance the environment or environmental law enforcement in the Party complained against, consistent with its law.

ANNEX 36A

CANADIAN DOMESTIC ENFORCEMENT AND COLLECTION

1.   For the purposes of this Annex, **"panel determination"** means:

    (a)   a determination by a panel under Article 34(4)(b) or 5(b) that provides that Canada shall pay a monetary enforcement assessment; and

(b)   a determination by a panel under Article 34(5)(b) that provides that Canada shall fully implement an action plan where the panel:

(i)   has previously established an action plan under Article 34(4)(a)(ii) or imposed a monetary enforcement assessment under Article 34(4)(b), or

(ii)   has subsequently determined under Article 35 that Canada is not fully implementing an action plan.

2. Canada shall adopt and maintain procedures that provide that:

(a)   subject to subparagraph (b), the Commission, at the request of a complaining Party, may in its own name file in a court of competent jurisdiction a certified copy of a panel determination;

(b)   the Commission may file in court a panel determination that is a panel determination described in paragraph l(a) only if Canada has failed to comply with the determination within 180 days of when the determination was made;

(c)   when filed, the panel determination, for purposes of enforcement, shall become an order of the court;

(d)   the Commission may take proceedings for enforcement of a panel determination that is made an order of the court, in that court, against the person against whom the panel determination is addressed in accordance with paragraph 6 of Annex 41;

(e)   proceedings to enforce a panel determination that has been made an order of the court shall be conducted by way of summary proceedings;

(f)   in proceedings to enforce a panel determination that is a panel determination described in paragraph l(b) and that has been made an order of the court, the court shall promptly refer any question of fact or any question of interpretation of the panel determination to the panel that made the panel determination, and the decision of the panel shall be binding on the court;

(g)   a panel determination that has been made an order of the court shall not be subject to domestic review or appeal; and

(h)   an order made by the court in proceedings to enforce a panel determination that has been made an order of the court shall not be subject to review or appeal.

3.   Where Canada is the Party complained against, the procedures adopted and maintained by Canada under this Annex shall apply and the procedures set out in Article 36 shall not apply.

4.   Any change by Canada to the procedures adopted and maintained by Canada under this Annex that have the effect of undermining the provisions of this Annex shall be considered a breach of this Agreement.

ANNEX 36B

SUSPENSION OF BENEFITS

1.   Where a complaining Party suspends NAFTA tariff benefits in accordance with this Agreement, the Party may increase the rates of duty on originating goods of the Party complained against to levels not to exceed the lesser of:

(a)   the rate that was applicable to those goods immediately prior to the date of entry into force of the NAFTA; and

(b)   the Most-Favored-Nation rate applicable to those goods on the date the Party suspends such benefits, and such increase may be applied only for such time as is necessary to collect, through such increase, the monetary enforcement assessment.

2.   In considering what tariff or other benefits to suspend pursuant to Article 36(1) or (2):

(a)   a complaining Party shall first seek to suspend benefits in the same sector or sectors as that in respect of which there has been a persistent pattern of failure by the Party complained against to effectively enforce its environmental law; and

(b)   a complaining Party that considers it is not practicable or effective to suspend benefits in the same sector or sectors may suspend benefits in other sectors.

ANNEX 41

EXTENT OF OBLIGATIONS

1.   On the date of signature of this Agreement, or of the exchange of written notifications under Article 47, Canada shall set out in a declaration a list of any provinces for which Canada is to be bound in respect of matters within their jurisdiction. The declaration shall be effective on delivery to the other Parties, and shall carry no implication as to the internal distribution of powers within Canada. Canada shall notify the other Parties six months in advance of any modification to its declaration.

2.   When considering whether to instruct the Secretariat to prepare a factual record pursuant to Article 15, the Council shall take into account whether the submission was made by a non-governmental organization or enterprise incorporated or otherwise organized under the laws of a province included in the declaration made under paragraph 1.

3.   Canada may not request consultations under Article 22 or a Council meeting under Article 23 or request the establishment of a panel or join as a complaining Party under Article 24 against another Party at the instance, or primarily for the benefit, of any government of a province not included in the declaration made under paragraph 1.

4.   Canada may not request a Council meeting under Article 23, or request the establishment of a panel or join as a complaining Party under Article 24 concerning whether there has been a persistent pattern of failure by another Party to effectively enforce its environmental law, unless Canada states in writing that the matter would be under federal jurisdiction if it were to arise within the territory of Canada, or:

   (a)   Canada states in writing that the matter would be under provincial jurisdiction if it were to arise within the territory of Canada; and

   (b)   the provinces included in the declaration account for at least 55 percent of Canada's Gross Domestic Product (GDP) for the most recent year in which data are available; and

   (c)   where the matter concerns a specific industry or sector, at least 55 percent of total Canadian production in that industry or sector is accounted for by the provinces included in the declaration for the most recent year in which data are available.

5.   No other Party may request a Council meeting under Article 23 or request the establishment of a panel or join as a complaining Party under Article 24 concerning whether there has been a persistent failure to effectively enforce an environmental law of a province unless that province is included in the declaration made under paragraph 1 and the requirements of subparagraphs 4(b) and (c) have been met.

6.   Canada shall, no later than the date on which an arbitral panel is convened pursuant to Article 24 respecting a matter within the scope of paragraph 5 of this Annex, notify in writing the complaining Parties and the Secretariat of whether any monetary enforcement assessment or action plan imposed by a panel under Article 34(4) or 34(5) against Canada shall be addressed to Her Majesty in right of Canada or Her Majesty in right of the province concerned.

7.   Canada shall use its best efforts to make this Agreement applicable to as many of its provinces as possible.

8.   Two years after the date of entry into force of this Agreement, the Council shall review the operation of this Annex and, in particular, shall consider whether the Parties should amend the thresholds established in paragraph 4.

ANNEX 45

COUNTRY-SPECIFIC DEFINITIONS

For purposes of this Agreement:

"territory" means:

(a)   with respect to Canada, the territory to which its customs laws apply, including any areas beyond the territorial seas of Canada within which, in accordance with international law and its domestic law, Canada may exercise rights with respect to the seabed and subsoil and their natural resources;

(b)   with respect to Mexico,

(i)   the states of the Federation and the Federal District,

(ii)   the islands, including the reefs and keys, in adjacent seas,

       (iii)   the islands of Guadalupe and Revillagigedo situated in the Pacific Ocean,

       (iv)   the continental shelf and the submarine shelf of such islands, keys and reefs,

       (v)   the waters of the territorial seas, in accordance with international law, and its interior maritime waters,

       (vi)   the space located above the national territory, in accordance with international law, and

       (vii)   any areas beyond the territorial seas of Mexico within which, in accordance with international law, including the *United Nations Convention on the Law of the Sea*, and its domestic law, Mexico may exercise rights with respect to the seabed and subsoil and their natural resources; and

(c)   with respect to the United States,

       (i)   the customs territory of the United States, which includes the 50 states, the District of Columbia and Puerto Rico,

       (ii)   the foreign trade zones located in the United States and Puerto Rico, and

       (iii)   any areas beyond the territorial seas of the United States within which, in accordance with international law and its domestic law, the United States may exercise rights with respect to the seabed and subsoil and their natural resources.

6

Border Environment Cooperation Commission and North American Development Bank

The NAFTA-related institutions described in previous chapters are trinational institutions involving all of the NAFTA countries, which is what one would expect in a regional trading arrangement. However, two additional institutions were created as a result of NAFTA that are bilateral, involving only the United States and Mexico. They are the Border Environment Cooperation Commission (BECC) and the North American Development Bank (NADB).

These two institutions are bilateral in nature because they were established specifically to deal with environmental problems along the U.S.–Mexico border. With a common border stretching approximately 2,000 miles, the United States and Mexico share the longest boundary between any two countries having widely disparate levels of economic development. That fact creates a number of challenges, one of them being the status of environmental conditions along the border.

Residents of Mexico have been attracted to the border region because of employment opportunities there. After the *bracero* program that allowed temporary entry of Mexican agricultural workers was terminated by the United States in 1964, Mexico initiated the Border Industrialization Program (maquiladora program) in 1965. That program permitted manufacturing plants established on the Mexican side of the border to import components and materials from the United States duty-free for assembly or processing. U.S. trade laws provided that the finished products could be imported into the United States with duty paid only on the value added in Mexico. Partly as a result of this program and the employment opportunities that it provided, the population of border communities increased from 4 million in 1980 to approximately 10 million in 1996 (USGAO 1996, 4).

As the population of the border region increased, and as industries expanded there, environmental conditions deteriorated. Much of the border region is arid or semiarid, and many of the border cities have to import water. Wastewater treatment and solid waste disposal have been substandard. In many instances untreated sewage and industrial waste have been discharged into rivers. Hazardous waste has often been dumped into the environment without sufficient treatment or safety measures to protect groundwater supplies.

Environmental pollution along the border is suspected to be a causal factor in several health problems. Neural tube birth defects, such as anencephaly and spina bifida, occur with greater frequency along the border than in other parts of the United States. Cases of Hepatitis A, a serious gastrointestinal virus that is transmitted by contaminated food and water, occur in the border region at rates 200 to 500 percent above the U.S. national average. The incidence of certain types of cancer and of tuberculosis is also much higher in the border region (USGAO 1999, 40).

The high degree of environmental pollution along the U.S.–Mexico border is partly the result of inadequate enforcement of environmental laws and regulations, particularly in Mexico. Mexico has lacked the resources to invest in adequate monitoring or enforcement, and because of other pressing problems has not been able to give environmental conditions the same priority that the United States does. The U.S. Environmental Protection Agency (EPA) estimated that in 1997 more than 30 percent of the population in major Mexican border cities lacked connections to sewage disposal systems, 12 percent lacked access to safe drinking water, and only 34 percent of the wastewater of these cities was treated (ibid., 16).

Even on the U.S. side of the border, however, environmental problems exist as a result of the poor economic conditions. If San Diego County is excluded, per capita income levels of the border counties are only about two-thirds of the U.S. average. Educational levels are relatively low and illiteracy rates are among the highest in the nation. Unincorporated villages, called *colonias*, often lack supplies of running water, sewage disposal systems, and solid waste disposal systems. An estimated 432,000 people lived in *colonias* in Texas and New Mexico in 1997 (ibid., 15).

Long before NAFTA, the United States and Mexico had cooperated to deal with the border environmental problems. They established the International Boundary Commission in 1889 to deal with water allocation issues along the border. In 1944 they signed the Treaty Between the United States and Mexico Relating to the Utilization of Waters of the Colorado and Tijuana Rivers and of the Rio Grande. That treaty established the International Boundary and Water Commission (IBWC), which has worked to alleviate pollution of rivers along the border and to facilitate wastewater treatment. In 1983 the United States and Mexico signed a framework agreement, the La Paz Agreement, that provided for cooperation between the EPA and Mexico's counterpart at the time, *Secretaria de Desarollo Urbano y de Ecologia*. Environmental problems along the border continued to worsen, however. With the prospect of increased population and increased economic activity in the border area as a result of NAFTA, those concerned about environmental conditions along the border became more and more insistent that the agreement must be accompanied by institutions devoted specifically to the border environment.

In recognition of this sentiment, early in 1992 the Bush administration negotiated with Mexico an integrated environmental plan for the U.S.–Mexico border area. This agreement committed the two governments to improve their enforcement of environmental laws and regulations, and to work together in various ways to address environmental problems along the border. After President Clinton took office, the Integrated Environmental Plan was supplemented by the Border Environment Cooperation Agreement. This agreement established both the BECC and the NADB. More recently, the United States and Mexico have agreed to Border XXI, an expanded planning and coordination system for border projects.

Border Environment Cooperation Commission

The BECC is headquartered in Ciudad Juarez, Chihuahua, Mexico. The governments of the United States and Mexico contribute equal amounts to the budget of the BECC ($1.7 million each in 1997). However, the BECC may receive contributions from other governmental entities, institutions, or foundations. The BECC has a ten-member board of directors equally balanced between representatives of the United States and of Mexico. The environment ministers of both countries are *ex officio* members, as are the U.S. and Mexican commissioners of the IBWC. Other directors represent states in the border region, localities in the border region, and members of the public who are residents of the border region. A general manager and a deputy general manager, who are appointed to renewable three-year terms, supervise the day-to-day operations of the BECC.

The board of directors and the general manager receive advice from an eighteen-member advisory council, the members of which are appointed by their respective governments to two-year renewable terms. The advisory council is composed of at least one representative from each of the U.S. and Mexican border states, plus three members of the public from each of the countries. At least one of the public representatives from each country is to be a member of a nongovernmental organization to ensure input from civil society.

The stated purpose of the BECC is "to help preserve, protect and enhance the environment of the border region in order to advance the well-being of people of the United States and Mexico" (NADB 1995). The BECC has several stated functions. It helps to coordinate environmental infrastructure projects in the border region (defined as 100 kilometers, or 62 miles, on either side of the border). The BECC works with states, localities, other public entities and private investors to design, develop, and implement such projects. It helps them to analyze both the environmental impact and the financial feasibility of such projects, and to arrange public and private financing for the projects. It also assists with analyzing the social and economic benefits of such projects, and helps to ensure that the public is both informed about the projects and participates in them (BECC 1996, 1).

A very important additional function of the BECC is certifying environmental infrastructure projects for financing by either the NADB or by other lenders. BECC certification is required for NADB financing, and is often required by other potential lenders as well. The BECC gives priority to projects dealing with water supply, wastewater treatment, and municipal solid waste management.

Technical Assistance Programs

In many instances, communities along the border need technical assistance in preparing project proposals for BECC certification. Accordingly, the BECC expends part of its resources in assisting communities to meet the project certification criteria. As of early 1999, BECC had approved technical assistance grants of approximately $13.2 million to assist with the development of environmental infrastructure projects in more than 70 communities (BECC-NADB 1999, 5).

The BECC has several different programs to aid communities in meeting project certification criteria. One of these programs is the Project Development Assistance Program (PDAP). The PDAP is funded primarily by the EPA to assist with projects related to water and wastewater treatment. The level of funding for the program in 1999 was $20 million. Under this program the BECC has assisted 67different communities with their development of 74 projects. Of the total $11.8 million expended, $11.1 million came from EPA funding to assist 62 communities, whereas $0.7 million came from the BECC's own funds to assist the remaining 5 communities (ibid.).

Another of the technical assistance programs is the Capacity Building Needs and Solid Waste Technical Assistance Program. The BECC has expended $1.4 million to assist with the development of 15 solid waste projects. In this program, funds from BECC's budget have been supplemented by funds from other sources, such as the Ministry of Social Development in Mexico (ibid.).

Because state and municipal public utility operators in Mexico sometimes lack basic technical skills, another BECC program, the management training program, attempts to remedy this deficiency. Through this program the BECC helps to organize training courses on water management and solid waste management to upgrade the skills of public utility managers (ibid., 5–6).

Two other BECC technical assistance programs are the Sustainable Development Program and the High Sustainability Recognition Program. The first of these programs attempts to ensure that its certified projects meet sustainable development criteria, that is, the needs of future generations are not compromised by present-day programs of environmental protection. Communities are encouraged to go beyond the sustainable development criteria required for project certification, and one incentive for doing so is the favorable publicity accorded by the High Sustainability Recognition Program. While participation in this program is optional, the recognition that it brings may be helpful in obtaining grant funds (ibid., 6).

Finally, in its technical assistance program, the BECC goes to great lengths to assure public support for projects through its public participation program. When projects are being considered for BECC certification, local steering committees are required. These steering committees work in many ways to fully inform and educate the public about the nature of the project and what its costs and benefits will be. The goal is to have broad-based public support for projects that will endure through their operation and maintenance phases (ibid.).

Project Certification Criteria

One reason for the high level of technical assistance made available by the BECC is that projects seeking certification must meet a number of stringent criteria in six different categories. Under the heading of general criteria, the project must fall within one or more of the BECC priority areas (water supply, wastewater treatment, municipal solid waste, or other related matters), and must be located within 100 kilometers of the border. The project must be thoroughly described in the application, justification for it must be stated, and the work tasks must be planned. The project must also conform to the terms of any international treaties and agreements to which either or both countries are parties (BECC 1996, 11).

To meet human health and environment criteria, projects must demonstrate that they provide a high degree of environmental protection and that they are designed to meet a human health and environmental need. The project must comply with all relevant environmental laws and regulations. Further, it must comply with cultural resource laws and regulations, dealing with archeological, historical, and ethnic issues. Also, each project application must be accompanied by an assessment of its environmental effects. If domestic law requires such an environmental assessment, that document may be submitted in fulfillment of this requirement (ibid., 14–16).

Under the heading of technical feasibility criteria, the BECC requires that projects incorporate technologies appropriate to the setting within which the project will take place. This means that the technology should not create much dependency on resources from outside the community, and should be capable of being operated and maintained by local personnel. The project should have a well-developed plan for operation and maintenance, including a training plan for required personnel. It should comply with all pertinent design regulations and standards (ibid., 17–20).

Another criteria category deals with financial feasibility and project management. This category gives rise to the need for much technical assistance, and still is problematic for many of the border communities. This category requires detailed financial information, including historical and pro forma financial statements, historical and pro forma operations and maintenance budgets, financial break-even analysis, and a capital improvement budget. Detailed demographic and economic information for the proposed service area must be provided. The applicant must analyze the sensitivity of the proposed project to changes in such variables as business cycles, exchange rates, interest rates, and so on. In addition, historical and pro forma rate and fee schedules must be submitted, as must a plan for how the project is to be organized and managed (ibid., 21–23). Clearly, several of these requirements are beyond the capabilities of many communities along the border without substantial technical assistance.

Each project must also satisfy certain community participation criteria. The project applicant must submit a comprehensive community participation plan. A required part of this plan is the establishment of a steering committee composed of the representatives of a broad range of community organizations. If the project affects both the United States and Mexico, the steering committee must have representatives from both countries. In addition to forming a steering committee, the applicant is required to meet individually with local organizations that will be affected by the project. The purpose of such meetings is both to inform the public about the project and to develop support for it.

The project applicant must also make the project proposal readily available to the public at least thirty days before the first public meetings on the proposal. At least two public meetings must be held in the community affected by the project. At these meetings a written document summarizing the project has to be made available to the public.

The applicant must document to the BECC in a written report that all of the measures in the participation plan have taken place. Further, this report must be able to affirm that the community understands the costs and benefits of the project as they relate to a range of issues, and that the community supports the project even though it may involve changes in user fees (ibid., 24–26).

Finally, the project must satisfy certain sustainable development criteria. Following the definition adopted at the 1992 Rio Environmental Summit, sustainable development is defined as development that meets the needs of the present without compromising the ability of future generations to meet their own needs. Project applicants must present evidence that the community has the ability to support and maintain the project over the long term, or if it does not, that a plan exists for developing such institutional and human capacity. Projects must conform to all relevant plans for local and regional conservation and development. They must manifest a "reasonable degree" of conservation of natural resources, and must also foster community development (ibid., 27–29).

Given the stringency of these project certification criteria and the documentation required to meet them, the technical assistance programs of the BECC and the NADB are critical. Many of the areas along the border most in need of environmental infrastructure development lack the human and institutional capacity required to put together a proposal that would meet all of the certification criteria. Therefore, an important role for both the BECC and the NADB is to supply the advisory services to help with project planning and preparation.

As of 30 June 1999, the BECC had 134 projects in the development stage. Fifty-four of these were on the U.S. side of the border, and 80 were on the Mexican side. Reportedly, as many as 30 of these projects could be certified within the following 18 months. Of the 27 projects already certified, 15 of them are in the United States and 12 are in Mexico. The BECC estimates that more than 7 million residents of the border region will benefit from these projects, which represent a total investment of $800 million (BECC 1999, 1).

North American Development Bank

The NADB was established at the same time, and by the same charter, as the BECC. While they are distinct and separate institutions, they work together to address the environmental infrastructure problems of the U.S.–Mexico border. Whereas the BECC is concerned primarily with initial project development, the role of the NADB is to facilitate financing of projects and to oversee their long-term implementation. All projects that the NADB helps to fund require BECC certification, but not all BECC certified projects receive NADB funding.

The NADB is headquartered in San Antonio, Texas. Its board of directors consists of three cabinet level officials from each country. The representatives of the United States are the secretary of the treasury, the secretary of state, and the administrator of the EPA. The counterpart officials from Mexico are the secretary of finance and public credit, the secretary of commerce and industrial development, and the secretary of social development. The chairmanship of the board of directors alternates annually between a U.S. member and a Mexican member. The board of directors appoints the managing director who serves as chief executive officer, and also the deputy managing director who serves as chief operating officer. These officers are appointed to three-year renewable terms. The positions alternate between nationals of the United States and Mexico, and at all times the nationalities of these two officials must be different. The NADB is relatively small for an international institution, having just over thirty employees, and total expenses for fiscal 1997 of approximately $4.4 million (NADB 1998, 32).

The NADB's capital has been contributed equally by the United States and Mexico. The initial authorized capital stock of the NADB was $3 billion. Of this amount, 15 percent or $450 million is paid-in capital, and the remaining $2.55 billion is callable capital. Paid-in capital is appropriated by the member countries and contributed directly to the NADB. Callable capital consists of funds that the countries have agreed to provide, if necessary, for the NADB to meet its outstanding debt obligations and guarantees. The surety provided by the callable capital has the effect of lowering the NADB's cost of funds in the capital markets. Under the terms of its charter, the outstanding loans and guarantees of the NADB cannot exceed the amount of its subscribed capital, reserves, and surplus.

An interesting feature of NADB capitalization is that only 90 percent of its authorized capital is designated for the funding of environmental infrastructure projects along the border. The remaining 10 percent is set aside to fund community adjustment and investment programs in the United States and Mexico. These projects are not limited geographically to the border region. The governments of the United States and Mexico were given leeway to develop these programs as they wished, independent of the NADB. The programs have developed differently in the United States and Mexico, as discussed later in this chapter.

Regular NADB Programs

Central to the purpose of the NADB is its loan and guaranty program. Through its loan program the NADB provides direct financing for environmental infrastructure projects in the border region that are judged to have reasonable prospects for repayment, but are having difficulty finding funding in private capital markets. Funding from other sources is required since the NADB cannot fund more than 50 percent of a project's total capital cost. In general, NADB financing is intended to bridge financing gaps not covered from other funding sources. NADB loans can have maturities of up to 25 years in length.

The NADB usually acts not only as lender, but also as investment banker helping to locate funding from both public and private sources and to structure a financial package that is both affordable and flexible enough to fit the specific needs of a community. The NADB works in concert with the BECC at the project proposal stage to provide advice to communities concerning their long-term infrastructure needs. NADB assistance to potential borrowers on the financial design of the projects improves the chances that the projects will meet the requirements of both BECC certification criteria and NADB loan evaluation criteria.

Besides making direct loans, the NADB can provide interim financing in the form of short-term loans until permanent funding is available, and can make loans through purchasing the bonds or other obligations of governmental entities. Also, the NADB can guarantee loans of up to 50 percent of the total capital cost of a project. In this way the NADB encourages other public and private sector lenders to participate in the project, since through its guarantee the NADB assumes part of the risk of the loan.

In addition to its core loan and guaranty program, the NADB has a number of complementary programs and services. An important one of these, instituted in 1996, is the Institutional Development and Cooperation Program (IDP). This program, which operates in conjunction with the BECC technical assistance program, is designed to strengthen the institutional capacities of public utilities in the border region. By helping these utilities to improve their rate structures, billing and collection systems, and other aspects of their operations, the IDP helps to put them on a more solid financial foundation and enhances their chances for future funding. In early 1999 this aspect of the NADB program was involved in 93 projects, 57 of which will be carried out in Mexico. Of these, 9 had been completed, 50 were in progress, and 34 were under design (BECC-NADB 1999, 7). The total amount of IDP funds committed as of mid-1999 was $5.15 million, 72 percent of which will be used to develop projects in Mexico (Lehman 1999, 7).

A new addition to the IDP inaugurated in 1999 is the Utility Management Institute. This is a professional development program for the managers and staff members of public utilities in the border area. Its goal is to increase the managerial and financial skill of professionals responsible for operating the public utilities along the border. The program also aims to develop a network of such professionals so that they can share their expertise as they address common problems.

Because economies of scale typically exist in the operation of public utilities, the NADB has a program to encourage regional projects that will serve more than one community. Developing independent water supplies and wastewater treatment facilities for small communities is inefficient if there are other communities close enough to share facilities. The NADB helps to negotiate and to implement regional agreements that provide for facilities of more efficient scale.

In order to help coordinate the activities of various institutions involved in border environmental infrastructure projects, and to bring about synergies among them, the NADB has established a cooperative credit agreement program. In doing so, the NADB hopes to avoid duplication of efforts, streamline application processes, and increase the amount of capital available for border infrastructure projects. The NADB has initiated formal relationships with, among others, the Mexican National Water Commission, various agencies of the border states, and with U.S. government agencies such as the EPA, the department of agriculture, and the department of commerce. By making use of the personnel and administrative networks of these agencies, the NADB is able to extend its reach beyond what it would be otherwise.

A major problem in the development of public utilities along the border has been the fact that the poor economic conditions of the communities involved have limited the viability of infrastructure projects. Rate structures sufficient to provide long-term funding for projects implied burdensome charges for the population served, and therefore failed to generate public support. In recognition of this problem, the NADB in 1997 established the Border Environment Infrastructure Fund (BEIF). The BEIF was set up to receive and administer grants from outside agencies that could be combined with loans or guarantees of the NADB to make otherwise unfeasible projects financially feasible. The U.S. EPA made an initial contribution of $170 million for this purpose. These funds may be used either to cover a portion of construction costs for water or wastewater projects, or to absorb a portion of rate increases over a five to seven year period. In this way the users of a system can have a gradual transition to the higher level of fees that would be required to finance an improved system. Because the EPA funding comes from the United States, the projects financed, whether in Mexico or the United States, must in some way have an impact on the U.S. environment. Communities must demonstrate financial need, as determined by an affordability analysis conducted by NADB, in order to qualify for BEIF funding. As of early 1999, $97.7 million had been authorized under this program to help fund ten different projects (ibid.).

Initially, Mexico could not take full advantage of NADB programs because of a provision in their Constitution that forbids states and municipalities in Mexico to borrow from foreign entities or in foreign currencies. Therefore, the states and municipalities on the Mexican side of the border could not receive NADB funds. Eventually, Mexico's Ministry of Finance and Public Credit suggested that a limited-purpose financial institution (*Sociedad Financiera de Objeto Limitado*, or SOFOL) be created at the federal level to receive the funds and then make the loans to the states and municipalities. This institution, called *Corporacion Financiera de America del Norte, S.A. de C.V. SOFOL*, is limited to making loans to finance environmental infrastructure. Because the SOFOL is a Mexican federal government institution, and because it converts funds into pesos before lending them, the constitutional problem has thereby been circumvented (NADB 1998, 6).

As of spring 1999, the BECC had certified twenty-seven environmental infrastructure projects. Twenty of these projects had requested financial assistance from the NADB, and the other seven had decided not to seek NADB support. Of the twenty projects requesting assistance, fourteen had been authorized for loans, guarantees, and/or grants of BEIF funds. These fourteen projects will involve a total investment of $408.5 million and should benefit an estimated 5 million border-area residents. The remaining six projects that were in the planning stage should involve an investment of about $192 million and benefit an additional 2 million people (BECC-NADB 1999, 10).

Community Adjustment and Assistance Program

Although the community adjustment and assistance program was not envisioned originally as part of the NADB, the United States and Mexico have agreed that up to 10 percent of the capital of NADB will be designated for community adjustment and investment projects. The U.S. Community Adjustment and Assistance Program (USCAIP) was established as a way of getting the requisite political support for NAFTA in the U.S. Congress. Congressman Esteban E. Torres of Los Angeles insisted that such a program be created as a condition of his support. Congressman Torres carried significant political influence in both the Hispanic community and among organized labor, having been heavily involved in labor organizations before running for Congress. During his time in Congress, Rep. Torres had interacted with members of the European Parliament, and had developed an appreciation for the regional development efforts of the European Union. Rep. Torres desired a new institution that would serve a different function from existing ones, whereas the administration did not. The resulting structure, which resulted from negotiations between the U.S. Department of Treasury and the office of Rep. Torres, is a rather unusual one (McKinney 1998).

The office of the USCAIP is located in Los Angeles, and officially is a branch of the NADB. However, the programs of the USCAIP are quite different from those of the rest of the NADB. The USCAIP is totally directed by a finance committee headquartered in Washington. This committee consists of representatives of the U.S. Department of Treasury, the U.S. Small Business Administration, the Economic Development Administration of the U.S. Department of Commerce, the U.S. Department of Housing and Urban Development, the U.S. Department of Agriculture, and the U.S. Department of Labor (ibid.).

The purpose of the USCAIP is to provide loans or loan guarantees that will help to retain or create private sector jobs in U.S. communities that have lost a significant number of jobs due to the NAFTA agreement. These communities can be located anywhere in the United States, not necessarily in the border region. In order to qualify for assistance, communities must show that they have lost a significant number of jobs as a result of NAFTA, and that they have a continuing need for transition assistance.

The USCAIP can make direct loans or loan guarantees directly to communities for projects that are expected to create jobs. For the most part, however, it has carried out its mandate by working with other agencies of the U.S. government. Specifically, the USCAIP has underwritten the cost of delivering programs of the Small Business Administration, and also those of the Business and Industry Program of the U.S. Department of Agriculture's Rural Business Program (ibid.).

In the relatively full employment economy experienced in the United

States since the passage of NAFTA, few communities have been able to meet the criteria required for direct loans from the USCAIP. For fiscal 1997 the approved budget of USCAIP was $497,025, while its actual expenditures were $355,300. Its budget for fiscal 1998 was approved for $455,126 (NADB 1998, 26). As of early 1999, the USCAIP had helped to finance 196 loans totaling $165.2 million. These loans financed projects that would create an estimated 2,766 new jobs, and help to preserve 2,387 existing jobs (BECC-NADB 1999, 8). Viewed in the context of the entire U.S. labor market, this had a minuscule effect.

As each of the member countries was given leeway to determine how to structure their community adjustment and investment programs (CAIP), Mexico's program has developed along distinctly different lines from that of the United States. The Mexican Ministry of Finance and Public Credit chose a federally operated investment bank, *Banco Nacional de Obras y Servicios Publicos, S.N.C.* (Banobras) to receive and administer the funds allocated by the NADB for this project. This institution has an existing network of offices throughout Mexico, and has had much experience in administering environmental and infrastructure projects, as well as urban development projects. Mexico has chosen to focus its CAIP activities on urgently needed environmental infrastructure projects. Thus far it is funding water, wastewater, and solid waste projects in the Mexican states of Zacatecas, Chihuahua, Sonora, and Oaxaca (NADB 1998, 27). By concentrating on environmental infrastructure projects, Mexico's CAIP activities are much more closely related to the types of projects that the NADB was initially envisioned to help finance.

Conclusion

For many years before NAFTA environmental conditions along the U.S.–Mexico border had received insufficient attention and had been allowed to deteriorate. A major benefit of the NAFTA debate and the resulting agreement is that they have focused attention on environmental and other problems in the border region that probably would not have been addressed in the absence of NAFTA.

Much of the pollution along the border has been the result of population growth and increased industrial production in the region. This increased production and trade has brought widespread economic benefits to the citizens of both the United States and Mexico. However, in some cases production costs that should have been borne by firms have spilled over into the environment in the form of pollution. Residents of the border region who suffer from this pollution have borne part of the production cost of goods that were sold artificially cheap to the citizens of both countries. Therefore, a strong case can be made for funding the cleanup of the border region out of general tax revenues.

The institutional arrangement established to deal with problems along the U.S.–Mexico border has been awkward. Two separate institutions, the BECC and the NADB, were established in large part so that both Mexico and the United States could host an institution. Other development banks function as unitary institutions without having separate entities, one to certify projects for funding and the other to arrange the funding. The BECC and the NADB have had to learn to work together during their early years, to define the separate nature of their activities, and to coordinate their actions. Gradually they are learning how best to work together and to function most effectively.

The resources available to the BECC and the NADB are hardly sufficient to address the environmental infrastructure problems along the U.S.–Mexico border. The U.S. General Accounting Office estimated in 1996 that $8 billion would be required during the succeeding 10 years to remedy deficiencies there. Since the time of that estimate industrial expansion and population growth along the border have placed additional demands on the environmental infrastructure. As of June 1999, the NADB had made loans to 7 projects totaling $11.1 million, and had provided BEIF construction grants of $119.3 million (USGAO 1999, 42). NADB commitments and projections for 21 BECC-certified projects amounted to about $200 million, about two-thirds of which will fund projects in Mexico (Lehman 1999, 7).

With the population of the border region projected to double to more than 20 million people during the next decade, the urgent need for additional funding is apparent. The BECC was originally authorized for $5 million of annual funding from each government, but the most that it has ever received in a year was $1.75 million from each government, and in each of the past four years funding has been reduced (Silva 1999). The ability of the NADB to respond to border infrastructure needs is greatly limited by its relatively small amount of paid-in capital. Of course sources of funding other than the NADB exist for border infrastructure projects, such as other EPA-funded programs, U.S. Department of Agriculture rural development funds, tax-exempt municipal bonds, state government funds, and some private funding. Even so, infrastructure expansion in the border region is hardly keeping pace with the needs generated by increasing industrialization and population growth.

The resources being made available to the border region through the BECC and the NADB, while far from sufficient to address the many problems that exist there, nevertheless are critically important. Some of the border communities are getting clean water supplies, adequate wastewater treatment, and solid waste disposal for the first time ever as a result of the activities of these institutions.

The USCAIP, while well intentioned, has been something of a distraction from the main purpose of the NADB. The job losses in the U.S. economy attributable to NAFTA have been very small compared to the normal job turnover resulting from technological change, changing preferences of consumers, etc. In addition, the economy has had much more net job creation since NAFTA went into effect. Trade adjustment assistance programs already in place, not to mention the special NAFTA-Trade Adjustment Assistance appropriated specifically to assist workers displaced by trade with Canada and Mexico, should have been sufficient to deal with the employment effects of NAFTA.

The USCAIP is, admittedly, somewhat different from other programs in that it provides assistance to specific firms at the project level. Other trade adjustment assistance programs in the United States are geared to assist either the individual worker or to provide general assistance to affected communities (McKinney 1999).

The USCAIP was originally envisioned as a transitional program that would terminate when its funds were exhausted. However, in a recent appropriation for the U.S. Treasury Department, $10 million in funds were included for USCAIP that will enable it to provide grants as well as loans (ibid.). The program may possibly endure and be broadened to cover firms affected by trade agreements other than NAFTA, particularly if a free trade agreement for the Americas materializes. As mentioned earlier, Mexico has chosen to use its CAIP funds in different ways from the United States, and in ways more in line with the original purposes of the NADB concept.

Both the BECC and the NADB were slow to get organized and to begin operations. The conditions that loan applicants must meet are burdensome, and could probably be streamlined without compromising the integrity of the process. The grant funds provided by the U.S. EPA have greatly improved the ability of the BECC and the NADB to carry out their mandates in view of the fact that many communities along the border lack the economic resources to engage in environmental infrastructure improvement without assistance. Further funding of this type is urgently needed and would greatly enhance the effectiveness of the BECC and the NADB as institutions that are trying to address the serious environmental needs of the border region.

Appendix 6.1
Charter of North American Development Bank and Border Environment Cooperation Commission

AGREEMENT BETWEEN
THE GOVERNMENT OF
THE UNITED STATES OF AMERICA AND
THE GOVERNMENT OF THE UNITED MEXICAN STATES
CONCERNING THE ESTABLISHMENT OF
A BORDER ENVIRONMENT COOPERATION COMMISSION
AND A NORTH AMERICAN DEVELOPMENT BANK

The Government of the United States of America and the Government of the United Mexican States *("the Parties"):*

CONVINCED of the importance of the conservation, protection and enhancement of their environments and the essential role of cooperation in these areas in achieving sustainable development for the well-being of present and future generations;

RECOGNIZING the bilateral nature of many transboundary environmental issues, and that such issues can be most effectively addressed jointly;

ACKNOWLEDGING that the border region of the United States and Mexico is experiencing environmental problems which must be addressed in order to promote sustainable development;

RECOGNIZING the need for environmental infrastructure in the border region, especially in the areas of water pollution, wastewater treatment, municipal solid waste, and related matters;

AFFIRMING that, to the extent practicable, environmental infrastructure projects should be financed by the private sector, but that the urgency of the environmental problems in the border region requires that the Parties be prepared to assist in supporting these projects;

AFFIRMING that, to the extent practicable, environmental infrastructure projects in the border region should be operated and maintained through user fees paid by polluters and those who benefit from the projects, and should be subject to local or private control;

NOTING that the International Boundary and Water Commission, established pursuant to the Treaty between the United States and Mexico Relating to Utilization of Waters of the Colorado and Tijuana Rivers and of the Rio Grande, signed at Washington February 3, 1944, plays an important role in efforts to preserve the health and vitality of the river waters of the border region;

RECOGNIZING that there is a need to establish a new organization to strengthen cooperation among interested parties and to facilitate the financing, construction, operation and maintenance of environmental infrastructure projects in the border region;

AFFIRMING the desirability of encouraging increased investment in the environmental infrastructure in the border region, whether or not such investment is made under the auspices of this Agreement;

CONVINCED of the need to collaborate with states and localities, nongovernmental organizations, and other members of the public in the effort to address environmental problems in the border region;

SEEKING to assist community adjustment and investment in the United States and Mexico;

REAFFIRMING the importance of the environmental goals and objectives embodied in the Agreement on Cooperation for the Protection and Improvement of the Environment in the Border Area, sign at La Paz, Baja California Sur, August 14, 1983; and

WISHING to follow upon the goals and objectives of the North American Free Trade Agreement, signed at Washington, Ottawa, and Mexico December 8, 11, 14, and 17, 1992, and the North American Agreement on Environmental Cooperation, signed at Mexico, Washington, and Ottawa September 8, 9, 12, and 14, 1993;

HAVE AGREED as follows:

INTRODUCTORY ARTICLE

The Parties agree to establish the Border Environment Cooperation Commission and the North American Development Bank, which shall operate in accordance with the following provisions:

CHAPTER I

BORDER ENVIRONMENT COOPERATION COMMISSION

Article I: **Purpose and Functions**

Section 1:   *Purpose*

(a)   The purpose of the Commission shall be to help preserve, protect and enhance the environment of the border region in order to advance the well-being of the people of the United States and Mexico.

(b)   In carrying out this purpose, the Commission shall cooperate as appropriate with the North American Development Bank and other national and international institutions, and with private sources supplying investment capital for environmental infrastructure projects in the border region.

Section 2:   **Functions**

In carrying out this purpose, the Commission may do any or all of the following:

(i)   with their concurrence, assist states and localities and other public entities and private investors in:

     (A)   coordinating environmental infrastructure projects in the border region;

     (B)   preparing, developing, implementing, and overseeing environmental infrastructure projects in the border region, including the design, siting and other technical aspects of such projects;

     (C)   analyzing the financial feasibility or the environmental aspects, or both, of environmental infrastructure projects in the border region;

     (D)   evaluating social and economic benefits of environmental infrastructure projects in the border region;

     (E)   organizing, developing and arranging public and private financing for environmental infrastructure projects in the border region; and

(ii)   certify, in accordance with Article II, Section 3 of this Chapter, applications for financing to be submitted to the North American Development Bank, or to other sources of financing that request such certification, for environmental infrastructure projects in the border region.

The Commission, with the concurrence of the United States Environmental Protection Agency and the Mexican Secretaria de Desarollo Social, may carry out these functions with respect to an environmental infrastructure project outside the border region upon finding that the project would remedy a transboundary environmental or health problem.

Article II: **Operations**

Section 1:   **Use of Resources**

The resources and facilities of the Commission shall be used exclusively to implement the purpose and functions enumerated in Article I of this Chapter.

Section 2:   *Requests for Assistance*

(a)   The Commission may seek and accept requests from states and localities, other public entities and private investors for assistance in carrying out the activities enumerated in Article I of this Chapter.

(b)   Upon receipt of a request for assistance pursuant to paragraph (a) of this Section, the Commission may provide any and all such assistance as it deems appropriate. In providing such assistance, or in making certifications pursuant to Section 3 of this Article, the Commission shall give preference to environmental infrastructure projects relating to water pollution, waste water treatment, municipal solid waste and related matters.

(c)   In providing such assistance, the Commission shall consult with the Advisory Council established pursuant to Article III, Section 5 of this Chapter, and, as appropriate, with private investors and national and international institutions, particularly the North American Development Bank.

Section 3:   *Applications for Certification*

(a)   The Commission may accept applications from states and localities, other public entities and private investors for certification of environmental infrastructure projects in the border region with respect to which an applicant will be seeking financial assistance from the North American Development Bank or other sources of financing requesting such certification.

(b)   The Commission may certify for such financing any project that meets or agrees to meet the technical, environmental, financial or other criteria applied, either generally or specifically, by the Commission to that project. To be eligible for certification, a project shall observe or be capable of observing the environmental and other laws of the place where it is to be located or executed.

(c)   For each project located in the border region and having significant transboundary environmental effects,

(1)   an environmental assessment shall be presented

as part of the application process, and the Board of Directors shall examine potential environmental benefits, environmental risks, and costs, as well as available alternatives and the environmental standards and objectives of the affected area; and

(2) the Board of Directors, in consultation with affected states and localities, shall determine that the project meets the necessary conditions to achieve a high level of environmental protection for the affected area.

(d) Upon certification of a project for financial assistance from the North American Development Bank, the Commission shall submit a proposal for such assistance to the Bank for its consideration.

(e) Upon certification of a project for financial assistance from another source of financing requesting such certification, the Commission shall submit a proposal for such assistance to that source for its consideration.

Section 4:   Relationship with the Public

The Commission shall establish procedures in English and Spanish:

(1) ensuring, to the extent possible, public availability of documentary information on all projects for which a request for assistance or an application for certification is made;

(2) for giving written notice of and providing members of the public reasonable opportunity to comment on any general guidelines which may be established by the Commission for environmental infrastructure projects for which it provides assistance, and on all applications for certification received by the Commission; and

(3) whereby the Board of Directors could receive complaints from groups affected by projects that the Commission has assisted or certified and could obtain independent assessments as to whether the terms of this Chapter or the procedures established by the Board of Directors pursuant to this Chapter have been observed.

Section 5: *Reimbursement, Fees and Charges*

(a) The Commission may arrange for reimbursement of the costs of furnishing assistance on terms which the Commission deems appropriate.

(b) The Commission may establish reasonable fees or other charges for its assistance, including the processing of applications for certification.

Article III: Organization and Management

Section 1: *Location of Offices*

The Commission shall have its offices in the border region.

Section 2: *Structure of the Commission*

The Commission shall have a Board of Directors, a General Manager, a Deputy General Manager, an Advisory Council and such other officers to perform such duties as the Commission may determine.

Section 3: *Board of Directors*

(a) All the powers of the Commission, including the power to determine its general operational and structural policies, shall be vested in the Board of Directors. The Board shall have ten directors:

    (1) the United States Commissioner of the International Boundary and Water Commission, who shall serve *ex officio*;

    (2) the Mexican Commissioner of the International Boundary and Water Commission, who shall serve *ex officio*;

    (3) the Administrator of the Environmental Protection Agency of the United States, or his/her delegate, who shall serve *ex officio*;

    (4) the Secretario de Desarollo Social of Mexico, or his/her delegate, who shall serve *ex officio*;

    (5) six additional directors having expertise in environmental planning, economics, engineering, finance, or related matters, consisting of—

(i)   a representative of one of the U.S. border states, appointed by the United States in such manner as it may determine;

(ii)   a representative of one of the Mexican border states, appointed by Mexico in such manner as it may determine;

(iii)   a representative of a U.S. locality in the border region, appointed by the United States in such manner as it may determine;

(iv)   a representative of a Mexican locality in the border region, appointed by Mexico in such manner as it may determine;

(v)   a member of the U.S. public who is a resident of the border region, appointed by the United States in such manner as it may determine; and

(vi)   a member of the Mexican public who is a resident of the border region, appointed by Mexico in such manner as it may determine.

Each of the Parties, on an alternating basis, shall select one of the directors as Chairperson of the Board of Directors for a one-year term.

(b) The Board of Directors may delegate to the General Manager authority to exercise any powers of the Board, except the power to:

(i)   certify environmental infrastructure projects in accordance with Article II, Section 3 of this Chapter;

(ii)   apply, either generally or specifically, technical, environmental, financial or other criteria to an environmental infrastructure project;

(iii)   determine the salary and terms of contact of service of the General Manager and the Deputy General Manager; and

(iv)   approve the annual program and budget and the annual report of the Commission.

(c) The Board of Directors shall hold quarterly regular sessions, and such other special sessions as may be called by the Board or the General Manager. At all regular sessions, the Board of

Directors shall hold at least one public meeting. One public meeting each year shall be designated the Annual Meeting of the Board.

(d)   A quorum for any meeting of the Board of Directors shall be a majority of the directors appointed by each of the Parties.

(e)   All decisions of the Board of Directors shall require the approval of a majority of the members appointed by each Party. A written record of such decisions shall be made public in English and Spanish.

(f)   The Board of Directors may adopt such rules and regulations as may be necessary or appropriate to conduct the business of the Commission.

(g)   Directors shall serve as such without compensation from the Commission, but the Commission shall pay them reasonable expenses incurred in attending meetings of the Board of Directors.

Section 4:   *General Manager*

(a)   The Board of Directors shall appoint a General Manager and a Deputy General Manager, neither of whom shall be a director. The General Manager and the Deputy General Manager shall each be appointed for a term of three years and may be reappointed. The General Manager and the Deputy General Manager shall cease to hold office when the Board of Directors so decides with respect to either officer. The offices of General Manager and Deputy General Manager shall alternate between nationals of the Parties. The General Manager and the Deputy General Manager shall be nationals of different Parties at all times.

(b)   The General Manager shall exercise all the powers delegated to him or her by the Board of Directors. The General Manager may participate in meetings of the Board, but shall not vote at such meetings. The General Manager shall be chief of the operating staff of the Commission and shall conduct, under the direction of the Board of Directors, the ordinary business of the Commission. Subject to the general control of the Board of Directors, the General Manager shall be responsible for the organization, appointment and dismissal of the officers and staff of the Commission.

(c) The General Manager, officers and staff of the Commission, in the discharge of their offices, shall owe their duty entirely to the Commission and to no other authority. The Parties shall respect the international character of this duty and shall refrain from all attempts to influence any of them in the discharge of their duties.

(d) In appointing the officers and staff, the General Manager shall, subject to the paramount importance of securing the highest standards of efficiency and technical competence, seek to achieve at each level a balanced proportion of nationals of each Party.

(e) The General Manager shall submit to the Board of Directors for its approval an annual program and budget for the Commission. The Advisory Council established pursuant to Section 5 of this Article shall receive at the same time as the Board of Directors drafts of the annual program and budget and may make comments to the Board on the same.

Section 5: **Advisory Council**

(a) The Advisory Council shall be composed of:

(i) at least one resident of each of the U.S. border states, totaling not more than six such representatives, who shall represent states or localities, or local community groups, to be appointed by the United States in such manner as it may determine;

(ii) one resident of each of the Mexican border states, who shall represent states or localities, or local community groups, to be appointed by Mexico in such manner as it may determine;

(iii) three members of the public, including at least one representative of a U.S. nongovernmental organization, appointed by the United States in such manner as it may determine; and

(iv) three members of the public, including at least one representative of a Mexican nongovernmental organization, appointed by Mexico in such manner as it may determine.

(b) Council members shall be appointed for a term of two years and may be reappointed. Each of the Parties shall select from among the members it appoints a Co-Chairperson of the Council. Council members shall serve as such without compensation from the Commission, but the Commission shall pay them reasonable expenses incurred in attending meetings of the Council.

(c)   The Council shall meet quarterly during the regular sessions of the Board of Directors, and at such other times as the Council, with the consent of a majority of the members appointed by each of the Parties, or the Board shall determine.

(d)   The Council may adopt such rules as may be necessary or appropriate to conduct the business of the Council.

(e)   The Council may provide advice to the Board of Directors or the General Manager on any matter within the scope of this Chapter, including certifications pursuant to Article II, Section 3, of this Chapter, and on the implementation and further elaboration of this Chapter, and may perform such other functions as directed by the Board.

Section 6:   *Relationship to the International Boundary and Water Commission*

(a)   The Commission may enter into arrangements with the International Boundary and Water Commission ("IBWC") regarding facilities, personnel and services and arrangements for reimbursement of administrative and other expenses paid by one organization on behalf of the other.

(b)   Nothing in this Chapter shall make the Commission liable for the acts or obligations of the IBWC, or the IBWC liable for the acts or obligations of the Commission.

(c)   The Parties shall call upon the Commission and the IBWC to cooperate, as appropriate, with each other in planning, developing and carrying out border sanitation and other environmental activities.

Section 7:   *Funding*

Each Party shall contribute an equal share of the budget of the Commission, subject to the availability of appropriated funds in accordance with its domestic legal requirements. The Commission shall establish an account or accounts to receive such contributions from the Parties.

Section 8:   *Channel of Communication*

Each Party shall designate an appropriate authority with which the Commission may communicate in connection with any matter arising under this Chapter.

Section 9:   *Annual Reports*

(a) The Commission shall submit to the Parties an annual report in English and Spanish on its operations. The report shall be prepared by the General Manager and shall be approved by the Board of Directors. The Advisory Council shall receive at the same time as the Board of Directors drafts of the annual report and may make comments to the Board on the same. The annual report shall include an audited statement of the Commission's accounts.

(b) Copies of the annual report prepared under this section shall be made available to the public.

Section 10:   *Limitations on Disclosure*

(a) Notwithstanding any other provision of this Chapter, the Commission, including its officers and staff, shall not make public information with respect to which a Party has notified the Commission that public disclosure would impede its law enforcement.

(b) The Commission shall establish regulations to protect from disclosure business or proprietary information and information the disclosure of which would violate personal privacy or the confidentiality of government decision-making.

(c) A party that requests assistance or submits an application to the Commission may request that information contained therein be designated confidential by the Commission, and may request an advance determination from the Commission as to whether such information is entitled to confidentiality pursuant to subsection (b) above. If the Commission determines that such information is not entitled to confidentiality pursuant to subsection (b) above, the party may withdraw its request or application prior to further action by the Commission. Upon such withdrawal, the Commission shall not keep any copy of the information and shall not make public that it received such a request or application.

Article IV: Status, Immunities and Privileges

Section 1:   Scope of Article

To enable the Commission to fulfill its purpose and the functions with which it is entrusted, the status, immunities and privileges set forth in this Article shall be accorded to the Commission in the territories of each Party.

Section 2:   Legal Status

(a)   The Commission shall possess juridical personality and, in particular, full capacity:
  (i)   to contract;
  (ii)   to acquire and dispose of immovable and movable property; and
  (iii)   to institute legal proceedings.
(b)   The Commission may exercise such other powers as shall be necessary in furtherance of its purpose and functions, consistent with the provisions of this Chapter.

Section 3:   Judicial Proceedings

The Commission, its property and its assets, wherever located, and by whomsoever held, shall enjoy the same immunity from suit and every form of judicial process as is enjoyed by foreign governments, except to the extent that the Commission may expressly waive its immunity for the purposes of any proceedings or by the terms of any contract.

Section 4:   Immunity of Assets

Property and assets of the Commission, wheresoever located and by whomsoever held, shall be considered public international property and shall be immune from search, requisition, confiscation, expropriation or any other form of taking or foreclosure by executive or legislative action.

Section 5:   *Inviolability of Archives*

The archives of the Commission shall be inviolable.

Section 6:   *Freedom of Assets from Restrictions*

To the extent necessary to carry out the purpose and functions of the Commission and to conduct its operations in accordance with this Chapter, all property and other assets of the Commission shall be free from restrictions, regulations, controls and moratoria of any nature, except as may otherwise be provided in this Chapter.

Section 7:   *Privilege for Communications*

The official communications of the Commission shall be accorded by each Party the same treatment that it accords to the official communications of the other Party.

Section 8:   *Personal Immunities and Privileges*

The directors, General Manager, Deputy General Manager, officers and staff of the Commission shall have the following privileges and immunities:

(i)   immunity from legal process with respect to acts performed by them in their official capacity except when the Commission expressly waives this immunity;

(ii)   when not local nationals, the same immunities from immigration restrictions, alien registration requirements and national service obligations and the same facilities as regards exchange provisions as are accorded by each Party to the representatives, officials, and employees of comparable rank of the other Party; and

(iii)   the same privileges in respect of traveling facilities as are accorded by each Party to representatives, officials, and employees of comparable rank of the other Party.

Section 9: *Immunities from Taxation*

(a) The Commission, its property, other assets, income, and the operations it carries out pursuant to this Chapter shall be immune from all taxation and from all customs duties. The Commission shall also be immune from any obligation relating to the payment, withholding or collection of any tax or customs duty.

(b) No tax shall be levied on or in respect of salaries and emoluments paid by the Commission to officers or staff of the Commission who are not local nationals.

Section 10: *Implementation*

Each Party, in accordance with its juridical system, shall take such action as is necessary to make effective in its own territories the principles set forth in this Article, and shall inform the Commission of the action which it has taken on the matter.

Article V: Consultations

Section 1: *Principle of Cooperation*

The Parties shall at all times endeavor to agree on the interpretation and application of this Chapter, and shall make every effort to resolve any matter that might affect the implementation of this Chapter.

Section 2: *Consultations*

Upon the written request of either Party or the Board of Directors in English and Spanish, the Parties shall consult regarding the interpretation or application of this Chapter. These consultations shall take place within 30 days after a written request for consultation.

Article VI: Termination of Operations

(a) The Parties, by mutual agreement, may terminate the operations of the Commission. A Party may withdraw from the Commission by delivering to the Commission at its principal office a written notice of its intention to do so. Such withdrawal shall become finally effective on the date specified in the notice but in no event less than six months after the notice is delivered to the Commission. However, at any time before the withdrawal becomes finally effective, the Party may notify the Commission in writing of the cancellation of its notice of intention to withdraw. The Commission shall terminate its operations on the effective date of any notice of withdrawal from the Commission.

(b) After such termination of operations the Commission shall forth-with cease all activities, those incident to the conservation, preservation, and realization of its assets and settlement of its obligations.

CHAPTER II

NORTH AMERICAN DEVELOPMENT BANK

Article I: **Purposes and Functions**

Section 1:   *Purposes*

The purposes of the North American Development Bank shall be:

(a) to provide financing for projects certified by the Border Environment Cooperation Commission, as appropriate, and, at the request of the Commission, to otherwise assist the Commission in fulfilling its purposes and functions;

(b) to provide financing endorsed by the United States, as appropriate, for community adjustment and investment in support of the purposes of the North American Free Trade Agreement; and

(c) to provide financing endorsed by Mexico, as appropriate, for community adjustment and investment in support of the purpose of the North American Free Trade Agreement.

Section 2: *Functions*

To implement its purposes, the Bank shall utilize its own capital, funds raised by it in financial markets, and other available resources and shall fulfill the following functions:

(a) to promote the investment of public and private capital contributing to its purposes;

(b) to encourage private investment in projects, enterprises, and activities contributing to its purposes, and to supplement private investment when private capital is not available on reasonable terms and conditions; and

(c) to provide technical and other assistance for the financing and, in coordination with the Commission, the implementation of the plans and projects.

In carrying out its functions, the Bank shall cooperate as appropriate with national and international institutions and with private sources supplying investment capital.

Article II: **Capital of the Bank**

Section 1: *Authorized Capital*

(a) The authorized capital stock of the Bank initially shall be in the amount of $3,000,000,000 in United States dollars and shall be divided into 300,000 shares having a par value of $10,000 each, which shall be available for subscription by the Parties in accordance with Section 2 of this Article.

(b) The authorized capital stock shall be divided into paid-in shares and callable shares. $450,000,000 shall be paid-in shares, and $2,550,000,000 shall be callable for the purposes specified in Section 3 (d) of this Article.

(c) The authorized capital stock may be increased when the Board of the Bank by a unanimous vote deems it advisable, subject to the domestic legal requirements of the Parties.

Section 2:   *Subscription of Shares*

(a)   Each Party shall subscribe to shares of the capital stock of the Bank. The number of shares to be subscribed by the Parties shall be those set forth in Annex A of this Agreement, which specifies the obligation of each Party as to both paid-in and callable capital.

(b)   Shares of capital stock initially subscribed by the Parties shall be issued at par. Other shares shall be issued at par unless the Board of the Bank decides in special circumstances to issue them on other terms.

(c)   The liability of the Parties on capital shares shall be limited to the unpaid portion of their issue price.

(d)   Shares of capital stock shall not be pledged or encumbered in any manner, and they shall be transferable only to the Bank.

Section 3:   *Payment of Subscriptions*

Payment of the subscriptions to the capital stock of the Bank as set forth in Annex A shall be made as follows:

(a)   As soon as possible after this Agreement enters into force pursuant to Article I of Chapter III, but no later than thirty days thereafter, each Party shall deposit with the Bank an Instrument of Subscription in which it agrees to pay in either Party's currency to the Bank the amount of paid-in capital set forth for it in Annex A, and to accept the obligations of callable shares ("Unqualified Subscription"). Payment of the paid-in capital shall be due according to a schedule to be established by the Board after entry into force of this Agreement.

(b)   Notwithstanding the provisions of paragraph (a) of this Section regarding Unqualified Subscriptions, as an exceptional case, a Party may deposit an Instrument of Subscription in which it agrees that payment of all installments of paid-in capital, and its obligations with respect to all callable shares, are subject to subsequent budgetary legislation ("Qualified Subscriptions"). In such an instrument, the Party shall undertake to seek to obtain the necessary legislation to pay the full amount of paid-in capital and to accept the full amount of corresponding

obligations for callable shares, by the payment dates determined
in accordance with paragraph (a) of this Section. Payment of an
installment due after any such date shall be made within sixty
days after the requisite legislation has been obtained.

(c)   If any Party which has made a Qualified Subscription has not
obtained the legislation to make payment in full of any
installment (or to accept obligations in respect of callable shares)
by the dates determined in accordance with paragraph (a) of
this Section, then a Party which has paid the corresponding
installment on time and in full, may, after consultation with the
Board of the Bank, direct the Bank in writing to restrict
commitments against that installment. That restriction shall not
exceed the percentage which the unpaid portion of the
installment, due from the Party which has made the Qualified
Subscription, bears to the entire amount of the installment to be
paid by the Party, and shall be in effect only for the time that
unpaid portion remains unpaid.

(d)   The callable portion of the subscription for capital shares of the
Bank shall be subject to call only when required to meet the
obligations of the Bank created under Article III, Section 2 (b)
and (c) of this Chapter on borrowings of funds for inclusion in
the Bank's capital resources or guarantees chargeable to such
resources. In the event of such a call, payment shall be made in
either Party's currency. Calls on unpaid subscriptions shall be
uniform in percentage on all shares.

Section 4:   *Capital Resources*

As used in this Chapter, the term "capital resources" of the Bank shall
be deemed to include the following:

(1)   authorized capital, including both paid-in and callable shares,
subscribed pursuant to Section 2 and 3 of this Article;

(2)   all funds raised by borrowings under the authority of Article V,
Section 1(a) of this Chapter to which the commitment set forth
in Section 3(d) of this Article is applicable;

(3)   all funds received in repayment of loans made with the resources
indicated in paragraphs (1) and (2) of this section;

(4)   all income derived from loans made from the aforementioned

funds or from guarantees to which the commitment set forth in Section 3(d) of this Article is applicable; and

(5) all other income derived from any of the resources mentioned above.

Article III: Operations

Section 1:   *Use of Resources*

The resources and facilities of the Bank shall be used exclusively to implement the purposes and functions enumerated in Article I of this Chapter.

Section 2:   *Methods of Making or Guaranteeing Loans*

Subject to the conditions stipulated in this Article, the Bank may make or guarantee loans to either Party, or any agency or political subdivision thereof, and to any entity in the territory of a Party, in any of the following ways:

(a)   by making or participating in direct loans with funds corresponding to the unimpaired paid-in capital and to its reserves and undistributed surplus;

(b)   by making or participating in direct loans with funds raised by the Bank in capital markets, or borrowed or acquired in any other manner, for inclusion in the capital resources of the Bank; and

(c)   by guaranteeing in whole or in part loans made to, or securities issued in connection with, projects.

Section 3:   *Grants*

(a)   Subject to the conditions stipulated in this Article, the Bank shall make grants to the United States or any agency or political subdivision thereof, and to any entity in the territory of the United States for purposes specified in Article I, Section 1(b) of this Chapter.

(b)   Subject to the conditions stipulated in this Article, the Bank shall make grants to Mexico or any agency or political subdivision thereof, and to any entity in the territory of Mexico for purposes specified in Article I Section 1(c) of this Chapter.

Section 4: *Limitations on Operations*

(a) The total amount outstanding of loans and guarantees made by the Bank in its operations shall not at any time exceed the total amount of the unimpaired subscribed capital of the Bank, plus the unimpaired reserves and surplus included in the capital resources of the Bank, as defined in Article II, Section 4 of this Chapter, exclusive of income of the capital resources assigned by decision of the Board of the Bank to reserves not available for loans or guarantees.

(b) The total amount of loans, guarantees and grants provided for the purposes specified in Article I, Section 1(b) of this Chapter, shall not exceed 10 percent of the sum of the paid-in capital actually paid to the Bank by the United States, and the amount of callable shares for which the United States has an unqualified subscription.

The total amount of grants made pursuant to Section 3(a) of this Article, plus 15 percent of the total amount of loans and guarantees made for the purposes specified in Article I Section 1(b) of this Chapter, shall not exceed 10 percent of the paid-in capital actually paid to the Bank by the United States.

(c) The total amount of loans, guarantees and grants provided for the purposes specified in Article I, Section 1(c) of this Chapter, shall not exceed 10 percent of the sum of the paid-in capital actually paid to the Bank by Mexico, and the amount of callable shares for which Mexico has an unqualified subscription.

The total amount of grants made pursuant to Section 3(b) of this Article, plus 15 percent of the total amount of loans and guarantees made for the purposes specified in Article I, Section 1(c) of this Chapter, shall not exceed 10 percent of the paid-in capital actually paid to the Bank by Mexico.

Section 5: *Direct Loan and Grant Financing*

In making grants or in making direct loans or participating in them, the

Bank may provide financing in the currencies of the Parties to meet the costs and expenses related to the purposes of the grant or loan.

Section 6:   *Rules and Conditions for Making or Guaranteeing Loans*

(a)   The Bank may make or guarantee loans, subject to the following rules and conditions:

    (1)   in considering a request for a loan or a guarantee, the Bank shall take into account the ability of the borrower to obtain the loan from private sources of financing on terms which, in the opinion of the Bank, are reasonable for the borrower, taking into account all pertinent factors;

    (2)   in making or guaranteeing a loan, the Bank shall pay due regard to prospects that the borrower and its guarantor, if any, will be in a position to meet their obligations under the loan contract;

    (3)   in the opinion of the Bank, the rate of interest, other charges and the schedule for repayment of principal are appropriate for the purposes or project in question; and

    (4)   in guaranteeing a loan made by other investors, the Bank shall receive suitable compensation for its risk.

(b)   in addition to the rules and conditions set forth in paragraph (a) of this Section, the following rules and conditions shall apply to loans or guarantees made pursuant to a certification from the Commission:

    (1)   the applicant for the loan or guarantee shall have submitted a detailed proposal to the Bank, and the Commission shall have presented a written report certifying the proposal;

    (2)   in making or guaranteeing a loan to a project, the Bank shall find that the project is economically/financially sound, and pay due regard to the prospects that the project will generate sufficient revenues, by user fees or otherwise, to be self-sustaining or that funds will be available from other sources to meet debt servicing obligations; and

    (3)   loans made or guaranteed by the Bank shall be for financing specific projects:

(c)   In addition to the rules and conditions set forth in paragraph (a) of this Section, loans and guarantees made for the purposes specified in Article I, Section 1(b) of this Chapter shall require art endorsement from the United States.

(d)   In addition to the rules and conditions set forth in paragraph (a) of this Section, loans and guarantees made for the purposes specified in Article I, Section (c) of this Chapter shall require an endorsement from Mexico.

Section 7:   *Optional Conditions for Making or Guaranteeing Loans*

(a)   In the case of loans or guarantees of loans to nongovernmental entities, the Bank may, when it deems it advisable, require that the Party in whose territory the project is to be carried out, or a public institution or a similar agency of the Party acceptable to the Bank, guarantee the repayment of the principal and the payment of interest and other charges on the loan.

(b)   The Bank may attach such other conditions to the making of loans or guarantees as it deems appropriate.

Section 8:   *Use of Loans Made or Guaranteed by the Bank*

(a)   The Bank shall impose no condition that the proceeds of a loan shall be spent in the territory of either Party.

(b)   The Bank shall take the necessary measures to ensure that the proceeds of any loan made, guaranteed, or participated in by the Bank are used only for the purposes for which the loan was granted, with due attention to considerations of economy and efficiency.

Section 9:   *Payment Provisions for Direct Loans*

Direct loan contracts made by the Bank in conformity with Section 5 and 6 of this Article shall establish:

(a)   All the terms and conditions of each loan, including among others, provision for payment of principal, interest and other charges, maturities, and dates of payment; and

(b)   The currency or currencies in which payment shall be made to the Bank.

Section 10:   *Guarantees*

(a)   In making any guarantee pursuant to Section 2(c) of this Article, the Bank shall charge a guarantee fee, at a rate determined by the Bank, payable periodically on the amount of the loan outstanding.

(b)   Guarantee contracts concluded by the Bank shall provide that the Bank may terminate its liability with respect to interest if, upon default by the borrower and by the guarantor, if any, the Bank offers to purchase, at par and interest accrued to a date designated in the offer, the bonds or other obligations guaranteed.

(c)   In issuing guarantees, the Bank shall have power to determine any other terms and conditions.

Section 11:   *Rules and Conditions for Making Grants*

(a)   Notwithstanding Article VI, Section 3 of this Chapter, and subject to the limitations specified in Section 4(b) of this Article, the Bank shall make grants for the purposes specified in Article I, Section 1(b) of this Chapter pursuant to an endorsement by the United States.

(b)   Notwithstanding Article VI, Section 3 of this Chapter, and subject to the limitations specified in Section 4(c) of the Article, the Bank shall make grants for the purposes specified in Article I Section 1(c) of this Chapter pursuant to an endorsement by Mexico.

Section 12:   *Relationship with Other Entities*

(a)   The Bank may make arrangements with other entities, including multilateral development banks, regarding facilities, personnel and services and arrangements for reimbursement of administrative expenses paid by either entity on behalf of the other.

(b)   Nothing in this Agreement shall make the Bank liable for the acts or obligations of an entity referred to in paragraph (a) of this Section, or any such entity liable for the acts or obligations of the Bank.

Article IV: **Currencies**

Section 1:   *Use of Currencies*

(a)   The Parties may not maintain or impose restrictions any kind upon the use by the Bank or by any recipient from the Bank, for payment in any country, of the following:

   (1)   currencies received by the Bank in payment of each Party's subscription to shares of the Bank's capital;

   (2)   currencies of the Parties purchased with the resources referred to in (1) of this paragraph;

   (3)   currencies obtained by borrowings, pursuant to the provisions of Article V, Section 1(a) of this Chapter, for inclusion in the capital resources of the Bank;

   (4)   currencies received by the Bank in payment on account of principal, interest, or other charges in respect of loans made from the funds referred to in (1), (2) or (3) of this paragraph; and currencies received in payment of commissions and fees on all guarantees made by the Bank; and

   (5)   currencies received from the Bank pursuant to Article V Section 4(c) of this Chapter, in distribution of net profits.

(b)   A Party's currency held by the Bank in its capital resources, which is not covered by paragraph (a) of this section, also may be used by the Bank or any recipient from the Bank for payments in any country without restriction of any kind.

(c)   The Parties may not place any restrictions on the holding and use by the Bank, for making amortization payments or anticipating payment of, or repurchasing part or all of the Bank's own obligations, of currencies received by the Bank in repayment of direct loans made from borrowed funds included in the capital resources of the Bank.

Section 2:   *Valuation of Currencies*

(a)   The amount of a currency other than the U.S. dollar paid for purposes of Section 3(a), (b) or (d) of Article II of this Chapter or Section 3 of this Article to discharge a U.S. dollar-denominated obligation shall be that amount which will yield to the Bank the U.S. dollar amount of such obligation.

(b)   Whenever it shall become necessary under this Chapter to value any currency in terms of another currency, such valuation shall be determined by the Bank after consultation, if necessary, with the International Monetary Fund.

Section 3:   *Methods of Conserving Currencies*

The Bank shall accept from either Party promissory notes or similar securities issued by the government of the Party, or by the depository designated by such Party, in lieu of any part of the currency of the Party representing the paid-in portion of its subscription to the Bank's authorized capital, provided such currency is not required by the Bank for the conduct of its operations. Such notes or securities shall be non-negotiable, non-interest-bearing, and payable to the Bank at their par value on demand. On the same conditions, the Bank shall also accept such notes or securities in lieu of any part of the subscription of a Party with respect to which part the terms of the subscription do not require payment in cash.

Article V: Miscellaneous Powers and Distribution of Profits

Section 1:   *Miscellaneous Powers of the Bank*

In addition to the powers specified elsewhere in this Chapter, the Bank shall have the power to:

(a)   borrow funds and in that connection to furnish such collateral or other security therefore as the Bank shall determine, provided that, before making a sale of its obligations in the markets of Party, the Bank shall have obtained the approval of that country and of the Party in whose currency the obligations are denominated;

(b)   invest funds not needed in its operations in such obligations as it may determine;

(c)   guarantee securities in its portfolio for the purpose of facilitating their sale; and

(d) exercise such other powers as shall be necessary or desirable in furtherance of its purposes and functions, consistent with the provisions of this Chapter.

Section 2: *Warning to be Placed on Securities*

Every security issued or guaranteed by the Bank shall bear on its face a conspicuous statement to the effect that it is not an obligation of any government, unless it is in fact the obligation of a particular government, in which case it shall so state.

Section 3: *Methods of Meeting the Losses of the Bank*

(a) In case of arrears or default on loans made, participated in, or guaranteed by the Bank, the Bank shall take such action as it deems appropriate. The Bank shall maintain appropriate provisions against possible losses.

(b) Losses arising in the Bank's operations shall be charged first, to the provisions referred to in paragraph (a); second, to net income; third, against its general reserve and surpluses; and fourth, against the unimpaired paid-in capital.

(c) Whenever necessary to meet contractual payments of interest, other charges, or amortization on the Bank's borrowings payable out of its capital resources, or to meet the Bank's liabilities with respect to similar payments on loans guaranteed by it chargeable to its capital resources, the Bank may call upon both Parties to pay an appropriate amount of their callable capital subscriptions, in accordance with Article II, Section 3 of this Chapter. Moreover, if the Bank believes that a default may be of long duration, it may call an additional part of such subscriptions not to exceed in any one year one per cent of the total subscriptions of the Parties to the capital resources, for the following purposes:

(1) to redeem prior to maturity, or otherwise discharge its liability on, all or part of the outstanding principal of any loan guaranteed by it chargeable to its capital resources in respect of which the debtor is in default; and

(2) to repurchase, or otherwise discharge its liability on, all

or part of its own outstanding obligations payable out of its capital resources.

Section 4:   *Distribution or Transfer of Net Profits and Surplus*

(a)   The Board of the Bank may determine periodically what part of the net profits and of the surplus of the capital resources shall be distributed. Such distributions may be made only when the reserves have reached a level which the Board considers adequate.

(b)   The distributions referred to in paragraph (a) of this section shall be made from the capital resources in proportion to the number of capital shares held by each Party.

(c)   Payments pursuant to paragraph (a) of this section shall be made in such manner and in such currency or currencies as the Board of the Bank shall determine. If such payments are made to a Party in currencies other than its own, the transfer of such currencies and their use by the receiving country shall be without restriction by either Party.

Article VI: Organization and Management

Section 1:   *Structure of the Bank*

The Bank shall have a Board, a Manager, and such other officers and staff as may be considered necessary.

Section 2:   *Board of the Bank*

(a)   All the powers of the Bank shall be vested in the Board. Each Party shall appoint three representatives to the Board of the Bank, who shall serve at the pleasure of the appointing Party. Board members shall be persons of recognized competence and experience. Each Party, on an alternating basis, shall select one of its representatives as Chairperson for a one-year term.

(b)   Each Board member shall appoint an alternate who shall have full power to act for him or her when he or she is not present. Alternates may participate in meetings but may vote only when they are acting in place of their principals. In unusual circumstances, when neither a Board member nor his or her alternate is able to attend a meeting, the Board member may designate a temporary alternate.

(c)   Board members shall serve as such without compensation from the Bank, but the Bank may pay them reasonable expenses incurred in attending meetings of the Board of the Bank.

(d)   The Board of the Bank shall meet at the principal office of the Bank as often as the business of the Bank may require.

(e)   A quorum for any meeting of the Board of the Bank shall require two representatives, alternates, or temporary alternates from each Party.

(f)   The Board of the Bank may appoint such committees as it deems advisable.

(g)   The Board of the Bank shall determine the basic organization of the Bank, including the number and general responsibilities of the chief administrative and professional positions of the staff, and shall approve the budget of the Bank.

Section 3:   Decision-Making

All decisions of the Board of the Bank shall require the assent of at least two representatives, alternates, or temporary alternates of each Party.

Section 4:   Manager and Staff

(a)   The Board of the Bank shall elect a Manager of the Bank who may serve pursuant to an agreement entered into pursuant to Article III, Section 12 of this Chapter. The Manager, under the direction of the Board of the Bank, shall conduct the business of the Bank and shall be chief of its staff. The Manager or his or her designee shall be the legal representative of the Bank. The term of office of the Manager shall be three years. The Manager may be elected to successive terms. He or she shall cease to hold office when the Board of the Bank so decides.

(b)   The Manager, officers and staff of the Bank, in the discharge of their offices, shall owe their duty entirely to the Bank and to no other authority. The Parties shall respect the international character of this duty and shall refrain from all attempts to influence any of them in the discharge of their duties.

(c)   In appointing the officers and staff the Manager shall, subject to the paramount importance of securing the highest standards of efficiency and technical competence, seek to achieve, at each level, a balance in the number of nationals from each Party.

(d)   The Bank, its officers and staff shall not interfere in the political affairs of either Party, nor shall they be influenced in their decisions by the political character of the Party or Parties concerned. Only economic/financial considerations shall be relevant to their decisions, and these considerations shall be weighed impartially in order to achieve the purposes and functions stated in Article I of this Chapter.

Section 5:   *Publication of Reports and Provision of Information*

(a)   The Bank shall publish an annual report containing an audited statement of its accounts. It shall also transmit quarterly to the Parties a summary statement of its financial position and profit-and-loss statement showing the results of its operations.

(b)   The Bank may also publish such other reports as it deems desirable to inform the public of its activities and to carry out its purposes and functions.

Article VII: Suspension and Termination of Operations

Section 1:   *Suspension of Operations*

In an emergency the Board of the Bank may suspend operations in respect of loans and guarantees until such time as the Board of the Bank may have an opportunity to consider the situation and take pertinent measures.

Section 2:   *Termination of Operations*

(a)   The Parties, by mutual agreement, may terminate the operations of the Bank. A Party may withdraw from the Bank by delivering to the Bank at its principal office a written notice of its intention to do so. Such withdrawal shall become finally effective on the date specified in the notice but in no event less

than six months after the notice is delivered to the Bank.
However, at any time before the withdrawal becomes finally
effective, the Party may notify the Bank in writing of the
cancellation of its notice of intention to withdraw. The Bank
shall terminate its operations on the effective date of any notice
of withdrawal from the Bank.

(b)   After such termination of operations the Bank shall forthwith
cease all activities, except those incident to the conservation,
preservation, and realization of its assets and settlement of its
obligations.

Section 3:   *Liability of the Parties and Payment of Claims*

(a)   The liability of the Parties arising from their subscriptions to
the capital stock of the Bank shall continue until all direct and
contingent obligations shall have been discharged.

(b)   All creditors holding direct claims shall be paid out of the
assets of the Bank and then out of payments to the Bank on
unpaid or callable subscriptions. Before making any payments
to creditors holding direct claims, the Board of the Bank shall
make such arrangements as are necessary, in its judgment, to
ensure a pro rata distribution among holders of direct and
contingent claims.

Section 4:   *Distribution of Assets*

(a)   No distribution of assets shall be made to either Party on
account of their subscription to the capital stock of the Bank
until all liabilities to creditors chargeable to such capital stock
shall have been discharged or provided for. Moreover, such
distribution must be approved by a decision of the Board of the
Bank.

(b)   Any distribution of the assets of the Bank to the Parties shall be
in proportion to payments on capital stock held by each Party
and shall be effected at such times and under such conditions as
the Bank shall deem fair and equitable. The shares of assets
distributed need not be uniform as to type of assets. No Party
shall be entitled to receive its shares in such a distribution of
assets until it has settled all of its obligations to the Bank.

(c)   A party receiving assets distributed pursuant to this Article shall enjoy the same rights with respect to such assets as the Bank enjoyed prior to their distribution.

Article VIII: Status, Immunities and Privileges

Section 1:   *Scope of Article*

To enable the Bank to fulfill its purposes and the functions with which it is entrusted, the status, immunities, and privileges set forth in this Article shall be accorded to the Bank in the territories of each Party.

Section 2:   *Legal Status*

The Bank shall possess juridical personality and, in particular, full capacity:

(a)   to contract;
(b)   to acquire and dispose of immovable and movable property; and
(c)   to institute legal proceedings.

Section 3:   *Judicial Proceedings*

Actions may be brought against the Bank only in a court of competent jurisdiction in the territories of a Party in which the Bank has an office, has appointed an agent for the purpose of accepting service or notice of process, or has issued or guaranteed securities.

No action shall be brought against the Bank by the Parties or persons acting for or deriving claims from the Parties. However, the Parties shall have recourse to such special Procedures to settle controversies between the Bank and its Parties as may be prescribed in this Chapter, in the by-laws and regulations of the Bank or in contracts entered into with the Bank.

Property and assets of the Bank shall, wheresoever located and by whomsoever held, be immune from all forms of seizure, attachment or execution before the delivery of final judgment against the Bank.

Section 4:   ***Immunity of Assets***

Property and assets of the Bank, wheresoever located and by whomsoever held, shall be considered public international property and shall be immune from search, requisition, confiscation, expropriation or any other form of taking or foreclosure by executive or legislative action.

Section 5:   ***Inviolability of Archives***

The archives of the Bank shall be inviolable.

Section 6:   ***Freedom of Assets from Restrictions***

To the extent necessary to carry out the purposes and functions of the Bank and to conduct its operations in accordance with this Chapter, all property and other assets of the Bank shall be free from restrictions, regulations, controls and moratoria of any nature, except as may otherwise be provided in this Chapter.

Section 7:   ***Privilege for Communications***

The official communications of the Bank shall be accorded by each Party the same treatment that it accords to the official communicating of the other Party.

Section 8:   ***Personal Immunities and Privileges***

All Board members, alternates, officers, and staff of the Bank shall have the following privileges and immunities:

(a) immunity from legal process with respect to acts performed by them in their official capacity, except when the Bank waives this immunity;

(b) when not local nationals, the same immunities from immigration restrictions, alien registration requirements and national service obligations and the same facilities as regards exchange provisions as are accorded by the Parties to the representatives, officials, and employees of comparable rank of the Inter-American Development Bank; and

(c) the same privileges in respect of traveling facilities as are
     accorded by the Parties to representatives, officials, and
     employees of comparable rank of members of the Inter-
     American Development Bank.

Section 9:   *Immunities from Taxation*

(a) The Bank, its property, other assets, income, and the operations
     it carries out pursuant to this Chapter shall be immune from all
     taxation and from all customs duties. The Bank shall also be
     immune from any obligation relating to the payment, withhold-
     ing or collection of any tax or customs duty.

(b) No tax shall be levied on or in respect of any salaries or
     emoluments paid by the Bank to Board members, alternates,
     officials or staff of the Bank who are not local nationals.

(c) No tax of any kind shall be levied on any obligation or security
     issued by the Bank, including any dividend or interest thereon,
     by whomsoever held:

   (1) which discriminates against such obligation or security
        by the Bank; or
   (2) if the sole jurisdictional basis for such taxation is the
        place or currency in which it is issued, made payable or
        paid, or the location of any office or place of business
        maintained by the Bank.

(d) No tax of any kind shall be levied on any obligation or security
     guaranteed by the Bank, including any dividend or interest
     thereon, by whomsoever held:

   (1) which discriminates against such obligation or security
        solely because it is guaranteed by the Bank; or
   (2) if the sole jurisdictional basis for such taxation is the
        location of any office or place of business maintained
        by the Bank.

Section 10:   *Implementation*

Each Party, in accordance with its juridical system, shall take such action as is necessary to make effective in its own territories the principles
set forth in this Article, and shall inform the Bank of the action which it
has taken on the matter.

Article IX: Interpretation and Arbitration

Section 1: Interpretation

The Parties shall at all times endeavor to agree on the interpretation and application of this Chapter, and shall make every effort to resolve any matter that might affect the implementation of this Chapter.

Section 2: Arbitration

In the event the Parties are not able to reach agreement on any question of interpretation of this Chapter within a reasonable time, either Party may request in writing the initiation of an arbitral proceeding. An arbitration panel shall be established in accordance with the following procedures:

(1) the panel shall be composed of three members;

(2) panelists shall be selected from the financial services roster established pursuant to Article 1414 of the North American Free Trade Agreement;

(3) the Parties shall endeavor to agree on the chairperson of the panel within 15 days of the delivery of the request for the initiation of the arbitral proceeding. If the Parties are unable to agree on the chairperson within this period, the Party chosen by lot shall select from the financial services roster within five days as chairperson an individual who is not a national of that Party; and

(4) within 15 days of selection of the chairperson, each disputing Party shall select a panelist from among the roster members who are nationals of the other Party.

Article X: General Provisions

Section 1: Principal Office

The principal office of the Bank shall be located in a place to be mutually agreed by the Parties so as to facilitate the operations of the Bank.

Section 2:   ***Relations with Other Organizations***

The Bank may enter into arrangements with other organizations with respect to the exchange of information or for other purposes consistent with this Chapter.

Section 3:   ***Channel of Communication***

Each Party shall designate an official entity for purposes of communication with the Bank on matters connected with this Chapter.

Section 4:   ***Depositories***

Each Party shall designate its central bank to serve as a depository in which the Bank may keep its holdings of such Party's currency and other assets of the Bank. However, with the agreement of the Bank, a Party may designate another institution for such purpose.

Section 5:   ***Commencement of Operations***

The Parties shall call the first meeting of the Board of the Bank as soon as this Agreement enters into force under Article I of Chapter III of this Agreement.

CHAPTER III

ENTRY INTO FORCE, AMENDMENT, DEFINITIONS AND OTHER ARRANGEMENTS

Article I: **Entry into Force**

This Agreement shall enter into force on January 1, 1994, immediately after entry into force of the North American Free Trade Agreement, on an exchange of written notifications certifying the completion of necessary legal procedures.

Article II: Amendment

The Parties may agree on any modification of or addition to this Agreement. In particular, the Parties shall from time to time consider whether to make such modifications of or additions to this Agreement as would be necessary to:

expand the functions of the Commission to include other kinds of environmental or other infrastructure projects;

expand the geographic scope of the Commission;

give the Commission the capacity to raise capital so that it might issue loans or guarantees for environmental or other infrastructure projects; or

change the environmental preferences expressed in Article II, Section 2(b) of Chapter I of this Agreement.

When so agreed, and approved in accordance with the applicable legal procedures of each Party a modification or addition shall constitute an integral part of this Agreement.

Article III: Relations to Other Agreements or Arrangements

(a)   Nothing in this Agreement shall prejudice other agreements or arrangements between the Parties, including those relating to conservation or the environment.

(b)   Nothing in this Agreement shall be construed to limit the right of any public entity or private person of a Party to seek investment capital or other sources of finance, or to propose, construct or operate an environmental infrastructure project in the border region without the assistance or certification of the Commission.

Article IV: Authentic Texts

The English and Spanish texts of this Agreement are equally authentic.

Article V: Definitions

For purposes of this Agreement, it shall be understood that:

"Bank" means the North American Development Bank established pursuant to Chapter II of this Agreement;

"Board of Directors" means the Board established pursuant to Article III, Section 3, of Chapter I of this Agreement;

"Board of the Bank" means the Board established pursuant to Article VI, Section 2, of Chapter II of this Agreement;

"Border region" means the area within 100 kilometers of the international frontier between the United States and Mexico;

"Commission" means the Border Environment Cooperation Commission established pursuant to Chapter I of this Agreement;

"Environmental infrastructure project" means a project that will prevent, control or reduce environmental pollutants or contaminants, improve the drinking water supply, or protect flora and fauna so as to improve human health, promote sustainable development, or contribute to a higher quality of life;

"Mexico" means the United Mexican States;

"Mexican border states" means Baja California, Chihuahua, Coahuila, Nuevo Leon, Sonora and Tamaulipas;

"National" means a natural person who is citizen or permanent resident of a Party, including:

1. with respect to Mexico, a national or a citizen according to Articles 30 and 34, respectively of the Mexican Constitution; and
2. with respect to the United States, "national of the United States" as defined in the existing provisions of the Immigration and Nationality Act.

"Nongovernmental organization" means any scientific, professional, business, non-profit or public interest organization or association which is neither affiliated with, nor under the direction of, a government;

"North American Development Bank" means the bank established by the Parties pursuant to Chapter II of this Agreement;

"United States" means the United States of America; and

"U.S. border states" means Arizona, California, New Mexico and Texas.

IN WITNESS WHEREOF, the undersigned, being duly authorized by their respective Governments, have signed this Agreement.

DONE at Washington and Mexico City, this 16th day and this 18th day of November 1993, in duplicate, in the English and Spanish languages.

FOR THE GOVERNMENT   FOR THE GOVERNMENT
OF THE   OF THE
UNITED STATES OF AMERICA   UNITED MEXICAN STATES

William Jefferson Clinton   Carlos Salinas de Gortari

ANNEX A

INITIAL SUBSCRIPTIONS TO THE AUTHORIZED CAPITAL STOCK OF THE BANK
(in shares of US $10,000 each)

	Paid-in Capital Shares	Callable Shares	Total Subscription
United States	22,500	127,500	150,000
Mexico	22,500	127,500	150,000
TOTAL	45,000	255,000	300,000

Bylaws of the
North American
Development Bank

These Bylaws are adopted under the authority of, and are intended to be complementary to, the Agreement Between the Government of the United States of America and the Government of the United Mexican States Concerning the Establishment of a Border Environment Cooperation Commission and a North American Development Bank and they shall be construed accordingly.

In the event of a conflict between the provisions of these Bylaws and the provisions of the Agreement, the provisions of the Agreement shall prevail. In the event of a conflict between these Bylaws and any rules and regulations adopted pursuant to the Agreement, the Bylaws shall prevail.

Section 1:   Principal Office of the Bank

The principal office of the Bank shall be located in San Antonio, Texas, United States of America.

Section 2:   Meetings of the Board

(a) The Board shall hold an annual meeting at such date as the Board shall determine.

(b) The Board may, in addition, hold special meetings when it so decides.

(c) At least one meeting of the Board each year shall be open to the public.

(d) The Board shall meet at the principal office of the Bank unless it decides that a particular meeting shall be held elsewhere.

(e) The Secretary shall notify each member of the Bank of the date and place of each meeting of the Board. Such notifications must be dispatched not less than 30 days prior to the date for any meeting, except that in urgent cases notice shall be sufficient if dispatched not less than 10 days prior to the date set for the meeting.

(f) A quorum for any meeting of the Board shall be two Board members or Alternates from each member of the Bank.

(g) Except as otherwise specifically directed by the Board, the Manager, together with the Chairperson and in cooperation with the host country and city, shall have charge of all arrangements for the holding of meetings of the Board.

Section 3:   *Attendance at Meetings*

(a) Meetings shall be open to attendance only by Board members and their Alternates or Temporary Alternates, such staff as may be required by Board members and their Alternates or Temporary Alternates, the Manager and such members of the staff as he/she may designate, and such other persons as the Board may invite.

(b) At each meeting of the Board, the Secretary shall present a list of the Board members, Alternates, or Temporary Alternates whose appointment has been officially communicated to the Bank.

Section 4:   *Agenda of Meetings*

(a) The Chairperson, with the assistance of the Manager, shall prepare an agenda for each meeting of the Board, and the Secretary shall transmit such agenda to each member of the Bank with the notice of the meeting.

(b) Additional subjects may be placed on the agenda for any meeting of the Board by any Board member provided that he/she shall give notice thereof to the Chairperson not less than 7 days prior to the date set for the meeting. In special circumstances, the Chairperson may at any time place additional subjects on the agenda for any meeting of the Board. The Chairperson shall give notice of the addition of any subjects to the agenda to each member of the Bank as soon as possible.

(c) The agenda shall be submitted by the Chairperson to the Board for approval at the beginning of each meeting.

(d) Prior to, or in the course of, any meeting, the Board may modify or eliminate items from the agenda.

(e) Any item included on the agenda for a meeting of the Board, consideration of which has not been completed at that meeting, shall, unless the Board decides otherwise, be automatically included on the agenda for the next meeting.

Section 5: *Chairperson*

(a) Each member of the Bank, on an alternating basis, shall select one of its representatives as Chairperson for a one-year term. The Chairperson may designate a Chairperson Pro Tempore, who, in the absence of the Chairperson, shall act in his/her place. The Chairperson shall communicate any such designation to the Secretary prior to any meeting of the Board. The Chairperson or his/her designee shall preside at all meetings of the Board.

(b) Beginning with the inaugural meeting of the Board, the Chairperson shall be a representative from the host country, who shall serve in this position until the end of the first annual meeting of the Board.

Section 6: *Secretary*

The Deputy Manager of the Bank shall serve as Secretary of the Board and shall be responsible for the preparation of a summary record of the proceedings of the Board.

Section 7: *Minutes*

(a) The Board shall keep a summary record (minutes) of its proceedings which shall be provided to each member of the Bank.

(b) Verbatim records will be reflected in the minutes only if a Board member requests that his/her remarks be taken down.

(c) Draft minutes will be circulated to all Board members as quickly as possible after meetings. Such minutes shall be presented to the Board for approval.

(d) Minutes approved by the Board shall be made available by the Bank for public viewing.

Section 8:   *Voting*

(a)   All decisions of the Board shall require the assent of at least two Board members from each member of the Bank. At any meeting the Chairperson may ascertain the sense of the meeting in lieu of a formal vote but he/she shall require a formal vote upon the request of any Board member. Whenever a formal vote is required the written text of the motion and/or resolution shall be distributed to the Board members.

(b)   At any meeting of the Board, the vote of any Board member must be cast in person by the Board member, his/her Alternate, or in unusual circumstances, by a formally designated Temporary Alternate appointed by a member for the purpose of attending and voting at the Board when both the Board member and his/her Alternate are absent.

Section 9:   *Voting Without Meeting*

(a)   Whenever the Chairperson, in consultation, as appropriate, with the Manager, considers that the decision on a specific question which is for the Board to determine should not be postponed until the next annual meeting of the Board and does not warrant the calling of a special meeting of the Board, the Chairperson shall request the Board to vote without meeting.

(b)   At the direction of the Chairperson, the Secretary shall transmit in writing to each member of the Bank by rapid means of communication the proposals relating to that question.

(c)   Votes on the proposals shall be transmitted to the Secretary in writing during such period as the Chairperson may prescribe.

(d)   At the expiration of the period prescribed for voting, the Secretary shall record the results, and report them to the Board. If the replies received do not include two Board members from each member of the Bank, which is required for a quorum for the Board, the motion shall be considered lost.

Section 10:   *Terms of Service*

(a)   Board members, Alternates, and Temporary Alternates may receive reimbursement for reasonable expenses incurred in attending meetings of the Board.

(b) The salaries, any other terms of remuneration, and any allowances of the Manager and Deputy Manager shall be determined by the Board and shall be included in their respective contracts.

Section 11: *Executive Committee*

(a) The Board shall have an Executive Committee composed of one Board member appointed by the Government of the United States of America and one Board member appointed by the Government of the United Mexican States. If a Board member who is a member of the Executive Committee is unable to attend any meeting of the Committee, that Board member may be represented by his or her Alternate, or any Temporary Alternate appointed for that purpose.

(b) The Executive Committee may meet from time to time as it deems appropriate to carry out the business of the Board between meetings of the Board.

(c) The Executive Committee shall inform the Board of its activities and consult the Board as necessary regarding those activities.

Section 12: *Authority of Manager and Deputy Manager*

The Manager, with the assistance of the Deputy Manager, shall conduct, under the direction of the Board, the current business of the Bank. The Board shall establish conditions (including provision for reporting), procedures and thresholds pursuant to which the Manager may submit various types of matters to it for consideration under an expedited procedure.

Section 13: *Rules and Regulations*

The Board shall adopt such rules and regulations, including financial regulations, as may be necessary or appropriate to conduct the business of the Bank.

Section 14: *Report of Manager*

At each annual meeting of the Board, the Manager shall submit an annual report on the operations and policies of the Bank.

Section 15:   *Financial Year*

The financial year of the Bank shall begin on 1 January and end on 31 December of each year.

Section 16:   *Budget and Audits*

(a)   The accounts of the Bank shall be audited in accordance with generally accepted accounting principles at least once a year by independent external auditors of international reputation chosen by the Board on the basis of a proposal by the Manager. On the basis of this audit the Manager shall submit to the Board for approval at its annual meeting a statement of accounts, including a general balance sheet and a statement of profit and loss.

(b)   The Manager shall prepare an annual administrative budget to be presented to the Board for its approval at its annual meeting.

Section 17:   *Official Languages*

(a)   All Board documents, including agendas, minutes and texts of motions and/or resolutions, shall be prepared in both English and Spanish, each text being equally authentic.

(b)   Simultaneous interpretation in English and Spanish shall be provided at all Board meetings.

Section 18:   *Amendment to Bylaws*

These Bylaws may be amended by the Board at any meeting thereof or by vote without a meeting as provided in Section 9.

7

Other Dispute Settlement Mechanisms

As explained in Chapter 3 of this book, general disputes arising from the implementation or interpretation of the NAFTA agreement are settled according to procedures spelled out in Chapter 20 of NAFTA. The process involves consultations first, then consideration of the issue by the Free Trade Commission, and, as a last resort, panel arbitration. Basically the same procedure is specified in Chapter 14 of NAFTA for settling disputes dealing with financial issues. The only difference is that in the case of a dispute over financial issues the roster of arbitrators from which the arbitration panel is chosen consists of persons having expertise specifically on financial issues.

As described in Chapters 4 and 5 of this book, different dispute settlement procedures are spelled out for dealing with disputes relating to either environmental or labor issues. In each case, the strong emphasis is on avoiding disputes or resolving them through consultation. For cases where the allegation concerns a partner country's failing to enforce its own environmental laws or labor laws, after a long and involved process these cases may also be taken to panel arbitration (though only for certain labor issues, and only for a persistent pattern of nonenforcement of environmental regulations), with trade sanctions or monetary fines as ultimate enforcement measures. Thus far no case has been taken to an arbitral panel, and given the political sensitivity of environmental and labor issues every effort will be made to deal with them in other ways.

Two other types of issues have dispute settlement provisions in NAFTA that depart significantly from those described above. Chapter 11 of the NAFTA agreement sets forth specific provisions for the settlement of disputes between foreign investors and the government of a member country. Chapter 19 of NAFTA specifies procedures for resolving disputes over member country application of antidumping and counter-vailing duty laws.

Chapter 11 Dispute Settlement Provisions

Chapter 11 of NAFTA carries much significance because it represents the first inclusion in a trade agreement of provisions allowing foreign investors to challenge a host government's investment regulations by taking the matter to binding arbitration. Of course, the investor may pursue remedies available in the host country's domestic courts if that seems more appropriate.

A major purpose of the investment provisions of NAFTA was to assure a climate of stability and to reduce uncertainty concerning decisions of whether to invest in partner countries. Historically, the foreign investment climate has been more predictable and friendly in the United States, and apart from some exceptional cases also in Canada, than in Mexico. Naturally, both the United States and Canada were interested in improving the climate for foreign investments in Mexico. Since a major reason for Mexico's entering into the NAFTA agreement had been to encourage foreign investment in Mexico, a convergence of interests existed on this issue.

According to the provisions for investor-state dispute settlement as spelled out in Chapter 11 of NAFTA, the aggrieved party must first attempt to settle the dispute through consultation and negotiation. Should that process fail, the investor must give notice of intent to ask for an arbitral panel at least ninety days before doing so. As part of the NAFTA agreement, each member country has agreed ahead of time to submit unresolved disputes to binding arbitration. The aggrieved party is required, as a condition of being able to take the matter to arbitration, to agree in writing to waive the right to pursue the matter through other avenues after it has requested an arbitral panel.

The investor rights set forth in Chapter 11 of NAFTA are quite far-reaching (although some exclusions and derogations on the part of each member country are spelled out in the agreement). The member countries are to accord investors from other member countries national treatment, that is, the same treatment received by domestic firms in the same industry. Further, NAFTA-country firms are entitled to most-favored-nation treatment, meaning treatment as good as that accorded to any other foreign firm. Should the treatment of foreign firms and domestic firms for some reason be different, then the NAFTA-member country is to extend the NAFTA-partner country investors the better of national treatment or most-favored-nation treatment. Finally, the NAFTA-country investor is to be accorded the minimum standard of treatment in accordance with international law.

In addition, Chapter 11 of NAFTA enjoins member countries from taking certain actions with respect to partner country investors. In general, it forbids export performance requirements, so that foreign firms cannot be required to export a portion of their production or to engage in trade balancing. Also, it rules out local content regulations or mandated preference for domestic sourcing. Likewise, the investment chapter forbids technology transfer requirements as a condition of foreign investment. Member country governments must allow conversion of the local currency at prevailing market rates and must permit repatriation of profits. The property of partner country firms must not be expropriated, either directly or indirectly, without fair compensation.

Arbitration of Investment Disputes

In order to take an investment case to panel arbitration, the investor must file the case within three years of the alleged infringement of the NAFTA agreement terms, and must claim to have suffered direct loss or damage as a result of the infringement.

In the case of investor-state arbitration, the arbitration panel consists of three persons. One arbitrator is appointed by each of the disputing parties, with the third, who serves as chair of the panel, being appointed by mutual agreement of the parties. The decision rendered by an arbitral panel is automatically enforceable in the domestic courts of the country involved.

No transparency requirements are specified concerning Chapter 11 cases, and their paper trail is difficult to follow. Some of them could go undetected because member country governments conceivably could settle the disputes and compensate the complaining parties without any public notification. In cases that do proceed to arbitration, the complaining party may choose to have the dispute settled according to either the World Bank's International Council for the Settlement of Investment Disputes Convention or the Arbitration Rules of the United Nations Commission on International Trade Law Arbitration Law. The NAFTA secretariat plays a very limited role in the process. It simply maintains a register of notices of arbitration and holds some documents for the record (Bogule and Alston 1999).

As of mid-1999, twelve Chapter 11 cases had been filed. Only one of these had been settled, nine were active, and two apparently had been dropped. U.S. firms have been by far the most frequent users of Chapter 11 provisions. Of the twelve cases, nine had been filed by U.S. firms. Five of these cases were against the Mexican government and four against the Canadian government. One case had been filed by a Mexican firm against the Canadian government, but was not pursued beyond the initial notice of intent to arbitrate. Canadian firms had filed two cases against the U.S. government.*

Chapter 11 Cases Filed by U.S. Firms Against the Mexican Government

One of the cases filed by a U.S. firm against the Mexican government involved an airport concession shop, but the case apparently was not pursued further after the notice of intent to arbitrate was filed. Three of the other cases by U.S. firms against the Mexican government dealt with waste management and disposal, and city maintenance.

In one of these cases, Metalclad Corporation is seeking $90 million in damages because Mexican state and local governments prevented Metalclad from reopening a hazardous waste landfill that it had purchased in the community of Guadalcazar in the state of San Luis Potosi. After Metalclad had invested in the facility, the government reportedly discovered that the landfill had the potential to damage underground streams and, consequently, declared the area an environmental zone and refused to allow the landfill to be reopened. Metalclad claims that the change in zoning was equivalent to expropriation or indirect expropriation of their property (Public Citizen 1999, 3).

In another case, Desechos Solidos de Naucalpan (a U.S. firm) is asking for $17 million in damages because the government of Mexico allegedly nullified an agreement of the company to manage solid waste disposal in the state of Mexico. In yet another case, USA Waste is claiming $60 million in damages in a dispute with Mexico over waste management and city maintenance.

In a case against Mexico that does not relate to waste disposal, U.S. businessman Marvin Feldman is seeking $50 million for losses incurred

*The summary of cases that follows is drawn from information provided (with some supplementation as noted) in Mann and von Moltke (1999).

as a result of Mexico's denial of excise tax rebates on cigarette exports. The claimant contends that his company, CEMSA, suffered loss of good-will and of export opportunities in addition to loss of the tax rebate, and that the Mexican government attempted to drive the company out of the business. The claimant further contends that the actions went against court decisions, and that they amounted to expropriation of funds to which the company was rightfully entitled.

Chapter 11 Cases Filed by U.S. Firms Against the Canadian Government

The cases filed by U.S. companies against the Canadian government deal with a variety of issues. The one that had been settled at the time of this writing was a case brought by Ethyl Corporation asking for $250 million for damages and compensation arising from a Canadian trade restriction banning the importation of MMT (methylcyclopentadienyl manganese tricarbonyl), an octane enhancer that is added to gasoline. MMT was not being produced in Canada, but substitute products were. Ethyl Corporation contended that the ban on MMT discriminated against the company in favor of producers of substitute products, and therefore violated Chapter 11's most-favored-nation provisions. Ethyl also claimed that since banning the additive reduced its business in Canada by about 50 percent, the effects on its goodwill, assets, and expected earnings were the equivalent of indirect expropriation.

One of the ingredients in MMT is manganese, and studies have indicated that manganese poisoning can cause serious neurological problems. Since no studies had been conducted specifically on the health effects of MMT, the use of MMT could not be banned under Canadian environmental laws. Because MMT was not produced in Canada, the Canadian government attempted to deal with the possible health risk by banning the importation and interprovincial trade of MMT. Ethyl claimed that the ban constituted an illegal performance requirement in that it would force the company to build a factory in every Canadian province in order to service the market (Public Citizen 1999, 2).

This case was never ruled on by an arbitration panel, but was settled out of court. In the final settlement of the case, the Canadian government withdrew the legislation that banned imports of MMT, wrote a letter stating that MMT had no proven adverse effects on the environment or on public health, and paid Ethyl Corporation $13 million.

In a case still pending at the time of this writing, S. D. Myers, Inc., a toxic waste disposal company in Ohio, is claiming losses of $30 million from an export ban imposed by the Canadian government on PCB (polychlorinated biphenal) waste from 1995 to 1997. The ban reportedly was imposed by the Canadian government out of concern that PCBs might end up in less developed countries where they could not be disposed of properly, and also that disposal standards of U.S. companies were substandard. S. D. Myers, Inc., claims the action was taken because it was not a Canadian company, and that the export ban prevented the company from operating in the same way that a Canadian company could have operated. It claims further that the regulation was unfair and discriminatory, and that the losses suffered from disruption of its operations amounted to indirect expropriation. An unusual aspect of this case is that, while it was filed under the terms of NAFTA's investment chapter, S. D. Myers, Inc., had no investment in Canada at the time that the alleged actions took place (*Financial Post* 1999). Furthermore, the firm currently would not be permitted to import PCBs into the United States as their importation has been banned by the U.S. Environmental Protection Agency since July 1997 (Public Citizen 1999, 4).

In another case, Sun Belt Water Company, Inc., of California is asking for $292 million in damages because the government of British Columbia changed its policy concerning water exports. Sun Belt had an agreement in conjunction with a Canadian joint venture partner, Snowcap Waters, Ltd., to export water from Canada to California. When the British Columbian government imposed a moratorium on water exports (which the Canadian government subsequently has done), the British Columbian government reached a settlement with the Canadian partner but allegedly would not negotiate with the U.S. partner. Sun Belt is seeking damages for lack of due process and lack of national treatment and most-favored-nation treatment.

An additional case filed by a U.S. company against the Canadian government involves a forestry company—Pope and Talbot, Inc.—that is based in Oregon but operates sawmills in British Columbia. Pope and Talbot is claiming damages of $130 million for the way in which the Canada–United States Softwood Lumber Agreement was implemented.*

---

*Public Citizen reports that Pope and Talbot is seeking $507 million in damages (Public Citizen 1999, 7).

The softwood lumber agreement arose out of a countervailing duty case filed in the United States charging that Canada was subsidizing lumber exports to the United States. Pope and Talbot contends that the Canadian government's method of allocating quotas and special levies among Canadian provinces in its implementation of the softwood lumber accord discriminated against them relative to other producers and interfered with their operation of their business.

Chapter 11 Cases Filed by Canadian Firms Against the U.S. Government

One of two cases that a Canadian company has filed against the U.S. government was filed by Loewen Group, Inc., a funeral services company. Loewen, a Vancouver-based company, derives more than 90 percent of its revenues from its U.S. operations. The firm is seeking damages of $725 million for discrimination, denial of justice, and "uncompensated expropriation" arising out of a civil court case in which a Mississippi jury ordered the company to pay $500 million in damages ($100 million of compensatory damages and $400 million of punitive damages) in a breach of contract suit. The company contends that a Mississippi law requiring the company to post bond amounting to 125 percent of the award (roughly equivalent to its net worth) in order to appeal the verdict forced it to settle the suit under duress. Loewen did settle the suit for $175 million, and has since filed for bankruptcy in the United States and Canada in order to reorganize financially (*BCD News* 1999, 1).

The other case involving a Canadian company against the U.S. government was filed by Methanex Corporation of Vancouver. Methanex is seeking $970 million that it estimates to be the cost imposed upon the company by the state of California's decision to phase out the use of methyl tertiary butyl ether (MTBE) as a gasoline additive. Methanex Corporation supplies methanol, an ingredient in MTBE, to the companies that produce it.

Originally, MTBE was thought to have positive effects on the environment because it makes gasoline burn cleaner and therefore reduces air pollution. However, the additive has been found to contaminate reservoirs and groundwater, and is possibly carcinogenic. Therefore, the governor of California ruled that its use would be phased out by the end of the year 2002. Methanex calculates that over the next 20 years its sales of methanol will be $970 million less because of that change in policy (*San Francisco Chronicle* 1999).

Assessment of Chapter 11 Dispute Settlement Provisions

The investor-state dispute settlement provisions of Chapter 11 of the NAFTA agreement are having far-reaching ramifications. The cases that have been filed under these provisions have raised fundamental questions about which there is much disagreement. Some of these questions concern the appropriate relationship between trade policy and environmental policy. Others concern the issue of how to provide legitimate property rights to foreign investors and at the same time protect the right of a sovereign state to make and enforce policies regulating what goes on within its borders.

Environmentalist groups are quick to point out that the two major national environmental initiatives taken by Canada since the signing of the NAFTA agreement that significantly affected business have been challenged under the terms of Chapter 11 (Mann and von Moltke 1999, 5). One of these policies (the MMT policy) has been reversed because of the Chapter 11 challenge, and the fate of the other (allocation of softwood lumber quotas) is pending. An environmental regulation in the United States is also being challenged under Chapter 11 provisions—the case of Methanex Corporation seeking damages from California's banning of the gasoline additive MTBE. These cases have caused the International Institute for Sustainable Development to charge that Chapter 11 provisions that were "designed to ensure security and predictability for the investors, have now created uncertainty and unpredictability for environmental (and other) regulators" (ibid., 7).

In addition to the uncertainty introduced into the regulatory process by Chapter 11 provisions, the possibility exists that corporations could, through its provisions, escape the liability of domestic civil court awards. If the Loewen Group is successful in collecting damages for the Mississippi civil court jury verdict against it, a dangerous precedent will have been set for interference in the effects of, if not the workings of, the legal systems of the member countries.

Perhaps it is premature to render an assessment of the Chapter 11 dispute settlement provisions, for the decisions of the arbitrators are still pending in every Chapter 11 case but one at the time of this writing. However, from the cases filed so far it seems that litigators are taking advantage of Chapter 11 provisions to gain advantages that were not intended when the agreement was negotiated.

The concept of indirect expropriation through the effect of domestic regulations may be a legitimate tool for preventing arbitrary discrimination against foreign firms by regulatory authorities. However, it is subject to abuse and may well need to be circumscribed to assure that it is used only for its intended purpose. As the MMT case in Canada and the MTBE case in California point out, there are instances in which precautions by regulatory authorities may be prudent even before firm scientific assessment of possible risks has been accumulated. In the MMT case, evidence exists that manganese poisoning causes serious neurological problems. The fact that studies concerning the effects specifically of MMT have not been conducted, even though it has been established that the manganese it contains is harmful, does not seem sufficient reason to make the ban of the additive contestable under the terms of Chapter 11. Likewise, if MTBE is considered a possible carcinogen, and has been discovered in reservoirs and groundwater, precautions taken by the government of California to reduce its concentration seem only prudent, and it is difficult to see why they should require compensating the additive's producers.

Because of Chapter 11 provisions, governments could be put in the position of having to compensate producers of polluting products for the elimination of these products from the environment. That certainly was not the intention of the signatories to the NAFTA agreement. In cases where definitive scientific evidence concerning the effects of pollutants exists, the provisions of Chapter 11 concerning environmental regulation are not problematic. However, since definitive evidence often is absent and takes time to accumulate, the amount of risk to be assumed by the populations of the member countries of NAFTA should be determined by the people through their democratically elected representatives, and not second-guessed by an arbitration panel.

The possible threat posed by Chapter 11 dispute settlement provisions to regulatory independence and to the effects of domestic court decisions (unless it is remedied) will be highly detrimental to the trade liberalization process. As the process of globalization intensifies, legitimate property right protections for foreign investors become increasingly important. However, if in trying to protect those property rights the integrity of regulatory processes or legal systems is undermined, a backlash against globalization will certainly develop. Some fine-tuning of the Chapter 11 provisions is called for to assure that protecting the rights of foreign investors does not result in undesirable side effects on regulatory and legal processes.

Disputes Arising from Antidumping and Countervailing Duty Cases

Chapter 19 of the NAFTA agreement sets forth the procedures for deal-ing with disputes relating to the application of antidumping and countervailing duty laws. Dumping is the selling of a product in a for-eign market either at a price below its total cost of production or below the price at which the identical product is sold in the home market. Each of the NAFTA countries has statutes making dumping illegal, and pro-viding for antidumping penalties to offset the dumping margin if a do-mestic industry is materially injured. In addition, each of the countries has legislation providing for the assessment of countervailing duties to offset foreign government subsidies that cause a domestic industry to be harmed.

Chapter 19 is carried over essentially intact from the United States–Canada Free Trade Agreement. In that agreement, the procedures for settling disputes concerning antidumping penalties and countervailing duties were considered to be a stopgap measure while negotiations con-tinued to establish a more permanent system. Canada had wanted to establish common competition and subsidy policies, thereby making it possible to suspend antidumping and countervailing duty actions among the member countries. That proved to be impossible for the United States, and instead a provision for binding arbitration panels was agreed as a temporary measure while negotiations for a more permanent solution continued. However, when the NAFTA agreement was negotiated the dispute settlement provisions of the United States–Canada free trade agreement dealing with trade remedies were carried over into the NAFTA agreement and made permanent.

Under the terms of these dispute settlement provisions, each country maintains its own antidumping and countervailing duty enforcement procedures. However, partner countries can challenge whether the ad-ministrative agencies responsible for carrying out these procedures have accurately and fairly applied their own laws and regulations. In fact, binational panel review replaces domestic judicial review of the admin-istrative agencies' actions.

Chapter 19 dispute settlement panels consist of five members selected from rosters maintained by each of the member countries. Panel mem-bers typically are lawyers, judges, former government officials, or oth-ers with expertise in trade dispute settlement. Each party selects two panel members who are nationals of the other party, and then the parties mutually agree on the fifth member. The chair of the panel must be a lawyer in good standing, as must a majority of the panel members.

In contrast to the Chapter 20 panel decisions, which deal with disputes over interpretation of the terms of the NAFTA agreement and are not binding on the parties, Chapter 19 decisions are binding. The panel may either affirm the administrative agency's determination, or remand it (return it for further action) to the agency. No provision exists for appealing a panel's decision in the domestic courts. There is an extraordinary challenge procedure under which it is possible, in highly unusual circumstances, to have the panel decision reviewed by another panel composed of retired judges. This procedure may only be used in cases where there is a perceived threat to the integrity of the panel process, such as gross misconduct or conflict of interest on the part of a panel member, or failure by the panel to apply an appropriate standard of review.

As of mid-1999, forty-nine panel reviews had been filed under the Chapter 19 provisions for dealing with antidumping and countervailing duty actions.* Nine of these challenged the determinations of Mexican agencies. One of the cases was still active, and three had been terminated at the request of the participants. Of the five decisions rendered by panelists, the Mexican agencies' decisions were ruled against in two cases, were affirmed in a third, and in the other two cases their decisions were partly affirmed and partly remanded.

Fourteen Chapter 19 cases had been filed challenging the determinations of Canadian agencies. Of these, three were still active, and four others had been terminated at the request of the participants. Of the six for which panel decisions had been rendered, three affirmed fully the decisions of Canadian agencies, and the other three partly affirmed and partly remanded their decisions.

Twenty-seven Chapter 19 cases had been filed questioning the determinations of U.S. agencies. Twelve of these were still active cases, and five others had been terminated at the request of the participants. One case was suspended pending panel selection, and another was stayed awaiting a decision in another case. Of the ten cases for which panel

---

*Information about Chapter 19 cases is available at the NAFTA secretariat web site (http://www.nafta-sec-alena.org/english/index.htm).

decisions had been rendered, four fully affirmed the agencies' determinations, one fully remanded the agency's decision, and the other five partly affirmed and partly remanded the agencies' decisions.

Assessment of Chapter 19 Dispute Settlement Procedures

When one considers the breadth of the economic relationship among the three countries of North America, the frequency of Chapter 19 cases seems rather modest. The fact that only forty-nine panel reviews of antidumping and countervailing duty determinations have been requested in more than five years (with eleven of those being withdrawn at the request of the participants before a panel decision was rendered) would seem to indicate that such disputes are not a major problem.

However, the Chapter 19 dispute settlement mechanism has been the target of criticism from different directions and for various reasons. Rugman and Anderson, pointing to the rather high remand rate (particularly if partial remands are included), suggest that the system needs modification. They object to the fact that panels can look only at the evidence submitted and on record, that they do not have to follow precedents set by other panels, and that the questions posed to them have been too narrow. They suggest establishing a different roster of panelists consisting of more highly qualified experts who could "investigate the real substance of a case and refer to the jurisprudence of related Panel decisions" (Rugman and Anderson 1997, 948).

Robert Howse, in a study conducted under the auspices of the C.D. Howe Institute in Canada, argues that, for complicated antidumping and countervailing duty cases, the dispute settlement procedures of the World Trade Organization (WTO) are preferable to those of NAFTA (Howse 1998). According to the terms of NAFTA, for the settlement of antidumping and countervailing duty disputes the disputing parties can choose either WTO or the NAFTA dispute settlement procedures, but by choosing one path the parties forfeit the use of the other. This is in contrast to the general dispute settlement procedures of NAFTA's Chapter 20, since those procedures deal with implementation or interpretation of the NAFTA agreement and therefore logically must be heard by a NAFTA panel.

According to Howse, the WTO procedures are preferable in the case of complex antidumping and countervailing duty cases, for a variety of reasons. In cases brought before the WTO, the definitions of dumping, subsidy, and material injury are more precise. Also in WTO cases, the panelists are experts drawn from a large number of countries so that the question of panelist nationality is avoided. Furthermore, according to Howse, the United States is less likely to disregard a WTO panel decision since the decisions are accorded a high level of legitimacy in the world community (Ibid.).

From another quarter, several industry associations in the United States have joined forces to try to exclude Chapter 19-type dispute settlement provisions from future trade agreements. They argue that, since the dispute settlement panels render judgments as to whether administrative agencies properly followed domestic law, the procedure illegitimately substitutes the panels' judgments for judgments normally rendered by domestic courts of law. Presumably, since WTO dispute settlement panels render judgments based upon international law as specified in the antidumping and countervailing duty codes of the WTO rather than interpretations of domestic laws, their judgments are not regarded as problematic. Amendments have been offered to proposed fast-track legislation that would prohibit future trade agreements from "limiting or transferring the jurisdiction or authority of a federal court" (Hall 1998, 3A).

Certainly some of the opposition to dispute settlement through NAFTA's trinational binding arbitration panels reflects genuine concern about the transfer of national sovereignty implied by the procedure. However, much of the opposition no doubt arises from the fact that certain industries have grown accustomed to using antidumping and countervailing duty measures as instruments of protection. These industries naturally resist having the effectiveness of protectionist measures diluted by panel review of domestic administrative agencies' decisions.

8

Summary and Conclusions

Regional institutions have been slow to develop in North America, compared to some other parts of the world, because formalized regional economic integration in North America is relatively new. Several reasons can be given for this fact. In the past the size disparities that exist among the economies of North America have inhibited institutionalized regional economic integration. The continent is dominated in many ways by the United States, which has an economy ten times larger than that of Canada and twenty-five times larger than Mexico's. This disparity, combined with an early history of U.S. incursions into Canada and Mexico's loss of much territory to the United States, have made both Canada and Mexico particularly sensitive to any arrangements that might weaken or threaten their national sovereignty. At the same time, the size and importance of the United States on the world stage have decreased its perceived need to develop, or to participate in, regional institutions.

In addition, disparities of economic development in North America have been a hindrance to regional economic integration. The fact that Mexico is at a much lower level of economic development than either the United States or Canada has created apprehension in Mexico about exposing Mexican industries to unrestrained competition from the technologically more advanced industries of the other two countries. Conversely, labor and environmental groups in the United States and Canada have been leery of competition from the low-wage industries of Mexico operating under less stringent pollution control measures.

A third reason for the later development of regional economic integration and a regional institutional structure in North America has been the philosophical paradigm from which the United States has operated. In general, the United States has been a proponent of a strong multilateral trading system, and has demonstrated a preference for trade liberalization within that setting. Only in the 1980s did the United States sign its first bilateral free trade agreement and open the door to regionalism within North America. In addition, the United States has had a stronger preference for private enterprise, with a minimum of regulation, than has been the case for much of the world. This philosophical stance has tended to minimize the perceived need for, and role of, regional institutions.

Even without formalized regional economic integration within North America, over time the region became increasingly integrated economically. Geographical proximity has provided powerful stimuli for what Clark Reynolds of Stanford University has termed the "silent integration" of increased trade and capital investment. Despite Canada's efforts at certain times to diversify the country's exports, Canada became increasingly dependent upon the large and dynamic market of the United States, and became the largest trading partner of the United States. Mexico attempted an industrialization policy that involved heavy protection of domestic industries, but over time experienced an increasing dependence on the U.S. market. Particularly after Mexico's import-substituting industrialization strategy was abandoned, the web of economic ties between the United States and Mexico became increasingly dense.

As explained more fully in Chapter 2 of this book, various strands of the theory of international institutions help to provide an explanation for the development of regional institutions within North America. The intensity of economic interactions among the countries of North America increased the demand for established rules, procedures, and dispute settlement mechanisms of the sort that regional institutions could provide. Hegemony by the United States could have been an alternative to these institutions, but philosophically the United States had no inclination to serve as hegemon in the region, and because of history, both Canada and Mexico would have resisted such a development in any case.

For certain situations, such as spillovers of environmental pollutants from one country to another, addressing the problems adequately requires regional planning and cooperation. In the case of matters having high emotive content such as environmental or labor issues, having an institution that is perceived to be impartial can be essential for cooperation. When a dispute arises between two member states, the third can often act as mediator or conciliator within the regional institution to facilitate agreement. Once regional institutions are established, they provide both economies of scale and economies of scope in decision making. As similar issues are dealt with repeatedly, the procedures and institutional memory inherent in an institution can lower the cost of decisions because less information has to be gathered to deal with each issue. Similarly, when the same institution deals with several types of issues, tradeoffs among issues may make agreements possible that would otherwise be impossible.

Among the major NAFTA-related institutions, the Free Trade Commission, although it is the governing body of NAFTA and supervises the implementation of the agreement, would have to be considered the least well developed and least transparent of the institutions. In contrast to the European Commission, which deals with a wide variety of regional economic integration issues, the Free Trade Commission is focused almost exclusively on trade facilitation matters. Of course NAFTA aimed for a much lower level of economic integration, with no harmonization of external tariffs, economic policies, or social policies, so a less elaborate institutional structure was required. Also, the countries of North America desired to avoid what was perceived to be an overly bureaucratized institutional framework in Western Europe.

On one level, one could say that the Free Trade Commission hardly exists as an institution. It has no physical location, since the proposed NAFTA coordinating secretariat has yet to be established, and has no staff of its own. The commission hardly has a virtual location, either, in that no web site exists for it, and only limited information about it can be found at the web sites of the member country trade ministries. By far the best source of information is the web site of Canada's Department of Foreign Affairs and International Trade. The national offices of the NAFTA secretariat do maintain a web site, but it reports only on the status and results of dispute settlement cases.

The annual meetings of the Free Trade Commission seem to be held mainly because the NAFTA agreement calls for them to take place at least once a year. The subsidiary bodies of the commission (working groups, committees, subcommittees) do serve an important purpose. By tackling issues of mutual concern and dealing with them before they become politicized, these bodies head off some trade problems. By increasing regional interaction and consultation on specific issues of concern, they increase the level of cooperation among the countries of North America. At the ministerial level, however, the Free Trade Commission is a relatively undeveloped institution. It has very limited interaction with the other NAFTA-related institutions.

Perhaps the most important function of the commission is its role in dispute settlement. The mandated consultation on matters in dispute, and the option of an arbitral panel as a last resort, no doubt facilitate the settlement of disputes even though panel arbitration has seldom been used. The dispute settlement procedures are particularly important for Mexico and Canada, the smaller countries in the relationship, since these procedures provide a forum for the settlement of disputes on an objective basis and move them away from arbitrary and unilateral actions by the dominant country in the region.

The Commission for Labor Cooperation and its affiliated national administrative offices have provided mechanisms through which cooperation and consultation on labor matters of concern to the countries of North America have been facilitated. The amount and quality of information about labor markets and labor conditions in North America are greater than ever before because of studies funded by this institution. However, the institutional structure established by the North American Agreement on Labor Cooperation (NAALC) provides for little in the way of remedial action, even in cases where labor abuses have been proven to have occurred.

Given the differences among the North American countries, in terms of culture, legal traditions, labor histories, and levels of economic development, the institutional framework that was established by the NAALC is probably as good as could have been attained. During their relatively brief existence, the labor-related institutions have not yet had much impact on labor conditions, nor have they done a great deal to promote the labor principles set forth in the agreement. However, a foundation has been laid upon which more robust institutions can be built over time for the benefit of labor in all three countries of North America.

Of all the NAFTA-related institutions, the most developed and active has been the Commission for Environmental Cooperation (CEC). The secretariat of the CEC has commissioned or carried out studies of important North American environmental issues that have received attention and analysis that they would not have received in the absence of this institution. The secretariat is collecting important data that will enable more accurate assessment and analysis of North American environmental conditions. In certain instances, such as the phasing out of some hazardous pesticides in Mexico, environmental conditions have been improved through the actions of the CEC.

With regard to "enforcement matters," during the first five and a half years of the agreement only twenty submissions alleging failure to enforce domestic environmental laws have been filed. Almost half of these were terminated as either having no merit or as not being valid under the criteria set forth in the North American Agreement on Environmental Cooperation (NAAEC). In only two cases has the development of a factual record on the matter been authorized.

No case alleging a "persistent pattern" of failure to enforce environmental laws has been filed. Private party access to this part of the dispute settlement procedure is denied. A member government must initiate such a case. Informal consultations among the member governments likely will preclude such cases, but the mere possibility of a case being taken to an arbitral panel no doubt makes the member governments more willing participants in the consultations on such matters.

The CEC has been a transparent institution in the sense that it keeps the public well informed about its activities. Its web site is highly developed and almost all relevant documents are readily available on it. The CEC receives input from civil society through its active fifteen-person joint public advisory committee. It receives further input in the United States and Canada from national advisory committees comprising private sector participants, and governmental advisory committees. Mexico has not yet formed either of these committees, but should be encouraged to do so. The CEC's interaction with civil society is further fostered by the grants that it extends to nongovernmental organizations through its North American Fund for Environmental Cooperation program.

A very important part of the CEC's long-term impact will be the program that it has established to work toward improving environmental conditions in North America. The CEC is engaging in path-breaking work to develop an analytical approach for studying the relationship between trade and environment within North America. The methodology being developed in this project should have applicability far beyond North America.

Because of the CEC's work program, information on the North American region is being systematically collected for the first time on subjects such as biodiversity and pollutant releases. Programs have been put into place to enhance regional cooperation in the conservation of birds in North America, to facilitate the trading of emissions credits as a way of controlling greenhouse gases, and to help small and medium-sized firms to prevent pollution. Projects have also begun between the United States and Mexico to protect the marine and coastal area ecosystems in the

Bight of the Californias, and between the United States and Canada to protect the ecosystem of the Gulf of Maine. Steps have been taken to increase cooperation among the countries of North America on environmental law enforcement and environmental regulation compliance.

Issues relating to trade and the environment are taking on increasing importance in regional trade negotiations, such as those for a free trade area for the Americas. They are also on the agenda for the next round of multilateral negotiations. These issues refuse to go away, and will have to be addressed. The pattern set by the CEC in analyzing and dealing with the intersection between trade issues and environmental issues should be useful to the rest of the world.

The bilateral institutions of the Border Environment Cooperation Commission (BECC) and the North American Development Bank (NADB) that developed out of NAFTA were sorely needed to deal with environmental problems along the U.S.–Mexico border. The fact that environmental pollution from one country spills over the border to affect citizens of the other country means that the problem cannot be dealt with effectively through governmental efforts of either country acting alone. Cooperation is essential. Furthermore, the fact that citizens in the border region have borne external costs from which consumers in both countries have benefited via lower prices provides a rationale for funding environmental cleanup through general tax revenues. The relative poverty of much of the border region makes external funding of environmental infrastructure projects essential.

The institutional structure that was established to deal with these problems has been awkward. The BECC was established to help develop and certify projects for funding, while the NADB was established to facilitate financing of projects and to oversee their implementation. This bifurcation of functions is uncharacteristic of other development banks, and has made the operation of the institutions more complicated than would have been the case in a unitary institution. In the United States, the NADB structure is further confused. In accordance with the NADB charter, 10 percent of the institution's funds are set aside for community adjustment and investment projects. The U.S. Community Adjustment and Investment Program, funded by NADB funds, functions essentially as a trade adjustment assistance program for NAFTA-affected communities. This aspect of its work could be better handled through the traditional trade adjustment assistance policy framework. Mexico, in contrast, has chosen to focus its community adjustment and investment resources on urgently needed environmental infrastructure projects.

While the BECC and NADB have been slow in getting started, their programs are making important differences to communities along the U.S.–Mexico border. With population in the border region projected to double in less than two decades (with two-thirds of the increase on the Mexican side of the border), improving environmental conditions there will be a great challenge. The creation of the BECC and the NADB as institutions to assist in this task can be considered one of NAFTA's significant contributions.

NAFTA's dispute settlement provisions relating to investment have turned out to be surprisingly controversial. The intent of NAFTA's investment chapter was to provide for a stable and attractive investment environment throughout North America by providing certain assurances to investors. In several ways it does this. The agreement forbids export performance requirements, trade balancing requirements, local content regulations, technology transfer requirements, and mandated preference for domestic sourcing. In the agreement NAFTA-member countries committed themselves to allow conversion of local currency at market rates, and to permit repatriation of profits. They also agreed that the property of partner-country firms would not be expropriated, directly or indirectly, without fair compensation. As further proof of their intention to protect property rights of foreign investors, the NAFTA countries agreed to submit unresolved investment disputes to binding arbitration.

The feature of the investment chapter that is proving most controversial is the concept of indirect expropriation and the way in which this concept is being employed in dispute settlement cases. Members of the legal profession are creatively using this concept to ask for damages allegedly resulting from pollution control regulations, or, in one case, from the verdict rendered by a state court system. At the time of this writing most of the cases had not been acted upon by arbitration panels. If the arbitrators' eventual decisions do require state or federal governments to compensate foreign firms for having changed their environmental regulations, or for the decisions rendered by domestic courts, a serious backlash can be expected. Such a development could have adverse effects upon multilateral trade negotiations as well, for the sovereignty issues related to investment regulation have already been a controversial issue in that forum. Some fine tuning of the NAFTA agreement definitely is needed here.

Disputes over antidumping and countervailing duty cases, while they have been relatively infrequent, have also given rise to some discontent. Chapter 19 of NAFTA provides for panel arbitration to rule on whether domestic administrative agencies responsible for carrying out antidumping and countervailing duty enforcement procedures have accurately and fairly applied their own laws and regulations. Some have suggested that the system could be improved by having panelists with higher qualifications, and allowing them more freedom to investigate the cases and to consider the precedents set by previous panels (Rugman and Anderson 1997). The dispute settlement mechanism of the World Trade Organization (WTO) is said to be preferable to that of NAFTA. For antidumping and countervailing duty cases it offers more precise definitions of dumping, subsidy, and material injury. Further, in the WTO a wider diversity of arbitration panelists is available (Howse 1998). Fortunately, NAFTA provides the option for disputing parties to use the WTO settlement procedures if they so desire, which makes the weaknesses in the NAFTA system less problematic than they would be otherwise.

In summary, the NAFTA-related institutions are for the most part rather minimalist institutions at a very early stage of their development. Those dealing with labor and the environment were created out of political necessity to gain legislative approval in the United States for the NAFTA agreement. By design all of the institutions were given limited power, and thus far have been given limited resources with which to work. To be sure, more institutionalization is not always preferred to less, and avoiding the bureaucratization of institutions that has characterized the European Union is a worthy goal for North America. Even so, the present underfunding of NAFTA-related institutions is a hindrance to their further development.

The NAFTA-related institutions were slow in getting organized, and almost six years after the implementation of the NAFTA agreement they have only begun to realize their potential. Even at their present stage of development they are serving a number of important functions. The institutionalization of trade rules and regulations, as well as dispute settlement procedures, has served to reduce uncertainty in trading relationships among the North American countries and has made possible a more efficient pattern of investment. Establishment of formal procedures whereby citizens can hold governments accountable for enforcement of their labor and environmental laws fosters compliance with those laws. Channels of government-to-government communication established by the NAFTA-related institutions, and the provision of more complete information to decision makers by the institutions, have reduced the costs and improved the quality of decisions. The level of trilateral cooperation in North America on a wide range of issues has never before been as great as it is today, and the NAFTA-related institutions are in large part responsible for this fact.

While the NAFTA-related institutions are relatively weak and undeveloped at this stage, they have laid a foundation upon which more robust institutions can develop in the future. As economic integration deepens within North America, the NAFTA-related institutions will take on increasing significance. While the institutions have attracted very little notice, they likely will be serving to facilitate cooperation and reduce conflict among the countries of North America long after the trade liberalization provisions of NAFTA have faded into the background.

Bibliography

Adams, Roy J., and Parbudyal Singh. 1997. Early experience with NAFTA's labour side accord. *Comparative Labor Law Journal* 18, no. 2.

Anderson, Sarah, John Cavanagh, and David Ranney. 1996. *NAFTA's first two years: The myths and the realities.* Washington, DC: Institute for Policy Studies.

Axelrod, Robert. 1983. *The evolution of cooperation.* New York: Basic Books.

Baker, Stephen, and Elizabeth Weiner. 1989. One tough hombre: Can President Salinas remake Mexico? *Business Week*, April 3.

Balls, Andrew, and Quentin Peel. 1999. Call for rules on global integration. *Financial Times*, July 12 , 4.

Bazar, Jason S. 1995. Is the North American Agreement on Labor Cooperation working for workers' rights? *California Western International Law Journal* 25, no. 2. Available in LEXIS-NEXIS Academic Universe.

Beauchesne, Eric. 1998. Bypass NAFTA to fight U.S., study urges: Americans more likely to accept WTO rulings, think-tank says. *The Ottawa Citizen*, July 3, final edition. Available in LEXIS-NEXIS Academic Universe.

Befort, Stephen F., and Virginia E. Cornett. 1996. Beyond the rhetoric of the NAFTA treaty debate: A comparative analysis of labor and employment law in Mexico and the United States. *Comparative Labor Law Journal* 17, no. 2. Available in LEXIS-NEXIS Academic Universe.

Bhagwati, J., and T.N. Srinivasan. 1996. Trade and environment: Does environmental diversity detract from the case for free trade? In *Fair Trade and Harmonization: Prerequisites for Free Trade?*, eds. J.N. Bhagwati and R.E. Hudec. Cambridge: MIT Press.

Bierman, Leonard, and Rafael Gely. 1995. The North American Agreement on Labor Cooperation: A new frontier in North American labor relations. *Connecticut Journal of International Law* 10, no. 2: 533–569.

Bogule, Feleke, and Jackie Alston. 1999. Phone conversations with Mr. Bogule of the U.S. Section and Ms. Alston of the Canadian Section of the NAFTA Secretariat, July 2.

Border Environment Cooperation Commission (BECC). 1996. *Project certification criteria.* Ciudad Juarez, Chihuahau, Mexico: Border Environment Cooperation Commission.

———. 1999. *BECC announces border needs assessment study and introduces new U.S. Advisory Council members.* Press release P17/PPU99, June 30.

Border Environment Cooperation Commission-North American Development Bank (BECC-NADB). 1999. *Joint status report: Spring 1999*. San Antonio, Texas. Available at http://www.nadbank.org/english/library/joint_status.

Brill, Edward A., and Stephanie L. Oratz. 1994. Labor accord put to the test; recent complaints have focused attention on a side agreement to NAFTA; hearings are scheduled. *National Law Journal*, September 19, C1.

Brown, D.K., A.V. Deardorff, and R.M. Stern. 1996. International labor standards and trade: A theoretical analysis. In *Fair Trade and Harmonization: Prerequisites for Free Trade?*, eds. J.N. Bhagwati and R.E. Hudec, 227–280. Cambridge: MIT Press.

Cable, V. 1996. The new trade agenda: Universal rules amid cultural diversity. *International Affairs* 72, no. 2: 227–246.

Canadian Department of Foreign Affairs and International Trade (CDFAIT). 1998. *NAFTA Operational Review*. Ottawa, Canada. Available at http://www.dfait-maeci.gc.ca/nafta-alena/review-e.asp.

Charnovitz, Steve. 1994. NAFTA's social dimension: Lessons from the past and framework for the future. *International Trade Journal* 8: 39–73.

———. 1996. The NAAEC and its implications for environmental cooperation, trade policy, and American treaty-making. In *NAFTA and the Environment*, eds. Seymour J. Rubin and Dean C. Alexander. The Hague: Kluwer Law International.

Canada says corporate claim on PCB ban valid. 1999. *Financial Post*, June 22, C2. Available in LEXIS-NEXIS Academic Universe.

Commission for Environmental Cooperation (CEC). 1995. *CEC secretariat report on the death of migratory birds at the Silva Reservoir (1994–95)*. Montreal, Canada. Available at http://www.cec.org/english/resources/publications/silindex.cfm.

———. 1997a. *Continental pollutant pathways: An agenda for cooperation to address long range transport of air pollutants in North America*. Montreal, Canada. Available at http://www.cec.org/english/resources/publications/polutindex.cfm.

———. 1997b. *NAFTA's institutions: The environmental potential and performance of the NAFTA Free Trade Commission and related bodies*, by John Kirton and Rafael Fernandez de Castro.

———. 1998a. *Four-year review of the North American Agreement on Environmental Cooperation: Report of the independent review committee*. Montreal, Canada. Available at http://www.cec.org/english/procurement.cfp3.cfm.

———. Secretariat. 1998b. *Determination pursuant to Article 14(1) of the North American Agreement on Environmental Cooperation SEM-97–005*. Available at http://www.cec.org.

———. 1999a. *25 environmental projects receive $1 million from CEC*. Press release, October 14. Available at http://www.cec.org/new/data.cfm.

———. 1999b. *Assessing environmental effects of the North American Free Trade Agreement (NAFTA): An analytic framework (phase II) and issue studies*. Montreal, Canada. Available at http://www.cec.org/english/resources/publications/eandt6.cfm.

———. 1999c. Ribbon of life: An agenda for preserving transboundary migratory bird habitat on the Upper San Pedro River. Available at http://www.cec.org/english/publications/sanped-e.cfm.

Commission for Labor Cooperation (CLC). 1998a. *Review of the North American Agreement on Labor Cooperation.* Dallas. Available at http://www.naalc.org/english/publications/review.htm.

———. 1998b. The employment of women in North America. Available at Available at http://www.naalc.org/english/publications/ewna.htm.

Compa, Lance. 1995. The first NAFTA labor cases: A new international labor rights regime takes shape. *U.S.–Mexico Law Journal* 3: 159–181.

———. 1997. Another look at NAFTA. *Dissent* (Winter): 45–50.

Connolly, C., and J. Tennant-Burt. 1997. The NAFTA labor agreement and U.S. employment-discrimination law. *Social Justice* 24, no. 1: 148–162.

Cook, Maria Elena. 1994. Regional integration and transnational labor strategies under NAFTA. In *Regional Integration and Industrial Relations in North America,* eds. Maria Elena Cook and Harry C. Katz, 142, 157. Ithaca, NY: Cornell University Press.

Cook, Maria Elena, Morley Gunderson, Mark Thompson, and Anil Verma. 1997. Making free trade more fair: Developments in protecting labor rights. *Labor Law Journal* 8 (August): 519–529.

Dean, David A. 1995. The labor supplemental agreement. In *Labor Law Development,* eds. Carol J. Holgren and Matthew Bender. New York: Matthew Bender.

Esty, Daniel C. 1994. Making trade and environmental policies work together: Lessons from NAFTA. In *Trade and the Environment,* vol. 1, eds. James Cameron, Paul Demoret, and Damien Geradin. London: Cameron May.

———. 1996. Revitalizing environmental federalism. *Michigan Law Review* (December), 95. Available in LEXIS-NEXIS Academic Universe.

EU calls for greater WTO-labor cooperation in WTO; India lashes out against new round. 1999. *BRIDGES Weekly Trade News Digest,* July 12, 1.

Ferrantino, Michael J. 1997. International trade, environmental quality and public policy. *World Economy* 20 (January): 43–73.

Fuentes, Manuel. 1995. The NAFTA labor side accord in Mexico and its repercussions for workers. *Connecticut Journal of International Law* 10, no 2. Available in LEXIS-NEXIS Academic Universe.

Fulton, Scott C., and Lawrence I. Sperling. 1996. The network of environmental enforcement and compliance cooperation in North America and the western hemisphere. *The International Lawyer* 30 (Spring): 111–140.

Gal-Or, Neomi. 1997. Multilateral trade and supranational environmental protection: The grace period of the CEC, or a well-defined role? *The Georgetown International Environmental Law Review* 9: 53–93.

Grieco, Joseph M. 1994. State interests and international rule trajectories: A neorealist interpretation of the Maastricht Treaty and European economic and monetary union. Paper prepared for delivery at the Symposium on Realism, May, Washington, DC.

———. 1995. Systemic sources of variation in regional institutionalization in Western Europe, East Asia, and the Americas. Paper prepared for delivery at the annual meeting of the American Political Science Association, August 31–September 3, Chicago, IL.

Grossman, Gene M. and Alan B. Krueger. 1995. Economic growth and the environment. *The Quarterly Journal of Economics* 110 (May): 353–377.

Haas, Peter M. 1992. Introduction: epistemic communities and international policy coordination. *International Organization* 46, no. 1: 1–36.

Hall, Kevin. 1998. Trade groups want end to NAFTA dispute panels. *Journal of Commerce* 29 (January), 3A.

Hart, Michael. 1990. A Canadian perspective on the 1987 Canada–United States Free Trade Agreement. In *Region North America: Canada, United States, Mexico* eds. Glen E. Lich and Joseph A. McKinney. Waco, TX: Baylor University.

Helfeld, David M. 1995. NAALC in the eyes of the beholder. *Connecticut Journal of International Law* 10, no. 2. Available in LEXIS-NEXIS Academic Universe.

Herzstein, Robert E. 1995. Labor cooperation agreement among Mexico, Canada, and the United States: Its negotiation and prospects. *US–Mexico Law Journal* 3: 121–131.

Howse, Robert. 1998, June. Settling trade remedy disputes: when the WTO forum is better than NAFTA. Commentary 81. Toronto: C.D. Howe Institute.

Johnson, P.M., and A. Beaulieu. 1996. *The environment and NAFTA: Understanding and implementing the new continental law.* Washington, DC: Island Press.

Kahler, Miles. 1995. *International institutions and the political economy of integration.* Washington, DC: Brookings Institution.

Keohane, Robert O. 1983. Theory of world politics: Structural realism and beyond. In *Political Science: The State of the Discipline*, ed. Ada Finifter. Washington, DC: American Political Science Association.

———. 1984. *After hegemony: Cooperation and discord in the world political economy.* Princeton, NJ: Princeton University Press.

———. 1998. International institutions: Can interdependence work. *Foreign Policy* 110 (Spring): 82–96.

Kindleberger, Charles P. 1981. Dominance and leadership in the international economy. *International Studies Quarterly* 25, no. 3: 242–254.

Kirton, John. 1997. The Commission for Environmental Cooperation and Canada–U.S. environmental governance in the NAFTA era. *The American Review of Canadian Studies* 27 (Autumn): 459–486.

Kirton, John, and Rafael Fernandez de Castro. 1997. *NAFTA'S institutions: The environmental potential and performance of the NAFTA Free Trade Commission and related bodies.* Montreal, Canada: CEC. Available at http://www.cec.org/english/resources/publications/insindex.cfm.

Lara-Saenz, Leonico. 1999. E-mail correspondence with author, July 12.

Lavalle, Marianne. 1994. Labor's charges test NAFTA rules in Mexico. *The National Law Journal*, September 19.

———. 1995. NAFTA jars labor laws; U.S., Mexico to discuss criticisms of Sprint's firing of employees. *The National Law Journal*, July 10.

Lehman, John P. 1999. *U.S.–Mexico border ten year outlook: Environmental infrastructure funding projections.* San Antonio, TX: North American Development Bank.

The Loewen Group files in U.S. and Canada. 1999, June 15. *BCD News and Comment* 34, no. 9. Available in LEXIS-NEXIS Academic Universe.

Lopez, David. 1997. Dispute resolution under NAFTA: Lessons from the early experience. *Texas International Law Journal* 32: 163–208.

Lucentini, Jack. 1998. Clinton in pro-trade move ends tariffs on brooms. *Journal of Commerce*, December 8, 3A. Available in LEXIS-NEXIS Academic Universe.

Makuch, Zen. 1994. The environmental implications of the NAFTA environmental side agreement: A Canadian perspective. In *Trade and the Environment* vol. 1, eds. James Cameron, Paul Demoret, and Damien Geradin. London: Cameron May Ltd.

Mann, Harold, and Konrad von Moltke. 1999. NAFTA's Chapter 11 and the environment: Addressing the impacts of the investor-state process on the environment. Winnipeg, Canada: International Institute for Sustainable Development. Available from http://www.iisd.ca.

Martin, Lisa L., and Beth A. Simmons. 1998. Theories and empirical studies of international institutions. *International Organization* 52, no. 4: 729–757.

McFadyen, Jacqueline. 1998, May. *NAFTA supplemental agreements: Four year review*. Washington, DC: Institute for International Economics.

McKinney, Joseph A. 1990. Introduction to *Region North America: Canada, United States, Mexico*, eds. Glen E. Lich and Joseph A. McKinney. Waco, TX: Baylor University.

———. 1998. Interview with Hugh Loftus, Director of Los Angeles Office of North American Development Bank, California, August 18.

———. 1999. Telephone interview with Hugh Loftus, July 16.

Merkin, William. 1990. Lessons from the United States–Canada negotiations for future consideration. In *Region North America: Canada, United States, Mexico*, eds. Glen E. Lich and Joseph A. McKinney. Waco, TX: Baylor University.

Murphy, Betty Southard. 1995. NAFTA's North American Agreement on Labor Cooperation: The present and the future. *Connecticut Journal of International Law* 10, no. 2: 403–426.

North American Agreement on Labor Cooperation (NAALC). 1993, September 13. Canada–United States–Mexico. Available at http://www.naalc.org/english/infocentre/naalc.htm.

North American Development Bank (NADB). 1995. *North American Development Bank: Charter and Bylaws*. San Antonio, Texas. Available at http://www.nadbank.org/english/library/charter and bylaws.

———. 1998. *Fiscal Year 1997 Annual Report*. San Antonio, Texas. Available at http://www.nadbank.org/english/library/annualreport.

North American Free Trade Agreement (NAFTA). 1992, December 8. Canada–United States–Mexico. Available at http://www.dfait-maeci.gc.ca/nafta-alena/agree-e.asp.

Orme, William A., Jr. 1993. *Continental shift: Free trade and the new North America*. Washington, DC: Washington Post Company.

Otero, Joaquín. 1995. The North American Agreement on Labor Cooperation: An assessment of its first year's implementation. *Columbia Journal of Transnational Law* 33, no. 3: 637–663.

Pérez-López, Jorge. 1995. The Institutional Framework of the North American Agreement on Labor Cooperation. *United States–Mexico Law Journal*, 3. Available in LEXIS-NEXIS Academic Universe.

Pomeroy, Lauran Okin. 1996. The labor side agreement under the NAFTA: Analysis of its failure to include strong enforcement provisions and recommendations for future labor agreement negotiated with developing countries. *The George Washington Journal of International Law and Economics* 29, no. 3. Available in LEXIS-NEXIS Academic Universe.

Public Citizen. 1999. NAFTA's corporate lawsuits. Briefing paper (April). Available from http://www.citizen.org.

Robinson, Ian. 1995. The NAFTA labor accord in Canada: Experience, prospects, and alternatives. *Connecticut Journal of International Law* 10, no. 2: 473–531.

Rubin, Seymour J., and Thomas R. Graham, eds. 1982. *Environment and trade.* Totowa, NJ: Allanheld, Osmun.

Rugman, Alan M., and Andrew D.M. Anderson. 1997. NAFTA and the dispute settlement mechanisms: A transaction costs approach. *World Economy* 20, no. 7: 935–951.

San Francisco Chronicle. 1999. Canadian firm sues California over MTBE; $970 million suit seeks to end gas-additive ban. June 18, final edition, 1. Available in LEXIS-NEXIS Academic Universe.

Saunders, J.O. 1994. NAFTA and the North American Agreement on Environmental Cooperation: A new model for international collaboration on trade and the environment. *Colorado Journal of International Environmental Law and Policy* 5, no. 2: 273–304.

Siebert, Horst. 1996. Trade policy and environmental protection. Supplement to *World Economy.*

Silva, Peter S. 1999. Oral presentation at NAFTA: The First Five Years International Economic Conference, November 4, at El Paso Branch of Federal Reserve Bank of Dallas.

Steinberg, Richard H. 1997. Trade-environment negotiations in the EU, NAFTA, and WTO: Regional trajectories of rule development. *The American Journal of International Law* 91. Available in LEXIS-NEXIS Academic Universe.

Sutter, Mary. 1998. Mexico asks arbitration to force open border. *Journal of Commerce* 24 (September). Available in LEXIS-NEXIS Academic Universe.

United States Department of Commerce (USDOC). 1999. *NAFTA Commission: Joint statement of ministers, five years of achievement.* Ottawa, Canada. April 3. Available at http://www.mac.doc.gov/nafta/joint.htm.

United States Department of Labor (USDOL). 1999. *NAO submissions: Status of submissions*, 3. Available at http://www.dol.gov/ilab/public/programs/nao/status.htm.

United States General Accounting Office (USGAO). 1993. *North American Free Trade Agreement: Assessment of the major issues.* GAO/GGD-93–137B. Washington, DC: U.S. Government Printing Office (GPO).

———. 1996. *International environment: Environmental infrastructure needs in the U.S.–Mexico border region remain unmet.* GAO/RCED-96–179. Washington, DC: GPO.

———. 1999. *U.S–Mexico border: Issues and challenges confronting the United States and Mexico.* GAO/NSIAD-99–109. Washington, DC: GPO.

United States International Trade Commission (USITC). 1990. Recent trade and investment reforms undertaken by Mexico and implications for the United States. *Review of Trade and Investment Liberalization Measures by Mexico and Prospects for Future United States–Mexican Relations, Phase I*, publication 2275. Washington, DC: GPO.

United States Trade Representative (USTR). 1997. Joint statement of trade ministers at the fourth NAFTA Commission meeting, Washington, DC, March 20.

———. 1998. Fifth meeting of the NAFTA Commission joint statement. Paris, France, April 29.

Vogel, David, and Alan M. Rugman. 1997. Environmentally related trade disputes between the United States and Canada. *The American Review of Canadian Studies* 27, no. 2: 271–292.

Waltz, Kenneth N. 1979. *Theory of international politics*. Reading, MA: Addison-Wesley.

Weintraub, Sidney. 1984. *Free trade between Mexico and the United States?* Washington, DC: Brookings Institution.

———. 1988. Mexican trade policy and the North American community. *Mexico Monograph Series* 10, no. 14. Washington, DC: Center for Strategic and International Studies.

———. 1990. A North American free trade area and the rest of the world. In *Region North America: Canada, United States, Mexico*, eds. Glen E. Lich and Joseph A. McKinney. Waco, TX: Baylor University.

———. 1997. Institutions and interactions. In *NAFTA at Three: A Progress Report*. Washington, DC: The Center for Strategic and International Studies.

Wendt, Alexander. 1994. Collective identity formation and the international state. *American Political Science Review* 88, no. 2: 284–396.

Web Pages of NAFTA-Related Institutions

Border Environment Cooperation Commission
http://cocef.org/englishbecc.htm

Canadian Department of Foreign Affairs and International Trade
http://www.dfait-maeci.gc.ca/

Canadian National Administrative Office
http://labour-travail.hrdc-drhc.gc.ca/doc/lab-trav/eng/

Mexican National Administrative Office
http://www.stps.gob.mx/index_12.htm

NAFTA Secretariat
www.nafta-sec-alena.org/english/index.htm

North American Commission for Environmental Cooperation
http://www.cec.org

North American Commission for Labor Cooperation
http://www.naalc.org

North American Development Bank
http://www.nadbank.org

United States Community Adjustment and Investment Program
http://www.nadbank-caip.org

United States National Administrative Office
http://www.dol.gov/dol/ilab/public/programs/nao/main.htm

United States Trade Representative
http://www.ustr.gov

Index

AFL-CIO, 50
Air Monitoring and Modeling Project, 96
Anderson, Andrew D.M., 234, 243
Antidumping cases, 232–35, 242–43
Antidumping penalties, 4, 5, 31, 232
Axelrod, Robert, 16

Bendesky, Leon, 114
Biodiversity Legal Foundation, 100
Border Environment Cooperation
  Commission (BECC), 161–68, 170,
  172, 175–77, 241–42
  Funding, 163
  Operations, 181–84
  Organization and management, 184–90
  Project certification criteria, 166–68
    Community participation, 167
    Financial feasibility and project
      management, 167
    Human health and environment
      criteria, 166
    Sustainable development criteria,
      167
    Technical feasibility criteria, 166
  Purpose and functions, 164, 180–81
  Technical assistance programs, 164–66
    Capacity Building Needs and Solid
      Waste Technical Assistance
      Program, 165
    High Sustainability Recognition
      Program, 165
    Project Development Assistance
      Program (PDAP), 165

BECC, Technical assistance
  programs (continued)
    Sustainable Development Program,
      165
Border Environment Infrastructure Fund
  (BEIF), 171–72, 175
Border Industrialization Program, 161
Bracero program, 161
Bramble, Barbara J., 114
Brittan, Sir Leon, 52
Buchanan, Pat, 33
Bush, President George, 7

Canada–United States Softwood Lumber
  Agreement, 228–29
Canadian Department of Foreign Affairs
  and International Trade, 31, 238
Canadian Environmental Assessment
  Act, 101
Canadian Fisheries Act, 101
Canadian Inter-governmental
  Committee, 38
Canadian National Administrative Office
  (NAO), 41, 45–46
Caribbean Barrier Reef, 101
Colonias, 162–63
CEC. See Commission for Environmen-
  tal Cooperation (CEC)
Centro Mexicano de Derecho Ambiental,
  95
Chapter 11 of NAFTA, 28, 224–31
Chapter 19 of NAFTA, 28, 31, 225,
  232–33, 243

Chapter 20 of NAFTA, 28–30, 234
CLC. *See* Commission for Labor
    Cooperation (CLC)
Clinton, President William J., 9, 12, 30,
    33, 90, 163, 216
Commission for Environmental
    Cooperation (CEC), 18–19, 21,
    90–122, 129–39
  Advisory committees, 105–06; 138–39
  Annual report, 134–35
  Assessment of, 115–17, 239–41
  Council, 92–93, 129–33
  Secretariat, 93–106, 133–38
  Work program, 110–13
    Biodiversity and ecosystems, 112
    Capacity building, 112–13
    Law and enforcement cooperation,
      113
    NAFTA effects, 110–12
    Pollutants and health, 112
Commission for Labor Cooperation
    (CLC), 18–19, 34–36, 58–64
  Council, 34–35, 58–60
  Cooperative activities, 60
  Secretariat, 35–36, 61–63
    Reports and studies, 62–63
    Structure and procedures, 61–62
Communications Workers of America,
    42
Community Adjustment and Assistance
    Program (CAIP), 172–77
Compliance monitoring, 18–19, 22
Confederation of Mexican Workers, 44
Constructivism, 22
Contingent protection, 4
Convention on Biological Diversity, 102
Countervailing duties, 4, 5, 31, 233

Decoster Farms, 45
Desechos Solidos de Naucalpan, 226
Dispute settlement, 10, 14, 17, 239–42
  NAAEC procedure, 106–09, 141–49
  NAALC procedure, 37–46, 68–77
  Under Chapter 11 of NAFTA, 224–31
  Under Chapter 19 of NAFTA, 232–35
  Under Chapter 20 of NAFTA, 28–30

Echlin, Inc., 44
Economic interdependence, 14–15
Endangered Species Act, 100
Environment Canada, 104
Environmental Protection Agency (EPA).
    See U.S. Environmental Protection
    Agency
Ethyl Corporation, 227

Federation of Goods and Services
    Companies of Mexico, 42
Feldman, Marvin, 226
Florida Tomato Exchange, 42
Fort Huachuca, 97–98
Free Trade Commission, 18, 24–32, 35,
    93, 115, 120, 132, 238–39
  Dispute settlement, 28–30
  Evaluation of, 31–32
  Meetings of, 24–27
  Operational review of NAFTA work
    program, 27–28

General Agreement on Tariffs and Trade
    (GATT), 3, 5–6, 9–10, 91
  Trade and environment committee, 91
  Tuna-dolphin case, 10
General Electric, 42
Generalized System of Preferences, 8
Grieco, Joseph M., 14, 20

Han Young, 44
Harmonized Agreement on the
    Environment, 118–19
Howse, Robert, 234
"Hub and spoke" system, 7
Human Rights Watch, 43–44

Immigration and Naturalization Service,
    46
Inter-American Development Bank,
    211
International Boundary and Water
    Commission (IBWC), 98, 163–64,
    179, 184, 188
International Institute for Sustainable
    Development, 230

International Labor Organization, 39, 44, 52

International Labor Rights Fund, 43–44

Joint Public Advisory Committee (JPAC). *See* North American Agreement on Environmental Cooperation (NAAEC)

Keohane, Robert O., 14
Kindleberger, Charles P, 15

Lake Chapala, 102
La Paz Agreement, 10, 105, 163
Loewen Group, Inc., 220–30
Lopez Portillo, Jose, 6

Maquiladora program. *See* Border Industrialization Program
Martin, Lisa L, 19
Maxi-Switch, 42
Medina, Luis, 47
Metalclad Corporation, 226
Methanex Corporation, 229–30
Mexican Ministry of Finance and Public Credit, 172, 174
Mexican National Association of Democratic Lawyers, 43
Mexican National Water Commission, 171
Mexican Secretariat of Labor and Social Welfare (Secretaria de Desarollo Social), 11, 181
MMT, 227, 230
Monetary enforcement assessment, 40–41, 46–47, 49, 75–76, 84–88, 148–49, 155–56, 159
MTBE, 229–231
Mulroney, Prime Minister Brian, 4

NAFTA coordinating secretariat, 25, 238
NAFTA coordinators, 27
NAFTA secretariat, 24–25, 29, 31, 226, 234, 239
National Association of Democratic Lawyers of Mexico, 43–44

National Audubon Society of the United States, 95
National Labor Relations Board (NLRB), 95
Neorealist school, 15
North American Agreement on Environmental Cooperation (NAAEC), 18, 91–94, 98–118, 123–60
Advisory committees, 105–6; 138–39
Governmental advisory committee (GAC), 106, 120,139
Joint public advisory committee (JPAC), 105–6, 120, 138
National advisory committee (NAC), 106, 120, 139
Article 13 reports, 94–98
Article 14 submissions on enforcement matters, 99–105
Article 15 factual records, 99, 101, 105, 137–38
Commission. *See* Commission for Environmental Cooperation (CEC)
Four-year independent review, 113–15
Recommendations, 118–22
Consultation and Dispute Resolution under Part V, 106–9, 141–49
Panel arbitration, 107–9, 142–49
Objectives, 124–25
Obligations, 125–28
Participation with broader environmental community, 113
Preamble, 123–24
Relation to other environmental agreements, 150
North American Agreement on Labor Cooperation (NAALC), 18, 33–89, 240
Commission. *See* Commission for Labor Cooperation (CLC)
Evaluation Committee of Experts, 39, 65–66, 87–88

North American Agreement on Labor
  Cooperation (NAALC) *(continued)*
Cooperation with International Labor
  Organization, 77–78
Cooperative Consultations and
  Evaluations, 64–67
Four-year independent review, 46–49
National Administrative Offices,
  36–51, 63–65
  Purposes and responsibilities, 37,
  63
  Submissions on enforcement
  matters, 41–46
Objectives, 33–34, 54–55
Obligations, 55–58
Panel arbitration, 40–41, 69–77
Preamble, 53–54
Principles, 34, 81–83
Resolution of disputes. *See* Dispute
  settlement
Significance of, 49–52
North American Biodiversity
  Information Network, 112
North American Development Bank
  (NADB), 161, 168–77, 178–222
Bylaws, 217–22
Capitalization, 169, 194–97
Institutional Development and
  Cooperation Program (IDP),
  170–71
  Utility Management Institute,
  170–71
Operations, 197–201
Organization and Management,
  205–7
Purposes and functions, 168, 193–94
North American Free Trade Agreement
  (NAFTA)
Development of, 3–13
Foundations of, 3–4
Launching of negotiations, 8
Provisions of agreement, 9

Occupational Safety and Health
  Administration (OSHA), 12

Omnibus Trade and Competitiveness
  Act, 4
Owen, Stephen, 114

Paradise Reef, 100
Path dependence, 19
Perot, Ross, 33
Pollution haven(s), 10, 21, 90
Pope and Talbot, Inc., 228–29
Prisoners' dilemma, 15

Race to the bottom, 90
Reagan, President Ronald, 4
Recissions Act of 1995, 100
Reynolds, Clark, 237
Rugman, Alan M., 234, 243

S.D. Myers, Inc., 228
Salinas de Gortari, President Carlos, 7, 9,
  216
San Pedro River Basin, 97–98, 101, 113
Shamrock Summit, 4
Sierra Club, 100
Signaling function, 20
Silva Reservoir, 95–96, 98, 116
Silver, Dr. Robin, 97, 101
Simmons, Beth A., 19
Snowcap Waters, Ltd., 228
Sociedad Financiera de Objecto
  Limitado, 172
Solec, Inc., 45
Sony Corporation, 43
Southwest Center for Biological
  Diversity, 97, 101
Special 301, 4
Sprint Corporation, 45
Summers, Clyde, 47
Sun Belt Water Company, Inc., 228
Super 301, 4

Time-inconsistency, 21
Torres, Esteban E., 173
Trade and Tariff Act of 1984, 3
Trade sanctions, 13, 46, 50, 91, 100,
  106, 109, 224

Transactions costs, 16–17
Trudeau, Pierre, 15
Turbio Basin Initiative, 95
Turner, John, 5

Union of Metal, Steel, Iron and Allied
    Workers, 43
Union of Telephone Workers of
    Mexico, 42
United Electrical, Radio, and
    Machine Workers of America,
    42–43
United Nations Commission on
    International Trade Law,
    225
United Nations Development Program,
    52
U.S.–Canada free trade agreement, 4–5,
    7–9, 232

U.S. Community Adjustment and
    Assistance Program. *See* Commu-
    nity Adjustment and Assistance
    Program (CAIP)
U.S. Environmental Protection
    Agency (EPA), 103, 162, 181,
    184
U.S. Senate Finance Committee, 4
U.S. Treasury Department, 176

Uruguay Round, 9, 25
USA Waste, 226

Verge, Pierre, 47
Voluntary export restraints, 4

Waltz, Kenneth N., 15
World Bank, 121, 225
World Trade Organization (WTO), 52,
    234, 243

About the Author

Joseph A. McKinney is a Ben H. Williams Professor of International Economics at Baylor University. He has also served on the faculty of the University of Virginia and has taught as a visiting professor at Seinan Gakuin University in Japan, Université de Caen in France, and Middlesex University in London where he was a Fulbright Senior Scholar. He is the author of many articles relating to international trade policy and has testified before state and national legislative committees concerning the NAFTA agreement.